Stratford-upon-Avon Studies
Second Series

General Editor: Jeremy Hawthorn

Professor of Modern British Literature,
University of Trondheim, Norway

The Nineteenth-Century British Novel

Editor: Jeremy Hawthorn

Edward Arnold

© Edward Arnold (Publishers) Ltd 1986

First published in Great Britain 1986 by
Edward Arnold (Publishers) Ltd, 41 Bedford Square, London WC1B 3DQ

Edward Arnold (Australia) Pty Ltd, 80 Waverley Road, Caulfield East,
  Victoria 3145, Australia

Edward Arnold, 3 East Read Street, Baltimore, Maryland 21202, U.S.A.

British Library Cataloguing in Publication Data

The Nineteenth-century British novel. ——
  (Stratford-upon-Avon studies. Second series)
  1. English fiction —— 19th century ——
  History and criticism
  I. Hawthorn, Jeremy   II. Series
  823′.009   PR861

ISBN 0–7131–6470–0

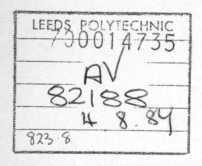

Text set in 10/11 pt Garamond Compugraphic
by Colset Private Limited, Singapore
Printed and bound in Great Britain by
Richard Clay plc, Bungay, Suffolk.

Contents

vi *Contents*

Preface

Faced with the claim that the nineteenth-century novel represents one of the supreme peaks of artistic achievement in the history of humanity many people who are by no means ill-disposed to it feel slightly uneasy – and uneasy in a way that they are not when the same claim is made for Renaissance painting or the Greek plastic arts, or even Elizabethan drama. Such an uneasiness can be traced to a number of possible roots: the feeling that the novel is too popular a genre to sustain such a claim; our vexed relationship with the nineteenth century which, like all parent–child relationships is riddled with neurotic elements; and a sense of Modernist superiority to the realist art of the past century.

And yet the claim must be conceded in essentials – conceded and explored. The contributions to the present volume seek to further this exploration in a variety of ways: through textual analysis and appreciation, through investigation into the literary roots of the novel's achievement in the nineteenth century, through study of readers and readings (both contemporary and subsequent), and through inquiry into the complex relationships of influence and reference which exist between the novels in question and various aspects of their time.

These are all complementary pursuits, and it is to be hoped that their collective result will be a fuller understanding of the greatness of the nineteenth-century novel – and perhaps less uneasiness in our acknowledgement of this greatness.

Note

Jane Austen was born in 1775 at Steventon in Hampshire where her father was rector. She lived all her life with her parents; with both until her father's death in 1805 and then with her mother until her own death. The household moved from Steventon to Bath in 1801, from Bath to Southampton in 1806, and from Southampton to the Hampshire village of Chawton in 1809. She died of Addison's disease at Winchester, where she had taken lodgings to be near her doctor, in July of 1817. Jane Austen never lived outside the south of England. She never married, though she had at least one proposal and one love affair that had nothing to do with the proposal. Her life is always described in biographical notes as 'uneventful', which outwardly it certainly was. She always had a close relationship with her large family, in particular with her sister Cassandra, a relationship which was of great importance to her development as a literary artist.

Jane Austen published only six novels: *Sense and Sensibility* (1811), *Pride and Prejudice* (1813); *Mansfield Park* (1814), *Emma* (1816), *Northanger Abbey* and *Persuasion* (posthumously, 1818). *Northanger Abbey* is, however, an early work, begun in 1797 and sold to a publisher in 1803, but not then published.

All Jane Austen's novels must be characterized as major works. They are still widely read and available in a number of editions. The standard edition is that by R.W. Chapman (1923–54) published by the Oxford University Press and constantly reprinted. R.W. Chapman has also edited *Jane Austen's Letters to her Sister Cassandra and Others* (London, Oxford University Press, second edn. 1952; reprinted 1979 with corr. text of last letter), the primary source of insight into Jane Austen's life.

A concise and readable biography is Elizabeth Jenkins, *Jane Austen. A Biography* (London, Gollancz, 1938, 1972) but the general reader may prefer David Cecil's elegant and amply illustrated *A Portrait of Jane Austen* (London, Constable, 1978). Some of the critical works on Jane Austen's novels also have short and informative biographical chapters, e.g. Mary Lascelles, *Jane Austen and her Art* (London, Clarendon Press, 1939; paperback 1963) and Christopher Gillie, *A Preface to Jane Austen* (London, Longman, 1974). The early criticism is collected and surveyed in B.C. Southam, *Jane Austen: the Critical Heritage* (London, Routledge, 1968).

Of modern studies, Mary Lascelles' book is invaluable and Christopher Gillie's *Preface* also has a useful section on 'Literary Background'. W.A. Craik, *Jane Austen: the Six Novels* (London, Methuen, 1965) is a sensible, work-by-work, introduction. It is worth noting that Jane Austen, perhaps more than other authors, has suffered under the New Critical search for irony. D.W. Harding, in an often reprinted article – 'Regulated Hatred: an Aspect of the Work of Jane Austen', *Scrutiny* VII, (1940) pp. 346–62 – introduced the view that Jane Austen 'really' disliked the world about which she seemed to write so lovingly and that she always undermined even her most attractive characters through irony. Marvin Mudrick's *Jane Austen. Irony as Defense and Discovery* (Princeton, Princeton University Press, 1952) presented a fully argued case for Jane Austen as an ironist. The view is today much less popular than it used to be. *Twentieth Century Interpretations of Pride and Prejudice*, ed. E. Rubinstein (Englewood Cliffs, Prentice-Hall, 1969) and *Jane Austen: 'Sense and Sensibility', 'Pride and Prejudice' and 'Mansfield Park'*, ed. B.C. Southam (London, Macmillan, 1976; Macmillan Casebook Series) are useful collections of modern critical views and articles.

1

Appreciating *Pride and Prejudice*

Stein Haugom Olsen

I

Jane Austen is a moralist and her interest is social morality. The issue which she always comes back to is that of the survival of rational social intercourse and civilized values. And the threat to this intercourse comes chiefly from one source: the young generation which is about to break away or take over the old order threatening the continuity of the society on which they depend for survival and meaningful human relationships; a threat which can only be neutralized by the socialization of the individual, the acceptance of the primacy of social over personal considerations. To define this issue and set the scene of her story Jane Austen employs two main tools. One is the construction of a highly specified social and economic background with well-defined social relationships. This social order is given; it is not attacked, questioned or endorsed. It is *there*, just as are the country houses and the improved landscapes around them, the villages and the market-towns. As an unproblematic given this social and economic order can be used to define the moral problems of the Austenian fictional world. For within this order, duties and privileges, obligations and responsibilities, what one is and what one deserves, can be given a precise definition. The ethical implications of social behaviour are immediately clear in this system and can be explored with a high degree of sophistication and complexity.

The society presented to the reader in *Pride and Prejudice* has a pyramidal structure. This society is not merely a social but also a moral order. The title 'gentleman' confers privileges and obligations and to each social position are attached duties and responsibilities. Thus, tied to Mr Darcy's high social and economic position is a range of duties which he cannot escape: 'As a brother, a landlord, a master, she considered how many people's happiness were in his guardianship! – How much of pleasure or pain it was in his power to bestow! – How much of good or evil must be done by him!' (p. 220).[1] There is no way in which Darcy can

---

[1] Page references are to the Oxford English Novels edition (London, 1970). References to other works by Jane Austen are also to the Oxford English Novels edition.

withdraw from these obligations and be just a private person. His very identity is tied to the image of the gentleman with wealth and responsibility, and he stands to be judged by his performance as a 'gentleman' in this social sense. It is noteworthy that there is, in Jane Austen's world, no distinction between the public and the private responsibilities of characters: 'As a brother, a landlord, a master', these responsibilities are of the same kind, governed by the same principles, and to be judged by the same standards. Indeed, Jane Austen concentrates on the moral behaviour of individuals in narrow private contexts, but the principles involved are general principles of social behaviour. Mr Bennet's failure as a husband and a father is a manifestation of his withdrawal from social responsibility and a result of his general avoidance of involvement and dismissive attitude to his human environment: 'For what do we live, but to make sport for our neighbours, and laugh at them in our turn?' (p. 323). Mr Bennet's irony and wit are ultimately irresponsible and socially disruptive, not only isolating himself from wife, children and society, but also undermining the possibility of his daughters entering into new, fruitful relationships, through marriage, to form new nuclei of social intercourse.

This moral system which assigns duties, responsibilities, privileges, and expectations to different social positions and functions – the gentleman, the husband, the father, the landlord, the clergyman and the officer – naturally builds on convention. It is not, however, a system of 'conventional morality' in any derogatory sense. It is, on the contrary, a living morality built on sympathy, affection, generosity and tolerance. If these sources of moral conduct dry up, the moral order withers and instead of promoting social cohesion, the social order becomes self-annihilating. Social conscience then turns into a desire merely to exercise power over others, to bully and dominate as with Lady Catherine: 'whenever any of the cottagers were disposed to be quarrelsome, discontented or too poor, she sallied forth into the village to settle their differences, silence their complaints, and scold them into harmony and plenty' (pp. 150–1). And respect for the social structure becomes merely creeping servility to rank and fortune as with Mr Collins. However, fully to understand the sources of this moral order, we must move on and consider Jane Austen's second tool of definition.

II

Given a social and economic structure which is also a moral order, what is needed to define the content of this order is a conceptual scheme or a vocabulary. The social order and the moral vocabulary used to define the values that sustain it are mutually dependent upon each other to acquire point and meaning. The reader is never left to private associations which may arise in connection with the different terms of the vocabulary; the meaning of every term is explored in the novel through different situations and events and their consequences for the social order. Always central to Jane Austen's moral vocabulary is a set of terms grouping themselves around the terms 'amiable'. In her works this term has an interesting ambiguity. On the one hand, it is connected with such concepts as 'agreeable', 'good breeding', 'civility', 'politeness' which have to do with the social interaction between individuals on a superficial level. Mr Wickham is amiable in this sense: '. . . he had all the best part of beauty, a fine countenance, a good figure, and a very pleasing address', and he shows 'a happy readiness of conversation – a readiness at the same time perfectly correct and unassuming' (p. 64). Amiability is here connected with the sort of good manners which a gentleman should possess, the social art of pleasing one's company through intelligent conversation and polished behaviour which is learnt through practice. It is in this social art Darcy is lacking. His cousin, Colonel Fitzwilliam, is used to bring this out. The Colonel is 'not handsome, but in person and address most truly the gentleman' (II, vii, 152) entering into conversation with 'the readiness and ease of a well-bred man'. Darcy, on the other hand, though 'a man of sense and education, and who has lived in the world, is ill qualified to recommend himself to strangers' because 'he will not give himself the trouble' of practising (p. 156).

On the other hand, 'amiability' is linked with such terms as 'general benevolence', 'universal goodwill', 'candour' (meaning 'free from malice: not desirous to find faults'), 'generosity', these terms being different expressions for the moral passion of sympathy. This notion of a moral passion which constitutes the foundation of moral behaviour is one of the basic features of eighteenth-century moral thought and it is the linchpin of Hume's moral philosophy. In Jane Austen's works it is the moral backbone of the social order and she always defines it through one or a pair of characters whom she endows with unreflective generosity. In *Pride and Prejudice* there is Jane Bennet, 'candid without ostentation or design', who takes 'the good of every body's character and make[s] it still better, and say[s] nothing of the bad' (p. 12). She shows 'a uniform cheerfulness of manner' (p. 17), and even Elizabeth is surprised at her 'universal good will' (p. 121). Realizing the value and prudence of this benevolent attitude when she has read and accepted Darcy's letter, Elizabeth regrets that she has 'often disdained the generous candour of my sister' (p. 185). This 'generous candour' manifests itself in a refusal to prejudge the character of an individual, finding excuses and explanations if somebody appears to behave in an unacceptable way: 'her mild and steady candour always pleaded for allowances, and urged the possibility of mistakes' (p. 124); and accepting offences without resentment or lasting ill will: 'We must not be so ready to fancy ourselves intentionally injured' (p. 122). There is also Bingley whose behaviour is distinguished sharply from that of his sisters. When Elizabeth arrives at Netherfield, having walked from Longbourn to visit Jane who is prevented from returning home by a cold, 'She was received . . . very politely by them [Mrs Hurst and Miss Bingley]; and in their brother's manners there was something better than politeness; there was good humour and kindness' (p. 28). When Bingley responds to Mrs Bennet's foolish outbursts and pointed attention he is always 'unaffectedly civil' (p. 39) and 'all grateful pleasure' (p. 93). Bingley's good breeding is expressive of his good will and tolerance:

> His ease and cheerfulness rendered him a most agreeable addition to their evening party; and he bore with the ill-judged officiousness of the mother, and heard all her silly remarks with a forebearance and command of countenance, particularly grateful to the daughter. (p. 306)

He has the ready tolerance of and consideration for others necessary for a society consisting of people with different and perhaps incompatible temper, interests, abilities, and education to function.

In *Emma* Mr Knightley makes a distinction between being 'amiable' in French and in English: a man 'may be very "aimable", have very good manners, and be very agreeable; but he can have no English delicacy towards the feelings of other people: nothing really amiable about him' (pp. 134–5). There is a contrast, Mr Knightley implies, between good manners, civility, politeness, on the one hand, and, on the other, benevolence, good will, and a 'delicacy towards the feelings of other people'. However, the *aimable* and the amiable are also connected in Jane Austen's works on a deeper level: benevolence manifests itself naturally in good manners. Civility is a way of showing consideration for others; it is a social mechanism to avoid hurting the sensibilities of one's fellow beings. *Genuine* good manners are not just manners but are closely linked to the moral passion of sympathy. Absence of good manners is morally reprehensible because it is socially divisive and a criterion of a deficiency in moral feeling. Darcy and the Bingley sisters dismiss the Longbourn/Meryton society and keep aloof from it: 'Elizabeth still saw superciliousness in their treatment of everybody, hardly excepting even her sister' (p. 17). By their superciliousness the Bingley sisters isolate themselves from the give and take of social intercourse, and, more seriously, their lack of benevolence and tolerance also makes them interfere with the foundation of the relationship, based on amiability, between Jane and Bingley, which would guarantee the survival of a morally sound society. Presence of good manners cannot, on the other hand, guarantee moral feeling. Wickham is *aimable* but he is not amiable.

Balancing the set of terms clustered around the concept of 'amiability' and dealing with the moral passion of sympathy and its manifestations, there is another set of terms grouped around the concept of 'propriety' and dealing with the conventional element in moral behaviour. 'Propriety' is, on the one hand, grouped with words like 'decorum' and 'form' which describe behaviour as conforming to accepted rules without carrying any implications about the ethical status of these rules. When Elizabeth arrives at Netherfield, having walked from Longbourn 'above her ancles in dirt, and alone, quite alone!' to visit Jane, she is criticized by Miss Bingley for showing 'a most country town indifference to decorum' (pp. 30–1). There are no moral implications in this judgement, only superficial social ones. This propriety is idle:

When my niece Georgiana went to Ramsgate last summer, I made a point of her having two men servants go with her. – Miss Darcy, the daughter or Mr Darcy, of Pemberley, and Lady Anne, could not have appeared with propriety in a different manner. (p. 188)

The attention to decorum shown by Lady Catherine would not have prevented Miss Darcy from disgracing her family in the way Lydia is later to disgrace hers. Furthermore, decorum and form unrelieved by sense is intolerable, ridiculous and self-defeating: it is Mr Collins: 'His air was grave and stately, and his manners were very formal' (p. 57). By doing everything in form, adhering blindly to what he believes is required of and due to the clergy, Mr Collins reduces form to absurdity.

'Propriety' is also allied to a set of concepts which throws light on the ethical function of decorum and social convention: 'restraint', 'moderation', 'respectability', 'respect', 'right', 'good principles'. This deeper significance of propriety is negatively defined: the 'total want of propriety so frequently, so almost uniformly betrayed by [Mrs Bennet], by [Elizabeth's] three younger sisters, and occasionally even by [her] father' (p. 176) is what the author describes:

> In vain did Elizabeth endeavour to check the rapidity of her mother's words, or persuade her to describe her felicity in a less audible whisper; for to her inexpressible vexation, she could perceive that the chief of it was overheard by Mr Darcy, who sat opposite to them. Her mother only scolded her for being nonsensical.
>
> 'What is Mr Darcy to me, pray, that I should be afraid of him? I am sure we owe him no such particular civility as to be obliged to say nothing *he* may not like to hear.'
>
> At length however Mrs Bennet had no more to say; and Lady Lucas, who had been long yawning at the repetition of delights which she saw no likelihood of sharing, was left to the comforts of cold ham and chicken. (pp. 89–90)

Propriety can be a self-denying subjection of selfish habits, impulses and desires to an accepted and acceptable social norm. Observing propriety will then be to fulfill a social contract which guarantees that one is, and is seen to be, showing consideration for the feelings, thoughts, and opinions of others. Mrs Bennet's conversation and behaviour is consistently indisciplined and inconsiderate. It is dictated exclusively by how she feels, not by how she thinks she will affect others. Her speeches are not a part of a social exchange; they are effusions without reference to others. This wholly selfish and unrestrained behaviour is socially disruptive. It not only creates a momentary isolation of the speaker and an embarrassment for the interlocutors, but it also marks the speaker as a socially disruptive element and thus sets off further negative consequences.

Impropriety at its extreme is a total lack of restraint, of socialization of private impulses and desires, and thus it is the manifestation of a total indifference to society and its requirements of consideration and respect for others. It is logically and psychologically correct, of course, that it is Mrs Bennet's favourite daughter, Lydia, who should be the representative of this attitude: 'Vain, ignorant, idle, and absolutely uncontrouled!' (p. 205). Lydia is wholly asocial, neither hearing what others have to say ('But of this answer Lydia heard not a word' (p. 197); 'If she heard me, it was by good luck, for I am sure she did not listen' (p. 287)), nor perceiving how they react to her behaviour, nor caring for their reaction: '[Elizabeth] blushed, and Jane blushed; but the cheeks of the two who caused their confusion, suffered no variation of colour' (p. 279). At this extreme, impropriety leads to social catastrophe. Lydia is threatened by isolation and exclusion from social intercourse altogether (the local gossipers speculate whether she will 'come upon the town' or be 'secluded from the world, in some distant farm house' (p. 273)) and she, and the Bennet family, is saved only through Darcy's intervention.

The connection between amiability and propriety is complex. Superficial civility stands opposed, yet related to, genuine propriety. Superficial civility stands in contrast to genuine propriety (e.g. Wickham's behaviour). Idle decorum stands opposed, yet related, to genuine propriety. Idle decorum stands in contrast to true amiability (e.g. the behaviour of Lady Catherine, Miss Bingley, and Mrs Hurst). There is, however, no opposition between superficial civility and idle decorum: it is quite possible to see both Wickham and the Bingley sisters as obeying social etiquette, and there is no deeper basis for either idle decorum or superficial civility which could be used to differentiate between them. Nor is there any opposition between true amiability and genuine propriety; these are in fact profoundly interdependent. True amiability is a social passion, but it is in Jane Austen's works associated with the more basic concept of affection. Jane and Bingley are not only amiable, but also people with strong affections: '. . . Jane united with great strength of feeling, a composure of temper and a uniform cheerfulness of manner' (p. 17). Now affection is a positive feeling in that it is the uniting force binding together man and woman, parent and child, brothers, sisters, and friends. It is his affection for Elizabeth, in particular, and Jane which redeems Mr Bennet; and Elizabeth acknowledges as a redeeming feature of Darcy that 'she had often heard him speak so affectionately of his sister as to prove him capable of *some* amiable feeling' (p. 184). On the other hand, affection is also a selfish and destructive feeling in that it breaks through the checks and balances of social convention: 'In vain have I struggled. It will not do. My feelings will not be repressed. You must allow me to tell you how ardently I admire and love you' (p. 168). It is in its origins an unsocialized passion: Darcy's affection for Elizabeth, or Lydia's for Wickham, they are not that different in their original nature. However, affection can develop in one of two directions. It can either degenerate into a totally asocial passion, focused on the object of affection to the exclusion of all other considerations, as with Lydia; or it can develop into a socially acceptable passion manifesting itself in an attitude of tolerance towards and consideration for other members of society, in fact, develop into true amiability, as it does with Darcy. This development is a socialization of affection and involves the subjection of this passion to social convention, to a set of principles determining to whom and on what grounds affection should be extended. 'Sympathy is not', as says one modern philosopher, 'a primitive animal feeling, but is an exercise of the imagination involving selfconsciousness and comparison',[2] i.e. it involves a sense of what one is, what is one's due, what others are, and what is their due. So affection becomes moral sympathy through a process of socialization, being subjected to such rules as in fact also constitute the basis of propriety.

Propriety, in its turn, is a social mechanism constituted by a set of conventions and principles of conduct to which behaviour should conform. Now the proper function of this mechanism is to restrain people's selfish impulses and desires and give one's behaviour a form acceptable to other members of society. It is at its best a mechanism serving the moral passion of benevolence. If the basis of affection on which this mechanism works is absent, then propriety degenerates into idle decorum. The link between principles of conduct and their moral source is then cut and one gets a Lady Catherine, a Miss Bingley or Mrs Hurst. Darcy is on his way down this slope when his affection for Elizabeth is aroused and changes the whole range of his attitudes and values. So propriety without amiability is empty, and amiability without propriety is asocial affection.

III

The problems which an attempt to appreciate *Pride and Prejudice* gives rise to can be focused by taking the title as a point of departure. The concept of pride is closely allied to the different senses of propriety. To propriety as idle decorum is correlated the sort of pride which has as its cognates 'arrogance', 'insolence', 'conceit': the Bingley sisters are 'proud and conceited' (p. 12). Just as idle decorum is the observance of rules of etiquette with no positive moral implications, arrogance and conceit are attitudes of superiority based on qualities of no relevance to the social and moral order. The Bingley sisters

> were rather handsome, had been educated in one of the first private seminaries in town, had a fortune of twenty thousand pounds, were in the habit of spending more than they ought, and of associating with people of rank; and were therefore in every respect entitled to think well of themselves, and meanly of others. (p. 12)

The Bingleys' money is idle; they have no estate with attendant obligations and responsibilities; they do not put their money to use in any other socially responsible way. Their pride is of rank and fortune unconnected to that social responsibility which should naturally be attached to wealth. There is, in *Pride and Prejudice*, a close connection between this type of improper pride and the neglect of one's social responsibilities. A full

[2] H.B. Acton, 'The Ethical Importance of Sympathy', *Philosophy* 30 (1955), p. 66.

acceptance of one's social obligations is only possible with a socially including attitude, while arrogance and conceit are socially disruptive and excluding. Lady Catherine, with the social responsibility and privileges of a large estate, fails her responsibilities and abuses her privileges, for example her method of settling the problems of her poor villagers, 'scold[ing] them into harmony and plenty' (p. 151), and her appointment of the nonsensical and obsequious Mr Collins to the living in her gift. Lady Catherine's attitude is excluding: 'Her air was not conciliating, nor was her manner of receiving them, such as to make her visitors forget their inferior rank' (p. 144). The effect of this arrogance is to create a splendid isolation which is lethal to the de Bourghs as a family. Lady Catherine's daughter is physically and spiritually a non-entity, 'pale and sickly; her features, though not plain, were insignificant; and she spoke very little, except in a low voice' (p. 145). There is nothing here to attract a lover; no warmth, affection, charm, intelligence, or sexual appeal, none of those fertilizing qualities which are necessary to ensure social continuity and renewal. The de Bourgh family is withering away.

Pride is, on the other hand, also given a positive meaning through an association with such concepts as 'responsibility' and 'respectability'. Proper pride involves a sense of responsibility, a sense of satisfaction in fulfilling the social obligations laid upon one by one's social position, together with a strong sense of what one's due is by virtue of this position and the way in which one fills it. Respect and deference are the expectation of those who have duties and perform them well. And respectability is the result of such social behaviour as one can rightly be proud of. This pride is a natural and necessary social attitude, a natural motive for beneficial social action:

> '[Pride] has often led him to be liberal and generous, to give his money freely, to display hospitality, to assist his tenants, and relieve the poor. Family pride, and *filial* pride, for he is very proud of what his father was, have done this. Not to appear to disgrace his family, to degenerate from the popular qualities, or lose the influence of the Pemberley House, is a powerful motive. He has also *brotherly* pride, which with *some* brotherly affection, makes him a very kind and careful guardian of his sister'. (pp. 72–3)

This kind of pride, attributed correctly to Darcy by Wickham in one of his cleverest moves to blacken Darcy's character, is not only compatible with amiability (which is what Wickham wants to deny). Amiability, as Elizabeth has to learn (being, as she is, deceived by Wickham's reasoning), constitutes a necessary ingredient of it. 'Indeed he has no improper pride', Elizabeth says in defence of Darcy when her father labels him 'a proud, unpleasant sort of man', for proper pride does not make a man unpleasant, 'He is perfectly amiable' (p. 335). Proper pride is a socially including attitude drawing society together.

And prejudice. 'Prejudice' is one of a family of terms which also have a distinctive Austenian flavour: 'reason', 'understanding', 'judgement', 'discernment', 'sense'; all concerned with man's intellectual capacities. 'Understanding' is not a part of the moral vocabulary of the novel, for a strong understanding is a morally neutral quality which can be employed destructively as by Mr Bennet in his ironic wit, for cold mercenary calculation as by Charlotte in capturing a husband, for evil deception and promotion of purely selfish aims as by Wickham. The notion of 'understanding' and its cognates are used to establish a different measuring rod applicable across ethical distinctions:

> Mr. Bennet was so odd a mixture of quick parts, sarcastic humour, reserve, and caprice, that the experience of three and twenty years had been insufficient to make his wife understand his character. *Her* mind was less difficult to develop. She was a woman of mean understanding, little information, and uncertain temper. (p. 3)

> [Elizabeth] with more quickness of observation and less pliancy of temper than her sister . . . (p. 12)

> In understanding Darcy was the superior. Bingley was by no means deficient, but Darcy was clever. (p. 13)

> Mr. Collins was not a sensible man, and the deficiency of nature had been but little assisted by education or society. (p. 61)

This scale along which characters are finely differentiated between the extremities of the silly and the clever, the nonsensical and the sensible, the stupid and the intelligent, is used as a basis for a further distinction which focuses the problem introduced by the difference in intellectual capacities between people:

> 'You begin to comprehend me, do you?' cried he, turning towards her.
> 'Oh! yes – I understand you perfectly.'
> 'I wish I might take this for a compliment; but to be so easily seen through I am afraid is pitiful.'
> 'That is as it happens. It does not necessarily follow that a deep, intricate character is more or less estimable than such a one as yours.' (p. 36)

Characters of strong understanding have motives and aims underlying their actions which it takes discernment and penetration to identify. A strong understanding makes for a complex character which presents to others a problem of judgement. Some of the major ironies of the novel are due to the difficulties that even characters of strong understanding have in penetrating the motives and aims of their clever fellow beings; e.g. Elizabeth's initial judgement of Darcy and Wickham together with her misjudgement of Charlotte; Darcy's misjudgement of Elizabeth (believing she is deliberately angling for him) and Jane (believing her indifferent to Bingley); Jane's wilful misjudgement of everybody as better than they are, complementing Elizabeth's wilful negative misjudgements; Bingley's lack of penetration allowing his sisters and Darcy to separate him from Jane.

Prejudice is contrasted with discernment. Discernment is the ability correctly to size up a character on the basis of his behaviour and background. Prejudice is the belief in one's own discernment regardless whether this has a sound basis or not. Prejudice, like improper pride, is socially disruptive. A society resting ultimately on the props of moral feeling (good will, amiability) and convention (propriety, good principles) requires the ability in at least some of its members to judge correctly the position and predicament of a person so as to be able to decide his responsibilities, duties, privileges and expectations. Only when this question is settled can moral feeling and moral evaluation become operative. Prejudice clouds the intellect thus blocking a fair appraisal of a person's duties and claims. The removal of prejudice, at least in those characters acting as the guardians of the social and moral order, is therefore a requirement essential for its survival.

IV

The reader is first confronted with Elizabeth occupied in trimming a hat, discussing with her sisters and mother the next ball. At the end of the book, a year later, she is the mistress of Pemberley, occupying the socially and morally most important position in this society. The novel covers the period of her growth from a girl to a woman, from the characteristic adolescent state of 'wilfully to misunderstand' everybody (p. 50), to a mature social being who has been taught to guide her judgements by social norms, who realizes the value of propriety and convention in regulating and promoting social intercourse, and who accepts the necessity of tolerance and understanding in a society of people with different abilities, interests, needs, and position.

The Bennet household is undisciplined:

' – Do your sisters play and sing?'
   'One of them does.'
   'Why did not you all learn? – You ought all to have learned. The Miss Webbs all play, and their father has not so good an income as yours. – Do you draw?'
   'No, not at all.'
   'What, none of you?'
   'Not one.'
   'That is very strange. But I suppose you had no opportunity. Your mother should have taken you to town every spring for the benefit of masters.'
   'My mother would have had no objection, but my father hates London.'
   'Has your governess left you?'
   'We never had any governess.'
   'No governess! How was that possible? Five daughters brought up at home without a governess! – I never heard of such a thing. Your mother must have been quite a slave to your education.'

Elizabeth could hardly help smiling, as she assured her that had not been the case.

'Then, who taught you? who attended to you? Without a governess you must have been neglected.'

'Compared with some families, I believe we were; but such of us as wished to learn, never wanted the means. We were always encouraged to read, and had all the masters that were necessary. Those who chose to be idle, certainly might.' (pp. 146–7).

This concern with formal education, embodied in the concept of 'the accomplished woman', recurs throughout the novel: in the discussion at Netherfield, in connection with Elizabeth's musical performance, in every mention of Miss Darcy before she appears. It is closely related to the notion of propriety and shares its ambiguity. Mrs Bennet's unrestrained ego-centric behaviour is of a piece with her lack of concern for her daughters' education. And with the Bennet sisters their lack of formal education reflects a general absence of discipline which also extends to more sub-stantial matters. Having been shocked into a clear perception of her family's weaknesses by Darcy's letter, Elizabeth reflects

In her own past behaviour, there was a constant source of vexation and regret; and in the unhappy defects of her family a subject of yet heavier chagrin. They were hopeless of remedy. Her father, contented with laughing at them, would never exert himself to restrain the wild giddi-ness of his youngest daughters; and her mother, with manners so far from right herself, was entirely insensible of the evil. (p. 189)

'In her own past behaviour': for while Kitty and Lydia suffer from the kind of moral indiscipline which leads to Lydia's elopement, Elizabeth herself has displayed indiscipline of an almost equally damaging kind. She has her father's wit and sense of irony, and also his tendency to make others the object of her wit rather than seeing them as fellow beings to be tolerated and lived with. Her attitude to people is wholly subjective: her judgements being based on her personal likes and dislikes, on how people, attitudes and actions appeal to her personally, she is unable to see a situation from what Hume called the point of view of the 'disinterested observer'; the necessary step for moral sympathy to come into play. When Charlotte represents to her how great the chance is that Bingley should remain unaware of Jane's regard for him, Elizabeth brusquely answers, 'If *I* can perceive her regard for him, he must be a simpleton indeed not to discover it too' (p. 18). When Jane informs her at the ball that Bingley will vouch for the 'good conduct, the probity and honour of his friend' she simply chooses to overlook his testimony: 'Mr. Bingley's defence of his friend was a very able one I dare say, but since he is unacquainted with several parts of the story, and has learnt the rest from that friend himself, I shall venture still to think of both gentlemen as I did before' (p. 86). By parity of reasoning, of course, she should equally distrust her own knowledge which is derived from Wickham and founded on nothing better than 'first impressions' of appearances: ' "To treat in such a manner, the godson, the friend, the favourite of his father!" – She could have added, "A young man too, like *you*, whose very countenance may vouch for your being amiable" ' (pp. 71–2). It is the essence of this uncritical attitude that it is dismissive of the claim of others to proper consideration and respect. On Charlotte's accepting Mr Collins offer of marriage Elizabeth finds it 'unaccountable! in every view unaccountable!' and she dismisses Jane's plea for Charlotte with a sharp retort: 'were I persuaded that Charlotte had any regard for him, I should only think worse of her understanding than I now do of her heart' (p. 121). This is an excluding attitude, anti-social in its rejection of people one cannot understand.

Elizabeth's socialization, her growth to a mature social being, takes place on these two levels: the subjection of taste to judgements based on objective social norms, and the reversal of her tendency to see people as objects for her wit rather than individuals to be tolerated and lived with. Darcy's letter is a model lesson on what is wrong with her judgement, giving a coherent and consistent interpretation of events which Elizabeth has seen merely as reinforcing her sympathies and antipathies, showing that the moral implications of these events are not those which Elizabeth wishes them to be. This lesson has an eye-opener effect; through its shock-like impact pieces of behaviour which Elizabeth has seen from her own egocentric viewpoint suddenly appear in their correct social and moral perspective:

> She perfectly remembered every thing that had passed in conversation between Wickham and herself, in their first evening at Mr. Philips's. Many of his expressions were still fresh in her memory. She was *now* struck with the impropriety of such communications to a stranger, and wondered it had escaped her before. She saw the indelicacy of putting himself forward as he had done, and the inconsistency of his professions with his conduct. (pp. 183–4)

> How differently did every thing now appear in which he was concerned! His attentions to Miss King were now the consequence of views solely and hatefully mercenary; and the mediocrity of her fortune proved no longer the moderation of his wishes, but his eagerness to grasp at anything. (p. 184)

At the same time she is forced to acknowledge the arbitrary way in which her opinions have been formed:

> Pleased with the preference of one, and offended by the neglect of the other, on the very beginning of our acquaintance, I have courted pre-possession and ignorance, and driven reason away, where either were concerned. Till this moment, I never knew myself. (p. 185)

After Darcy's letter she has to adjust her very perception of Wickham: 'She had even learnt to detect, in the very gentleness which had first delighted her, an affectation and a sameness to disgust and weary' (p. 206). And she makes an attempt at arguing her father into introducing some discipline into the Bennet household (pp. 204–5). She can no longer laugh at her sisters' silly behaviour. It is not an object of frivolous wit, it is a regrettable moral weakness (p. 203).

Having received, read, and assimilated Darcy's letter, Elizabeth's attitude to him is still one of dismissal:

> His attachment excited gratitude, his general character respect; but she could not approve him; nor could she for a moment repent her refusal, or feel the slightest inclination ever to see him again. (p. 189)

Then she goes with her uncle and aunt to see Pemberley and Darcy's character suddenly gains new depth and content. His social identity is established, an identity which reveals the inadequacy of judging him simply as 'the man who made himself agreeable no where' (p. 19). There he appears as the owner of Pemberley, 'the brother, the landlord, the master'. Pemberley itself is aesthetically expressive of the family's wealth, position and true gentility: 'She had never seen a place for which nature had done more, or where natural beauty had been so little counteracted by an awkward taste' (p. 215). Darcy's offer of marriage, she now comes to see, is not merely the offer of himself as an individual; it is the offer of a social role for her to fill; she will be the mistress of Pemberley: 'and at that moment she felt, that to be mistress of Pemberley might be something!'. (p. 215). Elizabeth's social and emotional development are tied together and are dependent on her corrected judgement. Her feelings for Darcy develop as she discovers his nature as a social being, and the recognition of Darcy's social identity is inextricably bound up with her discovery of the role she herself must play in this society, 'to be mistress of Pemberley might be something'. 'I believe,' says Elizabeth playfully to Jane about her love for Darcy, 'I must date it from my first seeing his beautiful grounds at Pemberley' (p. 332), and this, of course, is strictly true. One can feel correctly about an object only when one knows its characteristics and it is the confrontation with Pemberley which marks the decisive step in Elizabeth's revaluation of Darcy's character. Having seen Pemberley, which provides independent evidence that he is 'really amiable', Elizabeth is prepared to meet a reformed Darcy and recognize that his new-found civility is in character with his social identity. And as her new picture of Darcy develops, so do her feelings: 'She respected, she esteemed, she was grateful to him, she felt a real interest in his welfare' (p. 234). Lydia's elopement then puts in proper perspective the social propriety and moral rectitude which Darcy represents and Elizabeth can fully appreciate both his character and her altered feelings towards him,

> She began now to comprehend that he was exactly the man, who, in disposition and talents, would most suit her. His understanding and temper, though unlike her own, would have answered all her wishes. (p. 275)

For Elizabeth, Darcy starts out as an object for her dismissive and socially disruptive wit:

> 'It is such a spur to one's genius, such an opening for wit to have a dislike of that kind. One may be continually abusive without saying anything just; but one cannot be always laughing at a man without now and then stumbling on something witty.' (p. 199)

She ends by being involved with him in the deepest possible way, as an individual to be lived with, loved and respected. This movement from an isolating attitude to a tolerant and sympathetic one, is also reflected in her other relationships. Her sharp initial reaction to Charlotte's marriage and her reluctance to promise Charlotte a visit because she foresees 'little pleasure' in it (p. 130), mellow into an expectation of pleasure from seeing Charlotte again (p. 135) and, when she sees her at Hunsford, respect for the way in which Charlotte manages her husband and household (pp. 140–1, p. 150), renewed pleasure in her company (p. 151), and regret that she has to leave her to the society of Mr Collins (p. 192). Even her attitude to Wickham, who through his selfishness and moral depravity sets himself outside society, suffers a change, necessitated by circumstances, from her displeasure with him and desire never to see him again, to her acceptance of him as a brother: 'Come, Mr. Wickham, we are brother and sister, you know. Do not let us quarrel about the past. In future, I hope we shall be always of one mind' (p. 291). And it is Elizabeth who, at the end of the novel, encourages her husband to be reconciled to Lady Catherine.

VI

Simultaneous with the growth of Elizabeth is the development of Darcy. Though he is the owner of Pemberley he is not all that the owner of Pemberley ought to be. His father has been 'all that was benevolent and amiable' (p. 328), but the son, when the reader first meets him, is 'haughty, reserved, and fastidious, and his manners, though well bred, were not inviting' (p. 13). His attitude to people outside his immediate social circle is dismissive: at Meryton he 'had seen a collection of people in whom there was little beauty and no fashion, for none of whom he had felt the smallest interest, and from none received either attention or pleasure' (p. 13). Darcy's offensive manners and dismissive attitude are not merely superficial flaws but symptoms of a deepgoing moral weakness. His behaviour is in its essence anti-social.

If Georgiana should be protected against Wickham, so should any other 'young woman of character'. The responsibility for Wickham is inherited with the other responsibilities of Pemberley, and the realization that this is so, involves a recognition of a wider social framework on Darcy's part, a recognition that both he and Wickham have a place within this framework, and that it is his responsibility that Wickham is subjected to the norms and restraints of the framework. Social responsibilities and relationships become identified with personal ones.

Note

Editions used and cited in the text by page or line number are:

William Wordsworth and S.T. Coleridge, *Lyrical Ballads*, ed. R.L. Brett and A.R. Jones (London, Methuen, 1963, rvsd 1965). This prints the first texts of the editions of 1798 and 1800, together with Wordsworth's Preface of 1800 and the additions to the Preface of 1802; 'Michael', the final poem in the second volume of the 1800 edition, was subsequently revised and the text known to George Eliot different in detail but not in substance from that of 1800.

William Wordsworth, *Guide to the Lakes*, ed. Ernest de Sélincourt (Oxford and London, Oxford University Press, 1977). A reprint of de Sélincourt's 1906 edition of the Fifth Edition (1835).

Walter Scott, *The Black Dwarf* (London, Adam and Charles Black, 1896), standard ed., vol. V. First published 1816.

George Eliot, *Silas Marner*, ed. Q.D. Leavis, Penguin English Library (Harmondsworth, Middx, Penguin, 1967). First published 1861.

Criticism. The presence of Wordsworth in the nineteenth century has been often discussed though not yet satisfactorily synthesized. A good recent exploration is in Donald D. Stone, *The Romantic Impulse in Victorian Fiction* (Cambridge, Mass., and London, Harvard University Press, 1980); in particular ch. 5, 'Elizabeth Gaskell, Wordsworth, and the Burden of Reality', and ch. 6, 'George Eliot: the Romantic Legacy': Stone's notes to both chapters give useful suggestions for further reading. Jerome Thale, *The Novels of George Eliot* (New York, Columbia University Press, 1959) and U.C. Knoepflmacher, *George Eliot's Early Novels* (Berkeley, University of California Press, 1968) both discuss the relationship between Wordsworth and George Eliot; and the latter also has 'The Post-Romantic Imagination: *Adam Bede*, Wordsworth and Milton', *ELH* 34 (1967), 518–40. Rather general but not unsuggestive is John Speirs in *Poetry towards Novel* (London, Faber & Faber, 1971).

2

Statesman, Dwarf and Weaver: Wordsworth and Nineteenth-Century Narrative

Angus Easson

On 24 February 1861, as *Silas Marner* neared completion, George Eliot wrote to John Blackwood, her publisher, about his response to what he had seen so far: 'I don't wonder at your finding my story . . . rather sombre: indeed, I should not have believed that any one would have been interested in it but myself (since William Wordsworth is dead) if Mr. Lewes had not been so strongly arrested by it.' No doubt George Eliot had in mind the Wordsworth of *Lyrical Ballads* and of *The Excursion* (whether the story of Margaret or of the Solitary or of the various folk in Grasmere churchyard) and she emphasized the connection by her choice of an epigraph from 'Michael', which not only suggests the central role of the child but also, through Wordsworth's tragic pastoral, ways in which the story might be read. The presence of Wordsworth in nineteenth-century literature is a familiar enough idea, as is the vitality of that presence in the novel. Bayley has noted that it 'is arguable that the novelists rather than the poets of the nineteenth century are the real beneficiaries of the great Romantic endowment',[1] with no real sense that the argument would be contradicted, and George Eliot's *Adam Bede* makes the inheritance ironically explicit when Arthur Donnithorne (though enthusiastically endorsing the romance of 'The Ancient Mariner') dismisses most of *Lyrical Ballads* as 'twaddling stuff': Wordsworth's pathetic account in 'The Thorn' of the abandoned woman and dead child proves to be the emblematic concentration of Arthur's seduction of Hetty. *Silas Marner*'s epigraph ('A child, more than all other gifts/That earth can offer to declining man,/Brings hope with it, and forward looking thoughts')[2] stresses the Wordsworthian child of power, while the very nature of George Eliot's narrative, in which interior rather than exterior drama is crucial, has percolated from Wordsworth's generic and structural challenges to story-telling, whether in the sympathetic mockery of 'Simon Lee' ('and I'm afraid that you expect/Some tale will be related') and the comic frustrations of the

[1] John Bayley, *The Romantic Survival: a Study in Poetic Evolution* (London, Chatto and Windus, 1957), 1969 edition, p. 15.
[2] 'Michael', *Lyrical Ballads*, p. 231; Eliot quotes Wordsworth's later revision, her second line not appearing in 1800.

poet/narrator in 'The Idiot Boy' or in the shape and possibility of 'Michael', where the physical objects of the landscape, if interpreted aright, yield up a history:

> a straggling heap of stones!
> And to that place a story appertains
> . . . though it be ungarnish'd with events   (ll. 17–19)

Wordsworth did not, of course, effect this change in the novel single-handed. Nonetheless, I want to suggest, by a closer examination of two novels, the kinds of shifts that were undoubtedly taking place between the eighteenth- and nineteenth-century traditions and in which Wordsworth played a crucial mediating role. The connection between *Silas Marner: The Weaver of Raveloe* and Wordsworth's 'Michael' (his hero a 'statesman', one of those Lake District men who owned his own small parcel of land by which he maintained his family)[3] was made by George Eliot herself; the connection between *Silas Marner* and Walter Scott's *The Black Dwarf*, apart from an (apparently casual) brevity of form, lies in similarities of character and situation, even while their differences, the more marked for these surface likenesses, serve to illustrate what had happened in the novel between Scott and George Eliot. This is not simply a matter of dates, of course, since Scott, who published *The Black Dwarf* in 1816, had 'Michael' and the other *Lyrical Ballads* available to him. Rather, Scott represents, as is generally agreed, the culmination and the end of an eighteenth-century tradition of fiction (by no means the exclusive tradition), while George Eliot, only beginning her career in fiction in the 1850s, had worked out an aesthetic that took full advantage of the shifts in ideas about fiction in the earlier part of the century, so that from the first she wrote without the hesitations or influences that were the seedbed for her coevals Dickens and Thackeray twenty years before.

The shifts, none of them absolute, which I think it is commonly accepted took place between Victorian fiction and its predecessors, and which I want to exemplify by *Silas Marner* and *The Black Dwarf*, and to try to account for by the practice of a poem like 'Michael', are from the dramatic to the lyric in tone and technique; from the romantic to the realistic in plot and situation; and (more marginally) from the upper and middle classes to the common people for central characters and milieu. With the first, there is progress from a dominant plot structure, strongly influenced by the stage and its particular conventions, as the controlling organization of the work, to a stress upon feeling and the psychology of character, where, in Wordsworth's words, 'the feeling therein developed gives importance to the action and situation and not the action and situation to the feeling' (Preface, *Lyrical Ballads*, p. 248). With the second, what is likely or possible is stressed through 'incidents and situations from common life', even while the writer employs 'a certain

[3]Wordsworth, *Guide to the Lakes*, pp. 67–8.

colouring of imagination, whereby ordinary things should be presented to the mind in an unusual aspect' (Preface, 1802, *Lyrical Ballads*, p. 244). Clearly, in fictive terms, these three areas are interrelated; equally clearly I should emphasize that I am not denigrating the dramatic or the romantic as imaginative modes: Shakespeare, opera, and Scott himself provide supreme examples of the integration of both. Related to these fictive shifts was a new emphasis upon concerns such as Time and Childhood. While many Victorian narratives are retrospective and to some degree gain their 'colouring of imagination' through a nostalgic sense of the past, the slow passage of time is crucial to the process of interior change in terms both of psychological likelihood and temporal extensiveness: the alternatives in Victorian fiction are the temporal intensity of illness or else supernatural machinery, such as Dickens used respectively in *Martin Chuzzlewit* and *A Christmas Carol*. The handling of time allows for situations and characters that outwardly seem static and undramatic to be tackled. Time is vital in our response to 'Michael' or to *Silas Marner*: Michael's 60 years of pastoral activity, Marner's 15 years of isolation at the loom, are more than mere lapses of days, they are part of the men themselves and establish contexts in a way difficult to believe of the Dwarf, whose few months' sojourn on Mucklestane Moor (from Autumn 1706 to Spring 1707) gives no importance to where or how he lives. By rejecting the stage's tendency to compress time, writers could move from an often illusory freedom of physical action to the freedom of mental, emotional and spiritual action: a man could be totally bound by his class or his occupation, his struggle outwardly 'mere inconsistency and formlessness', yet still, as the Prelude to *Middlemarch* underlines, be revealed as a 'passionate ideal nature'. The Victorian novelists no longer needed to be afraid of reshaping narrative conceptions, even if they did not quite commit themselves to the 'eccentricity' of Wordsworth's narrative structure in 'Simon Lee' or 'Michael'. The way was found by abandoning the symmetry of mere plot and moving towards an 'organic' form through character development.

Credit might be claimed for the Gothic novel in psychological development and a stress on feeling, yet little of importance was done here that Wordsworth or other Romantics were not to do better. Even the Gothic response to scenery, as in Ann Radcliffe, is to landscape as painting, and the conventions of Gothic were familiar to Scott, who mocked their excesses through Dousterswivel in *The Antiquary*, even while prepared in the same novel to utilise their frisson so admirably in the Countess of Glenallan's nocturnal funeral (ch. 25). If Scott shows his 'Gothic' sensibility in the lowering sunset at the opening of ch. 6 or in the fresh morning at the beginning of ch. 7, yet the suggestion that the Dwarf might seem the demon of the coming storm stands as little more than a fancy gesture, the figure in the landscape that would provide the picture's title. Wordsworth enforced a new kind of response to nature: Greenhead Ghyll in 'Michael' provides 'an utter solitude' (l. 13), with 'rocks and stones, and kites' (l. 11), and the heap of stones is only given significance, as the poem goes on to reveal the meaning of the sheepfold, by its informing human history. There is no such meaning, either proposed by characters within the work or implanted by the author himself, in the Dwarf's cottage, remarkable though it is as a building feat, and object of superstition by its mysteriously rapid construction though it may be. Silas Marner at Raveloe is alienated: 'Nothing could be more unlike his native town, set within sight of the wide-spread hillsides, than this low, wooded region, where he felt hidden even from the heavens . . . There was nothing here, when he rose in the deep morning quiet and looked out on the dewy brambles and rank tufted grass, that seemed to have any relation with that life centring in Lantern Yard' (p. 63). If Silas 'felt', the feeling is scarcely a response to landscape; rather it is a response to an effect which has its origin in himself. The hills near his native town may remind him and us of those to which 'I will lift up mine eyes from whence cometh my strength', even while the bramble, though dewy, and the grass in its rankness, unnoticed by Marner, placed in the account by the author, hint at difficulty and sterility. Though at this moment the landscape enforces Marner's individual sense of loss and desolation, this place is to become a haven, Lantern Yard is to prove a false 'altar-place of high dispensations'. Their metamorphosis, though, is not through Silas's appreciation of landscape, which may demand a certain cultivation, of the kind the Black Dwarf, educated and wealthy, might have, but through the cultivation and response of the reader who has been taught to read such detail by the *Lyrical Ballads*. This move to the lyric and inward was attended with the thought that Wordsworth saw as the essential adjunct of the truism that 'all good poetry is the spontaneous overflow of powerful feelings' (Preface, *Lyrical Ballads*, p. 246), and in his thinking Wordsworth developed the structure and symbol which George Eliot recognized explicitly as an inheritance.

The Black Dwarf, published in 1816, the first within the fictional frame of the *Tales of My Landlord*, is a work of considerable power – despite the various strictures upon it, including those of Scott himself and of the 'friendly critic' of Scott's 1830 Preface which determined Scott to huddle to a conclusion in half the story's projected length: the handling of the humorous but never foolish Hobbie Elliot; the linking of the Jacobite conspiracy to the personal violence of the border robber Westburnflat; Isabella Vere's appeal for aid to the Dwarf, are all finely done. As the title insists, the Dwarf himself is in some way crucial to the whole. In Scott's own Preface (to which I shall return) he is termed, stressing his active importance, an 'agent' in the story, and an 'ideal being' in the sense of a fictional creation based on a 'real' prototype. The Black Dwarf, otherwise Elshender the Recluse or Canny Elshie or the Wise Wight, proves in the event to be the landowner Sir Edmund Mauley, linked by his past to both Vere of Ellieslaw, father of Isabella, and to Earnscliff, Isabella's eventual husband. The Dwarf's initial and apparently central role in the tale is that of misanthrope. He appears, without apparent antecedents, on Mucklestane Moor and sets about building a house from the stones scattered there (being assisted in labour and in materials by Hobbie Elliot, Earnscliff, and others). Believed by the superstitious locals to have more than natural powers, he performs cures, but only, it seems, as a reinforcement of his misanthropy, since he claims these apparent acts of good are productive of greater evil: Westburnflat's restoration means the robber can destroy Hobbie Elliot's house and carry off not only property but also Grace Armstrong, Hobbie's bride-to-be. Yet if the Dwarf seems bent on mischief, his misanthropy is also curiously tempered: having been instrumental in Grace Armstrong's kidnapping, he voluntarily secures her safe release; gives Hobbie Elliot gold in compensation of his material losses; and prevents Isabella Vere from contracting a marriage against her will. Isabella's visit to the Dwarf to beg his help is a scene of great power, melodramatic yet highly effective in context, and part of Scott's typical cumulative dramatic force. There is a real sense of moral crisis here, since we know, though it is knowledge we may have scarcely digested, that Isabella is the daughter of the Dwarf's betrothed who married his supposedly true friend, Ellieslaw. All is explained: the Dwarf's mystery is tied to his betrayal by Ellieslaw and to his sense of guilt for an act of manslaughter (the victim being Earnscliff's father). At the end, by the power of money and the claims of the past, the Dwarf can intervene at the very altar to prevent Isabella's forced marriage before he retires from the world, his part in the action done, his whereabouts known only to the faithful steward Ratcliffe. In the chapel scene the stage sense of catastrophe and revelation, with all the characters gathered, is predominant, and the plot sense, with all ends tied up, however contrived and final, is paramount.

Scott was habituated to the dramatic in narrative: a novel like *Ivanhoe*, diffuse though its elements and temporal span may seem to make it, is essentially a three-act dramatic comedy, of The Tournament, The Siege, and The Rescue of Rebecca. In *The Black Dwarf* this dramatic aspect is superficially underlined by 10 epigraphs (out of 18) being from plays; more significant is the dramatic clue in the epigraph which heads the fourth chapter, in which the Dwarf's appearance, the building of his shelter, and his behaviour are detailed. It comes from Shakespeare's *Timon of Athens*:

> I am Misanthropos, and hate mankind;
> For thy part, I do wish thou wert a dog,
> That I might love thee something. (ch. 4, p. 21)

Timon is the key to Elshie's character and behaviour, his outward deformity (not, of course, shared by Timon) apparently reflecting his inward deformity, though Scott is also at pains to make clear both self-loathing and something unbalanced in the Dwarf, who became, as Ratcliffe suggests, 'the most ingenious self-tormentor' (p. 112), mistaking the scoff and sneer and laughter (though of the rabble and the brutal vulgar and the common people) for the 'true sense which the world entertained of him' (p. 113) – evidence one might be forgiven for feeling had some force in it. Like Timon, he scorns the courtesies of the world. Hobbie suggests that at least thanks might be a return for his labour at building the

Dwarf's cottage: ' "Thanks!" exclaimed the Dwarf, with a motion expressive of the utmost contempt. "There, take them and fatten upon them! Take them, and may they thrive with you as they have done with me, as they have done with every mortal worm that ever heard the word spoken by his fellow reptile! Hence; either labour or begone!" ' (p. 24) His retirement, his expressed contempt for men and the conventionally valued powers of mind and feeling, his concern to do the world good to produce more evil, are all in Timon's vein. Westburnflat is surely worked up from the hint of Shakespeare's three Bandits to whom Timon gives gold providing they punish mankind (unlike them, Westburnflat is not near persuaded, by Elshie's conduct, from his occupation), while Hubert Ratcliffe parallels Timon's faithful Steward, so that it is not only upon character and situation but also upon action that Scott models himself. And as with Timon's retreat, one notices how quickly Elshie's desolate place becomes a place of traffic, though at least Scott has, arguably, reason in the Dwarf's choice of place, since Mauley wishes to see the monument to his betrothed raised at his instigation in Ellieslaw's house, though it then becomes part of the plot's unlikeliness that Ellieslaw, despite Elshie's notoriety in the neighbourhood, the open presence of Ratcliffe in his household, and the raising of the monument, has, until the chapel scene, assumed Mauley to be dead and indeed has no previous knowledge of the Black Dwarf, who dwelt so close at hand.

Scott's use of Shakespeare's Timon raises questions of identity. Scott might seem not to be accepting the logic of his own creation. Is Elshie the complete misanthropist? Or is he mad, driven insane by his own deformity and the world's mockery, compounded with society's injustice? As a Timon-figure, he should have no grace for anyone, though his soliloquies do suggest, even as they hint at his past and of the motives of his behaviour, that he inwardly struggles to subdue a nature both better and more truly himself. Ratcliffe insists that the Dwarf, though 'disordered', is not mad in his 'common state of mind', which is 'irregular, but not deranged', and claims that Elshie only with great ingenuity can reconcile 'to his abstract principles of misanthropy a conduct which flows from his natural generosity and kindness of feeling' (pp. 114–15). His misanthropy and madness spring, then, from an unnatural suppression of his true nature; his generous acts (the rose and promise given to Isabella that she redeems; the release of Grace Armstrong; the gold given to Hobbie) arise from that same nature's humanity and sanity. Yet if this explains the seeming inconsistencies in this misanthrope (whose misanthropy is better established in the early chapters than his conduct is explained in the late and compressed narrative of Ratcliffe), the issue stands of the Dwarf's role as agent. What need is there for the Dwarf? His centrality is stressed alike by the novel's title and by his prominence in the story. We might of course view the work in terms of Harry E. Shaw's classification of novels like *Quentin Durward* as 'disjunctive',[4] where, though the hero's action 'is the organising principle

[4]Harry E. Shaw, *The Forms of Historical Fiction: Sir Walter Scott and His Successors* (Ithaca and London, Cornell University Press, 1983), ch. 4 and in particular pp. 155–9.

for the novel, it leads to but does not embody the novel's historical meaning and effect' (p. 155). *The Black Dwarf* shows, typically of Scott, turning-points: Hobbie, longing for adventure though essentially law-abiding, is the figure of the settled Whig future as against the reiver West-burnflat, the last of the Border raiders, and whom, indeed, Scott acknowledges in a note (p. 364) to be an anachronism by 40 or 50 years; while a shift in politics consolidated by the 1707 Act of Union, though minor compared to the out-turn of the Young Pretender's rebellion in *Waverley*, occurs when the very real possibility of a successful Jacobite uprising is let slip. The two elements of community and politics are interconnected, since Hobbie is the more strongly impelled to defeat the political rebellion because of Ellieslaw's involvement in the apparent free-booting attack on Hobbie's house, itself encouraged by Westburnflat's abettors because Hobbie, being a loyal Whig, was not prepared to give up his weapons and so constituted a threat to the Jacobite enterprise. These threads, in which the Dwarf has no concern, for he is neither part of this community nor involved with politics, are yet interwoven with the Dwarf's actions, whether the cure of Westburnfleet; the release of Grace Armstrong; or the defeat of the uprising as part of Isabella's rescue, from a marriage itself designed to secure Sir Frederick Langley's political commitment. Further, Scott's control of these threads and his intermingling of them, so that they become interdependent is masterly. (Does Hobbie help suppress the uprising because of personal grievance or because of attachment to the Dwarf or because of his Whig politics? The answer is, all three.) Yet the question must again be asked: why the Dwarf? He is, as Scott intended, an agent as the story goes, but is it necessary he be a dwarf? Or is he necessary to the story at all? The final crisis of the chapel scene lacking Elshie would not be so effective, with its contrast of the living dwarf and the dead woman's monument (its statue in turn reflected in the living beauty of Isabella), but clearly other catastrophes might have been devised. True, his past history means there is some suspense as to whether Elshie will indeed fulfil his promise of help. Again, the physical sense of the Dwarf emphasizes the stage and clearly only such a creature would feel as he does and would have chosen to dwell in this particular place. Yet to stress the Dwarf's motives raises the question of whether the main actions in his past, the act of manslaughter when defending his friend and the betrayal by his friend and betrothed when suffering the penalty of that defence, require him to be a dwarf. Scott's conception of the Dwarf in stage terms, of the external, the physical, the rhetorical, is enforced by Elshie's exit speech:

'I thought,' he said, 'that tears and I had done; but we shed them at our birth and their spring dries not until we are in our graves. But no melting of the heart shall dissolve my resolution. I part here, at once and for ever, with all of which the memory (looking at the tomb) or the presence (he pressed Isabella's hand) is dear to me. Speak not to me! attempt not to thwart my determination! it will avail nothing; you will hear of and see this lump of deformity no more. To you I shall be dead ere I am actually in my grave, and you will think of me as of a friend disencumbered from the toils and crimes of existence.' (p. 128)

Scott's dramatic mode insists that events control character: the Dwarf is agent and is removed, essentially unchanged except for the revelation of his true social status. There is a potential in the prototype, even in Scott's conception of the Dwarf, which is not seized upon, whereas George Eliot can make a not dissimilar character central to her narrative and make him someone whose development and growth is part and parcel of the seriousness of theme and aesthetic conception.

To read *Silas Marner* in close proximity to *The Black Dwarf* emphasizes obvious similarities. Silas is ugly, his physical appearance frightening the boys who peer through his cottage window; he is isolated, living away from the main settlement of Raveloe; and for a time he performs cures. There is like conformation too in the plots, the triangle and betrayed loyalties of Silas, William Dane, and Sarah matching, without the extremity of manslaughter or imprisonment, the love betrayed of the Dwarf, Ellieslaw, and the betrothed. These likenesses, though, are more apparent than real and by superficial comparison help to point up what has happened, over 40 years, to the possibility of the novel. Scott's 1830 Preface, with its account of David Ritchie, the Dwarf's prototype, the 'real' from which the 'ideal being' of Elshie was derived, highlights the differences between the two stories as well as the narrative problems Scott was not able to cope with or else not prepared to challenge.

The Preface tells of Ritchie, the Dwarf's original, the son of a slate-quarry labourer, who was trained as a brushmaker. The physical likeness of Ritchie is reproduced in the Dwarf, along with details of character, he being of a 'jealous, misanthropical, and irritable temper' (p. xx), though in the Dwarf these are romanticized by his class and history. Scott also refers to Ritchie's interest in gardening, devotion to the beauties of nature, and his emotional response to the idea of a future state. Knowing what the nineteenth-century novel could do, we might well feel a sense of excitement at the potential of David Ritchie and of disappointment when we realize how Scott has virtually ignored it. There is a problem in handling passive characters and like Timon in the wilderness, Ritchie offers essentially a static figure. Yet narrative lies not just in physical action and George Eliot's depiction of Silas, also in many respects passive, proves how even with passivity there can be crisis, as in the drawing of lots in Lantern Yard, or event, as in the broken water pot. Scott's shift from Ritchie, the brushmaker, to Sir Edward Mauley, the deformed yet rich gentleman, is indicative of his need to transform his materials to a romantic level (in a largely pejorative sense: not here Wordsworth's 'a certain colouring of imagination') and his failure to realize the *donée*'s potential. Partly the treatment stems from Scott's idea of what may constitute the central as opposed to a subordinate character, though it stems also from neither having a model of how to set about realizing that potential other than through conventions of the stage and earlier fiction nor the wish to break with those conventions. The brushmaker had not, for Scott, been realized as the central figure of a serious action: for George Eliot the weaver had, through figures like Wordsworth's statesman Michael. Elshie is given the freedom of action and the power of a gentleman and yet this seems at odds with the vividly established misanthrope of the opening. From plot hints thrown out in Elshie's speeches, it is clear that Scott did not establish the Dwarf and then, having run into an impasse with a static character, tack on the plot. Still, the narrative seems huddled and overweighted by the later revelations, and even if the novel had run its full intended course, it is difficult to believe the effect would have been essentially different. Rather as with *Oliver Twist*, the power of Scott's tale does not lie in the unravelling of plot mysteries. Elshie's character and situation initially impress and their dark suggestiveness seems dissipated by the flummery of Sir Edward Mauley. Even at the plot level, Scott has not fully utilized the example of Shakespeare, as George Eliot may be thought to have done. Eliot early reveals Silas's origins and Godfrey's marriage, so that the reader, like the Shakespearean audience, watches process in the light of knowledge. In Scott everything is tied in, and yet there is no real explanation or exploration of the Dwarf. Although in *Silas Marner* we never learn what happened to William Dane and even Lantern Yard has disappeared,[5] that disappearance is not part of a mystery, however it may puzzle Marner, for by a force given in the narrative and in the commentary, this lost physical place is apprehended as belonging to a life that is no longer significant for Silas: Lantern Yard, while ceasing to be physical reality, yet remains a symbol.

Wordsworth knew that there may be found a 'tale in every thing'; including (indeed, especially) in a David Ritchie; even if the course of that narrative may not necessarily be as we expect it. Simon Lee is a grotesque, with his swollen ankles and little body half awry, but he is to be accepted as the tale itself, not as the prelude to some kind of gratuitous excitement. The anecdote of severing the root is seemingly trivial, yet in the complexity of outcome – the narrator's embarrassed recognition of Simon Lee's impotence, the sense of tears in the nature of things – thought can bring significance. 'Michael', we are assured, is a story 'ungarnish'd with events'. Its narrative structure might seem to turn upon and culminate in the sending of Luke to the city and his failure there. It is an event carefully prepared for: yet how briefly, even summarily, his career in the city is treated, so that we are turned back upon Michael and the meaning of that failure for Michael. In *Silas Marner*, the weaver's 'return to life' depends upon an interrelationship between his whole life and events and feeling. Objects, in a characteristically Wordsworthian way, become informed with human significance, from the nature of their use, as with the familiar example of Silas's earthenware pot (p. 69). When Scott finally admits us into the Dwarf's cottage (ch. 16), what significance do the objects in it

---

[5] It is, presumably, only a coincidence, though an intriguing one, that it is from a brushmaker that Marner asks for Lantern Yard (p. 240).

have? 'Wooden shelves, which bore a few books, some bundles of dried herbs, and one or two wooden cups and platters, were on one side of the fire; on the other were placed some ordinary tools of field-labour, mingled with those used by mechanics' (p. 117). The details are realistic, but what tale do they tell? What books? What is the life lived here? Compare the significant detail of Michael's life as shepherd and of his household. The sheep, the storms, the household routine are part of a realism, but one which underpins the meaning of being a statesman in the Lakes and of the marginal yet close-knit existence that Michael's commitment to his land preserves and Luke's failure will destroy, a realism moving into symbol that finds its clearest and fully explicit meaning in the sheepfold. The same careful detailing of Silas's life also chronicles a process of change: 'Strangely Marner's face and figure shrank and bent themselves into a constant mechanical relation to the objects of his life, so that he produced the same sort of impression as a handle or a crooked tube, which has no meaning standing apart' (p. 68). Yet Eliot also makes clear, in the broken pot, that there can be a relationship with objects beyond their utility. In *The Black Dwarf*, the rose Elshie gives Isabella is a token, perhaps an allusion also to her beauty (and to her dead mother's), but as it functions in the plot, a button or a ring or a glove or a weed would have served as well. The rose has no significant necessity; even its perishable quality is irrelevant, since the Dwarf will respond to a single petal, however faded. For Michael and for Silas Marner, whether consciously (Michael rather than the narrator talks of covenants at the sheepfold) or unconsciously, things have qualities and are extensions of their personalities. Michael's land provides him with his livelihood, yet he is tied to the property beyond its cash value. He has put himself into it and holds it in trust. And that extension of self, which trust makes unegotistical, is confirmed by time, as with the statesmen Wordsworth describes in *The Guide to the Lakes*, who had 'a consciousness that the land, which they walked over and tilled, had for more than five hundred years been possessed by men of their name and blood' (p. 68). Michael too has that consciousness which is bound up with the poem's crisis and its meaning:

> if these fields of our
> Should pass into a Stranger's hands, I think
> That I could not lie quiet in my grave. (ll. 240–2)

The significant narrative use of time can be highlighted by a conjectural calculation, which Wordsworth does not make explicit, of time spans in 'Michael'. Wordsworth as narrator heard the story 'while I was yet a boy' (l. 27); since Michael dies aged 91, his birth can be dated about 1670–80, and his parents would be born about 1630–40, his grandparents in the sixteenth century, each generation holding the land for the next. This span, underlying the poem, gives Michael his place in the natural scheme, like rocks or fields, as Marner is established in his 30 years at Raveloe, with his long withering and gradual return to life, and as the Dwarf in six months, merely the temporal span in which the action is played out, cannot be, whatever Sir Edward Mauley's past associations with the Veres. In narrative, this dedication of Michael and of Marner serves to enforce symbolic values; the sheepfold is a centre of Michael's land, its incompletion a witness of Michael's desolation. Even money, though no equivalent to the land for Michael or to Eppie for Marner, is treated significantly and significantly differently by Scott on the one hand and by Wordsworth and George Eliot on the other. For Scott, money is a plot manipulator, without raising issues of source or value: Grace Armstrong is freed by the Dwarf's gold; Hobbie is recompensed, with no sign of difficulty, by a bag of gold; Vere is defeated by the power of Elshie's gold, and its power is taken for granted. For Michael, the security called in provokes a crisis in which the sum has little importance except as it focuses on the value of land and of child. Either way, the decision is hard, though Michael prefers to risk Luke, since the son may redeem the land: the land, once gone, never could be redeemed. Yet Michael recognizes that his choice may mean, as it does, losing son and land both. With Marner, the money is a symptom of his withered humanity and also marks, very obviously, the transition from his old to new life, both in the community's response to him in his loss and famously when Marner, believing his gold has returned, 'stretched forth his hand; but instead of hard coin with the familiar resisting outline, his fingers encountered soft warm curls' (p. 167). The gold has gone and the child has come.

The child, evoked by the Romantics as a creature of power and transformed by the Victorians into a creature of emotions, was used by both as a test. The child's importance in Romanticism is rightly a commonplace, and George Eliot's epigraph enforces her inheritance. This commonplace may be given new force when we note Scott's unresponsiveness to its possibilities. Wordsworth's Michael is given, in old age, the child that offers new life and continuity; Silas is given Eppie; but Elshie's 'child' is Isabella, a young woman, and her influence on Elshie, though significant for the plot, hardly changes his life. *Silas Marner* has plot in the ordinary sense: Godfrey's marriage and Dunsey's theft; the eventual discovery of the thief and the claim on the child; all skilfully handled. Yet this action, instead of being the dominant interest, feeds into the novel's central emotional and moral courses of Marner's restoration, while the narrative crisis lies in Eppie's decision to stay with her true rather than go to her biological father, a decision that links back into all that Silas is. Eppie refuses to be a lady (p. 230), where Scott, one conjectures, would be inclined to see the recognition as Eppie's 'reward' and her elevation to quality as the correct fictional decision.

The crises in Marner's life, as in Michael's, are clearly marked and are tied in to character, time, property, and a child. What is the moral crisis for Scott? Chiefly, Elshie's decision to aid Isabella. Yet Scott has pre-empted much of the interest by the Dwarf's earlier promise to do so, come what may, while the motives for Elshie to renege on that promise are scarcely digested by the reader, from Ratcliffe's narration, before the interview takes place. Wordsworth's narrative pacing, the elaborated establishment of Michael's way of life, the detailed accounts of Luke's birth and child-hood, the lengthy accounts of family and the stress on sheepfolds and covenants, may seem oddly proportioned, yet the crisis, centred not in Luke's loss but in Michael's response, has been prepared for:

> There is a comfort in the strength of love;
> 'Twill make a thing endurable, which else
> Would break the heart:–Old Michael found it so. (ll. 457–9)

Scott's failure is partly a matter of narrative distribution, of the points at which information is given, but it is also a failure in analysis and in close detailing of process. Although the Dwarf's veiled references to the past show Scott well aware of the plot's structure from the beginning, Scott, like George Eliot, has chosen a potentially static character, whose isolation seems to preclude the activity of encounter and conflict. Eliot knows of ways to articulate this character, where Scott could only rely upon reve-lation, artificial connectedness, and extremes of romantic passion. Eliot finds (a common enough observation, but one to re-emphasize here) the inner growth of a humble character, infused with all her conviction of the spiritually organic, which itself feeds from the Romantic poetic of organic form. It is useful to ask why *The Black Dwarf* is so short. Scott says he intended it to be twice the length, its hasty termination being his response to the 'friendly critic' (p. xxiv) who found the idea of the Solitary too revolting and more likely to disgust than to interest the reader, allowing Scott to joke at the end of his Preface, with an abuse of metaphor that still surfaces in critical writings, that he has 'perhaps produced a narrative as much disproportioned and distorted as the Black Dwarf who is its subject' (p. xxiv). That 'friendly critic' and Scott himself responded with the expectations of an older sensibility. By the time the novel appeared, Scott's conventions in narrative, fictional character, and milieu had all been challenged and that challenge was absorbed by the Victorians. The challenge had come not exclusively but crucially in Wordsworth: in 'Simon Lee'; in 'The Idiot Boy'; in 'The Thorn'; and, most clearly for *Silas Marner*, in 'Michael'.

Let me try to pull together Wordsworth's part in the differences I have been tracing. Wordsworth made the ordinary a central and serious subject for fictional narrative. In the Preface to *Lyrical Ballads*, Wordsworth, as well as stressing common life, linked feelings and ideas, so that he might investigate 'the fluxes and refluxes of the mind when agitated by the great and simple affections of our nature' (p. 247). It is not that Scott *can't* handle ordinary people: famously, he can, as in Mucklebackit's response to Jonathan Oldbuck on the day of Steenie's burial (*The Antiquary*, ch. 34). But Wordsworth shifts the ordinary from the periphery, dignifies it without romanticizing, and establishes a new idea of heroism.

And together with this new milieu, Wordsworth shows a new way to conduct narrative. If the events, the outcome, the meaning of 'Michael' depend upon Luke's actions and Luke's fate, then what Luke does is summarily treated indeed. Five and a half lines dispose of the youth from the beginning of his dissipation to its end:

> Meantime Luke began
> To slacken in his duty, and at length
> He in the dissolute city gave himself
> To evil courses: ignominy and shame
> Fell on him, so that he was driven at last
> To seek a hiding-place beyond the seas. (ll. 451–6)

Is this (and Luke's disappearance, so far as any direct mention goes) the culmination of 450 lines? Even preparation for Luke's departure has dealt rather with his parents' and above all with his father's feelings for the son and for the land. The tale is not of Luke's adventures, but of love of person and place. Luke is most important not as prodigal or failure, but as a child, the late born and long hoped for, seemingly God-given son (the parallels with Abraham and Isaac are clear). In the lines that George Eliot uses for her epigraph, we are reminded that:

> a child, more than all other gifts
> That earth can offer to declining man
> Brings hope with it, and forward-looking thoughts,

though her omission of the next two lines:

> And stirrings of inquietude, when they
> By tendency of nature needs must fail

serves to underline her transformation as well as her uses of Wordsworth. In Luke's upbringing, Wordsworth depicts a toughness, harshness even, as when the boy is reproved for failing in tasks beyond his powers, whereas George Eliot's account is softer, within the context of comedy. But the shape and proportion of Wordsworth's narrative; the stress upon feeling; the shift to realism in social realization, even while the detail (of the spinning wheels, the lamp, the sheepfold) is so much more than merely realistic, since it serves to establish a world of values, covenants, connections in a landscape involved with feeling – these provide, not simply a tale to give cultivated persons the pleasurable sensations that might be derived from 'Rope-dancing, or Frontiniac or Sherry' (Preface, *Lyrical Ballads*, p. 257), but a serious presentation of a man and his passions integrated in place and time. These features help stress, juxtaposed with George Eliot's achievement in *Silas Marner*, the importance of Wordsworth not only in Romantic poetry, but also in nineteenth-century narrative. Without decrying Scott or saying George Eliot could not otherwise have been a great writer, I think it fair to claim that *Silas Marner* could not have been written, certainly not written as it is, without Wordsworth, nor indeed could so much else in Victorian fiction.

Note

Emily Brontë (1818–48) was born at Thornton in Yorkshire, the fourth daughter in a family of five daughters and one son. Three of the daughters, Charlotte, Emily, and Anne, became well-known novelists. Their father, Patrick Brontë, was an Irish clergyman whose wife died in 1821, leaving the six children motherless. In 1825, the two older girls died from illness contracted at Cowan Bridge School, and the remaining four children drew closer together, creating an enormous cycle of stories and poems centred around the imaginary countries of Gondal and Angria. These stories greatly influenced the themes and characters in *Wuthering Heights*.

Though Emily Brontë spent six months as a governess in 1836 and later in 1842 travelled to Brussels with her sister Charlotte, she was basically a recluse and profoundly unhappy away from the moors and the family home at Haworth. She died in 1848 at the age of thirty.

Wuthering Heights, originally published under the pseudonym Ellis Bell, received mostly negative commentary when it first appeared in 1848. Critics were repelled by its passionate intensity and unorthodox morality, though most acknowledged the novel's power and originality. Today *Wuthering Heights* is recognized as one of the great works of nineteenth-century fiction.

The following is a selection of the main books used for this article:

Emily Brontë, *Wuthering Heights* (New York, W.W. Norton, 1963). This Norton Critical Edition includes contemporary reviews and an excellent selection of essays on the novel.

Emily Brontë, *The Complete Poems of Emily Jane Brontë*. ed. C.W. Hatfield (New York, Columbia University Press, 1941).

Stevie Davies, *Emily Brontë: the Artist as a Free Woman* (Manchester, Carcanet Press, 1983), an original and perceptive interpretation of Brontë and her work.

Elizabeth Th. M. Van Laar, *The Inner Structure of Wuthering Heights: Study of an Imaginary Field* (Paris, Mouton, 1969), a detailed analysis of the novel's imagery, including the four elements, weather, dreams, windows, and the Bible.

Winifred Gérin, *Emily Brontë: a Biography* (Oxford, Clarendon Press, 1971).

3

'This Shattered Prison': Versions of Eden in *Wuthering Heights*

Marjorie Burns

Images of Eden, that enclosed and favoured realm, appear throughout the novel *Wuthering Heights* in recurring patterns of innocence and unity, seduction and fall. Yet Eden itself is not mentioned directly. We have instead incidents that imitate the Eden story (though always in ways that challenge traditional accounts) and frequent references to paradise, purgatory, heaven, and hell – parallel realms associated with Eden and, like it, representative of bliss or despair, harmony or disruption.

Although Thrushcross Grange, with its walled park and cultivated fruit trees (most notably the apple tree traditionally associated with the Fall) is an easy parallel to Eden, the rough and pandemonic Heights also has its Edenic side. Only here can the bonding of Catherine and Heathcliff flourish, a bonding which is destroyed when the Grange and its mannered society come in touch with their energetic and idiosyncratic world. This does not mean, however, that we should read *Wuthering Heights* as a simple reversal, as a variation on Blake's *The Marriage of Heaven and Hell* with its idealized devils and its dissatisfying angels. Though there is clearly something of an inversion in Emily Brontë's depiction of these two households (the violent has its loyalty and innocence, the peaceful its imperfections and falsity), the entrance of Edgar into the Heights is no less disruptive than Heathcliff's entrance into the Grange. Both men serve as tempters in each other's realm, Edgar with an offer of order and civility that has no place in the restless world of Wuthering Heights and Heathcliff (more clearly a serpent figure) with unhampered energy and vengeful intent, scaling the walls of the Linton Park.

The first clear parallel to the Eden story occurs at Thrushcross Grange. This is a world that suggests peace, civilization, and adherence to established order. Tea is taken in the parlour; books are perused at leisure; servants, attentive but somewhat vaguely depicted, move in the background. There is an innocence of labour here for the ruling Lintons, not even the 'pleasant labour' of Milton's Garden of Eden. Work is carried out – trimming and planting and maintenance – but removed from sight. It is a domesticated, easeful world of ponies and lapdogs, a world named for the thrush.

We first see Thrushcross Grange from the outside, through one of Emily Brontë's recurrent windows, and it seems a haven. The children, Catherine and Heathcliff, on their night-time escape, their 'ramble at liberty', creep like two dark, wild forces 'through a broken hedge', grope their way up the path, perch on the basement, and peer into the house through the window that divides them from the Lintons.

> Ah! it was beautiful – a splendid place carpeted with crimson, and crimson-covered chairs and tables, and a pure white ceiling bordered by gold, a shower of glass-drops hanging in silver chains from the centre, and shimmering with little soft tapers. Old Mr and Mrs Linton were not there. Edgar and his sister had it entirely to themselves; shouldn't they have been happy? We should have thought ourselves in heaven! (ch. 6)

Heaven, indeed, to two berated, unloved scamps! And yet our appreciation, though drawn to the warmth and light, remains with the world that Catherine and Heathcliff have travelled through, that essence of the Heights and the moors that they carry with them, for there is pettiness in paradise, and discontent. Edgar and Isabella, the inhabitants of this Eden, are less than ideally represented. 'And now, guess what your good children were doing?' says Heathcliff. 'Isabella . . . lay screaming at the farther end of the room, shrieking as if witches were running red hot needles into her'. Edgar stood by the hearth 'weeping silently' and on a table sat yelping a little dog which 'they had nearly pulled in two between them'.

Envy and admiration for the world of the Grange fades. We see that Isabella and Edgar, the 'petted things', are pets themselves, domesticated, pampered, and soft as puppies, pale creatures who ride to church in the family carriage, 'smothered in cloaks and furs' (ch. 7). 'When would you catch me wishing to have what Catherine wanted?' says Heathcliff, 'or find us by ourselves, seeking entertainment in yelling, and sobbing, and rolling on the ground, divided by the whole room? I'd not exchange, for a thousand lives, my condition here for Edgar Linton's at Thrushcross Grange' (ch. 6).

And yet, in a sense, this is exactly what Heathcliff will later attempt to do, for from this first confrontation comes further contact and increased and troubling interaction between the two households. Just as familiarity with the Lintons will irrevocably and unhappily alter Catherine and Heathcliff's future, bringing class consciousness and worldly values into their lives, so too will their entrance into the Grange's luxurious and sheltered world ultimately lead to the collapse of Linton privilege and Linton complacency.

Though the final effects of Grange and Heights affiliation is reciprocally destructive, the first invasion unquestionably comes from Catherine and Heathcliff. It is their action that sets the disruptive series of events into motion. Edgar, when he comes to visit Wuthering Heights, will do so by invitation, by employing all the proper methods of society, and he'll visit by day. But Catherine and Heathcliff are trespassers. They invade by night, uninvited and intent on mischief, and the world they invade is clearly suggestive of paradise.

In context of the Eden story, are we expected, then, to see Catherine and Heathcliff as Satan figures? The answer, like most answers about *Wuthering Heights*, is a somewhat complicated yes and no – yes, in that they have entered the sanctum of the Grange, broken through the barrier hedge, and disturbed the stale air of that world (and disturbed it in ways that will have increasingly unpleasant repercussions). We can carry the analogy further, keeping in mind *Paradise Lost*, which, Winifred Gérin tells us, was a great favourite of Emily Brontë's father, Patrick Brontë. The night 'ramble at liberty', which brings them for the first time to Thrush-cross Grange, comes after a description of Mr Earnshaw's death and Hindley's coming to power at Wuthering Heights. Heathcliff, the usurping foundling preferred by Mr Earnshaw, loses his position as the favoured, chosen son; and becomes an outsider and a rebel. In this he is like Satan, who (in Christian tradition and *Paradise Lost*) broods over 'Christ's celestial legitimacy'[1] and becomes the rebel angel. Heathcliff, along with Catherine, now plans revenge. The two of them vow 'to grow up as rude as savages' (which is, of course, to refuse to grow up at all). Like Satan, their revolt to a large extent is a revolt against a religious regime, against Sundays spent 'reading sermons, and being catechised' or being 'set to learn a column of Scripture names' (ch. 6). The night of the ramble, these two 'unfriended creatures', like a pair of Milton's exiled angels, have been banished from the warmth and comfort of the 'sitting-room' to the 'wash-house', a place clearly chosen for its pervading discomfort. From here they escape, as the exiled Satan does from hell, and visit the para-disiacal Grange.

'We thought we would just go and see whether the Lintons passed their Sunday evenings standing shivering in corners, while their father and mother sat eating and drinking, and singing and laughing, and burning their eyes out before the fire', says Heathcliff. Now, with the door to the Heights bolted behind them, they make their way into Eden, rebellious and indifferent to what trouble they might create.

It is not that simple, of course. How seriously can we take two such small devil figures who are, in fact, nothing more than mistreated and mis-behaving children, children who enter Eden in a state of revolt and resent-ment and whose greatest crimes are curiosity, the making of 'frightful noises' to 'terrify' the Linton children, and Heathcliff's 'recommenced cursing'? As Satans they are imperfectly bad, just as the inhabitants of Paradise are imperfectly good and Paradise itself (with its quarrelling inhabitants and its 'devil' dog guarding the grounds) is a good bit less than ideal.

In this first invasion of Thrushcross Grange, Eden and the Eden story are skilfully suggested but purposely left inexact and incomplete. However,

---

[1]Sandra M. Gilbert and Susan Gubar, *The Madwoman in the Attic* (New Haven and London, Yale University Press, 1979), p. 297.

the failure of the Grange to reach perfection does not, in itself, make Wuthering Heights a paradise by contrast. When we turn to the Heights and attempt to gauge that unruly and contrary household by an Eden measuring stick of its own, we run up against a new set of complexities, a new set of contradictions. It is unquestionably easier to see the hellish qualities of that 'infernal house' than it is to see the Edenic. Though it lies on the heights above the Grange, as Milton's Eden lies above the 'subjected Plain' to which Adam and Eve are later banished, Wuthering Heights is clearly not paradisiacal in any conventional sense. 'Wuthering', we are told, is a regional adjective depicting 'atmospheric tumult', and 'the excessive slant of a few stunted firs at the end of the house' and 'a range of gaunt thorns all stretching their limbs one way, as if craving alms of the sun' (ch. 1) in no way suggest the grace and fecundity one expects in a Garden of Eden.

Add to this an undeniable element of nastiness – beyond the wind and weather – a nastiness which has always been present at the Heights, even before Mr Earnshaw's death, and which is perhaps best exemplified by the servant Joseph, who endures almost uncannily from generation to generation, bullying and berating with 'religious curses' and prophecies of doom. In Lockwood's words, Wuthering Heights is 'a perfect misanthropist's heaven' (ch. 1). It is here, in scenes reminiscent of Goethe's 'Witch's Kitchen' (infernal and comic at once), that he is threatened by the Cerebus trio of dogs within the house and finally attacked by two of these hell hounds ('They suffer no resurrection') when he attempts to leave. Nonetheless Heathcliff's insistence that he would 'not exchange for a thousand lives' his situation at Wuthering Heights, and Catherine's girlhood dream, her rejection of Heaven in preference to the moors, must turn us back to the Heights as a rough and vivid home, a shelter of time or place that in its way too serves as an Eden. As adults, as the mistress of Thrushcross Grange or as master of both the Grange and the Heights, they never again experience the freedom of spirit and the passionate unity they knew as children. 'The greatest punishment we could invent for her', says Nelly of Catherine, 'was to keep her separate from him' (ch. 5). In the same way, Heathcliff cannot imagine wishing to be 'divided by the whole room' from Catherine, as the young Lintons are from each other when we first see them through the window of Thrushcross Grange. And though Heathcliff may covet and claim the horse belonging to the temporarily dispossessed and rather unappealing Hindley, there is no envy in his feelings for Catherine. 'When would you catch me wishing to have what Catherine wanted?'

But this assured and unquestioned loyalty cannot last. Heathcliff, after trespassing into Thrushcross Grange, is dragged away and has the door 'secured' behind him. The larger world of the Grange has invaded Catherine and Heathcliff's private world, and the two are driven apart. In the eyes of the Lintons, Heathcliff has no right to Catherine or to the privileges of her class. He is a 'gypsy', a 'castaway', a 'wicked boy, at all events . . . quite unfit for a decent house', while Catherine is 'Miss Earnshaw' (the name and status emphasized by repetition) and worthy of Linton respect and Linton attention.

Once at the Grange, Catherine is tempted by the world, and in yielding to this temptation ('for she was full of ambition') she brings about a fall from innocence as thorough as any in Genesis or *Paradise Lost*, though hers, as Gilbert and Gubar point out, is not so much a religious fall *from* grace as it is a fall *into* grace in its social sense.[2] Luxury seduces her. Catherine eats the foods of Thrushcross Grange, the 'plateful of cakes' and drinks the spiced, warm 'tumbler of negus'. And Heathcliff watches, this time separated by the window through which he and Catherine had earlier peered together. The taming of Catherine has begun, a process which will bring her to leave behind her rough girlhood ways and take up manners and clothing that require inhibited motion and artificial posturing. The girl who five weeks before raced barefoot in the dark from 'the top of the Heights to the park' (ch. 6) is now hampered by fashion and airs ('clothes and flattery') and seems to have fulfilled Mrs Linton's fearful prediction on seeing her wounded ankle, 'She may be lamed for life!' (ch. 6). When we see her next, she is no longer 'a wild, hatless little savage jumping into the house, and rushing to squeeze us all breathless'. Now there alights 'from a handsome black pony a very dignified person with brown ringlets falling from the cover of a feathered beaver, and a long cloth habit which she was obliged to hold up with both hands that she might sail in' (ch. 7).

With Catherine's return, the values of Thrushcross Grange enter Wuthering Heights. Now comes the period of Catherine's 'double character'. 'In the place where she heard Heathcliff termed a "vulgar young ruffian", and "worse than a brute", she took care not to act like him; but at home she had small inclination to practise politeness that would only be laughed at' (ch. 8). Edgar visits, bringing with him a continuation of luxury, comfort, and an artificiality of manners that allows her to say, in attempting to talk herself into accepting his proposal, 'I love the ground under his feet, and the air over his head, and everything he touches, and every word he says', unconvincing platitudes, as Nelly is quick to recognize. Edgar, Catherine sees, will be rich; and by marrying him she can become 'the greatest woman of the neighbourhood' (ch. 9).

This is the temptation Edgar presents; this is the attraction that brings Catherine to duplicity 'without exactly intending to deceive anyone' (ch. 8) and allows her to betray Heathcliff and her own heart. It is Edgar now who is the invader, whose influence disrupts an established good. As a classical figure of satanic destruction, however, Edgar makes a poor showing. His visits to the Heights are not intentionally destructive any more than Heathcliff and Catherine's first visit to the Grange had been. Edgar neither recognizes nor understands the bond that has held Catherine and Heathcliff together. He is, in fact, only minimally aware of Heathcliff's presence at Wuthering Heights. And yet we have his off-handed gibe about Heathcliff's shaggy locks, and there is as well a suggestion of predatory nastiness in Nelly's depiction of Edgar's courtship: 'He possessed the power to depart, as much as a cat possesses the power to leave

[2]Gilbert and Gubar, *Madwoman*, p. 255.

a mouse half killed, or a bird half eaten' (ch. 9). But whatever his intentions, the unity of Catherine and Heathcliff is ultimately destroyed by this invasion of Grange manners and Grange opinion. Inevitably Heathcliff and Catherine grow further and further apart. There comes the night when Heathcliff overhears Catherine saying, 'It would degrade me to marry Heathcliff now', and the fall is complete.

It doesn't matter that Catherine goes on to confess that Heathcliff is 'more myself than I am' or that her love for Edgar is merely temporary 'like the foliage in the woods' or that by marrying Edgar, she hopes she 'can aid Heathcliff to rise'. Her argument has no more validity than the argument of the fallen Eve, assuring Adam of a 'Godhead; which for thee/Chiefly I sought'.[3] The damage is done. Heathcliff, more dramatically though less willingly than Catherine, abandons Wuthering Heights and the childhood it represents. By his own means, he will gain the wealth and outer trappings of civilization that Catherine has come to value, and in doing so, he will re-enact the tale of our first 'parents'. Like Adam, he will share in her fall – will bite the fruit she has bitten and take on with her the knowledge of good and evil.

For Catherine and Heathcliff the knowledge they acquire is the knowledge of adult society. The innocence they lose is the innocence of childhood, and their Eden has been childhood itself. To those familiar with Emily Brontë's poetry there is nothing surprising in this. Golden-haired girls and dark, melancholy boys 'all doomed alike to sin and mourn'[4] appear throughout the poems, as does the word 'Eden' in reference to the unfallen state of childhood. It is a particularly appropriate term in the Gondal poems for the 'paradise lost' island of Ula ('Ula's Eden sky').

> I thought of many a happy day
> Spent in her Eden isle,
> With my dear comrades, young and gay,
> All scattered now so far away,
> But not forgot the while![5]

By specifically associating Eden with childhood Emily Brontë is following a convention of the times. In an age uneasy with adulthood, or with the sense of moral failure that comes with adulthood, only the child or childlike – Mr Dick in *David Copperfield*, for example – are seen as innocent. To put it simply (and borrowing from William Empson), 'The child has not yet been put wrong by civilization, and all grown-ups have been'.[6]

It is only in her poetry, however, that Emily Brontë expresses the usual nineteenth-century sentiment about childhood and its Edenic nature:

---

[3]John Milton, *Paradise Lost*, Book IX, ll. 877–8.
[4]Brontë, *Poems*, p. 122.
[5]Brontë, *Poems*, p. 149 and 193.
[6]William Empson, *Some Versions of Pastoral* (Norfolk, Connecticut, New Directions Books, 1960), p. 248.

'Dear childhood's Innocence', 'the pure light of childhood's morn', the 'darling enthusiast, holy child'. *Wuthering Heights* is another matter. Sentimental references to children are markedly lacking in this novel where violence and spite are the norm and where the children are as violent and spiteful as the adults. Nonetheless childhood innocence does exist in *Wuthering Heights*. It exists in Catherine and Heathcliff before their night visit to the Grange under the dairy woman's cloak. It exists in all the children figures that dominate and haunt *Wuthering Heights*, a novel full of children and the memories and ghosts of children. They come in pairs: Catherine and Heathcliff, Isabella and Edgar, young Cathy and Linton; and finally Cathy and Hareton. We have, as well, the short-lived pairing of Nelly and Hindley ('foster' siblings in their early years) and the brief coalition of Catherine and Hindley at Heathcliff's arrival. Even Frances and Hindley (though less clearly) fit this pattern in their childlike and pettish rule of the Heights, a rule more suggestive of 'playing house' than anything appropriately adult. 'Like two babies' (ch. 3) is Catherine's girlhood description of her brother and his wife.

All these children, all these pairs, begin with innocence; but innocence is not the same as docility or sweetness of temper, as Emily Brontë well knew; and she demonstrates this conviction by creating (most consistently in the first generation) children who are vivid but not particularly likeable: Catherine 'too mischievous and wayward for a favourite', Heathcliff 'not insolent to his benefactor' but 'simply insensible' (ch. 5) and those 'petted things', the pale and indulged Lintons. Our first view of the Grange children is of a weeping Edgar and a shrieking Isabella in the aftermath of the quarrel in which 'they had nearly pulled [the little dog] in two'. Nor is this behaviour simply the result of Grange indulgence. Catherine and Hindley, though less accustomed to luxury, acted much the same when the child 'dark almost as if it came from the devil' (ch. 4) arrived from Liverpool and Hindley – as weak spirited as Edgar – fell to blubbering over the loss of his violin and Catherine, for spite, made faces at the foundling. Even Heathcliff and Catherine, our main child pair and our main focus, are no improvement. We may side with these two, attributing their particular failings to high spirits and defiance in the face of tyranny, but it would be hard to make a case for their moral superiority. They, even more clearly than the others, repudiate the Victorian ideal of a sweet and compliant childhood.

More needs to be said about these child couples. By creating such matched pairs of siblings or playmates of the opposite sex, Emily Brontë is again following a nineteenth-century convention. Such boy/girl couples allowed for a type of innocent mating, small Adams and Eves in a prelapsarian state (*play*-mates, in fact), and the literature is full of examples: Tom and Maggie Tulliver in *The Mill on the Floss*, Pip and Estella in *Great Expectations*, Graham and Polly in *Villette*, or Carroll's 'Sylvie and Bruno'. In *Wuthering Heights*, however, the focus on the child or child couple is carried further than usual by both the sheer number of these pairs and also by the early loss of the adult generation. This is a world where adults seem peripheral, a world where the older generation neatly and quietly dies off before the main action begins. It is a mythopoetic world that stands for more than itself, where a small cast of players on a small stage is enough to represent the fate of the race. This is why concern for progenitors and descendants alike is so often absent in the novel; why Heathcliff, having no ties with past or future, needs no last name; and why the setting is purposefully narrow and the outside world beyond the Grange or Heights ill defined and of no real importance. (Where does Heathcliff come from? Or Frances? Where does Hindley go when he leaves the Heights? Or Heathcliff? Or Isabella?) The answers to such questions have no place in the story; they are beyond the range of our concern.

On one level it is as though the children in *Wuthering Heights* spring unaccompanied and untended into the world. Even young Cathy begins as 'an unwelcomed infant' wailing while 'nobody cared a morsel' (ch. 16). Parents are notoriously absent, indifferent, or easily lost to death. What, for example, do we see of the older Lintons? Never more than shadow figures, they are there in the background, owners of the attacking dog and servants, vague temporary support, host and hostess who conveniently take ill and fade from the picture, allowing Edgar and Isabella to come prematurely into possession of Thrushcross Grange, just as Hindley and Frances come unprepared and unguided into possession of Wuthering Heights. Inexperienced, youthful – and often thoughtless and selfish – they step into adult roles, no more ready to rule the Grange or Heights than the newly created Adam and Eve were ready to rule the Garden. For each of us, Emily Brontë seems to be saying, the world is created anew, and we ourselves are Adams and Eves alone in our Edens of childhood, and each of us alone confronts the Fall.

What follows for Catherine after Heathcliff's departure is illness and resignation. In the period of her convalescence she is invited to the Grange by Mrs Linton. 'But the poor dame had reason to repent of her kindness' (ch. 9), for Catherine's second stay at the Grange brings death to the older generation, much as Heathcliff's arrival at Wuthering Heights, though less directly or quickly, seems to herald the end of Mr and Mrs Earnshaw. Catherine marries, enters the drowsy seclusion of Thrushcross Grange and so becomes imprisoned. The Eden world of the Grange appears once again to be intact and reigned over by a new Mr and Mrs Linton. A cycle has completed itself. But once again the surface peace of this pale, complacent world is disrupted. The quiet and 'deep and growing happiness' (ch. 10), that Nelly, our somewhat unreliable narrator, claims to see in this newly-wed couple, is invaded, threatened, and lost.

The story picks up again when Heathcliff reappears after a three-year absence, outwardly a gentleman 'worthy of any one's regard'. His first visit to Thrushcross Grange is based, he tells us, on a wish to have only 'one glimpse of [Catherine's] face' (ch. 10); yet again his presence will upset the status quo, and this time the effects will reach deeper and wider, collapsing the inherited structure of both households. His reappearance is clearly satanic and his subsequent visits equally so.

'On a mellow evening in September, I was coming from the garden with a heavy basket of apples', says Nelly. 'It had got dusk, and the moon looked over the high wall of the court, causing undefined shadows to lurk in the corners of the numerous projecting portions of the building' (ch. 10). A voice calls out; Nelly, fearful, turns and sees 'a tall man dressed in dark clothes, with dark face and hair'. His fingers are on the latch, 'as if intending to open for himself'. Heathcliff has returned, and a reluctant Nelly is sent to inform Catherine of his presence. The dark setting, the dark man in the garden, the apples, Nelly's strong reluctance to dispel the 'wonderously peaceful' scene in the parlour, and Heathcliff's statement that he is 'in hell' until word can reach Catherine all have echoes of the Eden story, and these echoes, especially of Satan in the garden, will continue. It is here in the garden that Heathcliff meets Isabella and from here elopes with her, and here again he hangs her dog. During Catherine's final illness, he again waits in the garden, as he will later wait for word of Catherine's death and for a chance to visit her corpse. 'Last night, I was in the Grange garden six hours, and I'll return there to-night; and every night I'll haunt the place, and every day, till I find an opportunity of entering' (ch. 14).

This emphasis on Satan and rebellious satanic figures stems from Emily Brontë's earliest literary experiences. In Byron 'Emily found the champion of unsociable man', writes Winifred Gérin, but Satan in *Paradise Lost* had an even stronger influence. 'The sense of thwarted power in the fallen angel, conscious of his lost rights, stirred her to admiration and sympathy'.[7] From this come both the 'holy child' figure 'doomed to be/Hell-like in heart and misery'[8] in Emily Brontë's poetry and Heathcliff in *Wuthering Heights*. From the first, as a 'dirty, ragged' foundling, Heathcliff is associated with the demonic, but after his return as an adult until the close of the novel, the Satan/devil/serpent imagery increases prodigiously. The adult Heathcliff is a 'devil', a 'hellish villain', 'a lying fiend, a monster, and not a human being'. Even Catherine recognizes this side of Heathcliff, warning Isabella that he is an 'unreclaimed creature' and adding to Nelly that the idea of offering Heathcliff a wife is 'as bad as offering Satan a lost soul' (ch. 11).

The 'vagabond', the 'gipsy', even the 'imp of Satan' that Heathcliff was called as a child had no impact like this. Now we have the conscious man, the adult, aware of the injury he inflicts and planning it with care. Nonetheless, the story that follows Heathcliff's return, though it focuses on adult characters and is seen through adult eyes, is not so removed from the earlier part. Everything relates back to the novel's primary event: Catherine and Heathcliff's separation and fall. The hopes and failures of their childhood give rise to the specific temptations and failures of their adulthood. More falls are to come, all centred on choices made by the main characters as children. There are, in fact, good reasons for feeling that we

[7]Gérin, *Brontë*, pp. 46–7.
[8]Brontë, *Poems*, p. 121.

never leave the children behind even as we continue with their adult stories. Lockwood dreams of Catherine the ghost child, not Catherine the adult. The child that existed before still exists as a force or a spirit capable of manifestation and influence. Even Nelly has a vision of Hindley as a child, her 'early playmate', who some moments later seems to blend with the 'elf-locked' Hareton at the gates of Wuthering Heights. There is as well a persistent childishness in the now grown-up characters that makes it difficult to feel much has changed. Unlike the older Lintons and Earnshaws, this generation will never seem fully adult. The married Edgar and the full-grown Isabella are still referred to as 'childish'. ('Spoiled children', Catherine terms them.) And Catherine herself is 'no better than a wailing child' in her illness, engaging in what Nelly dismisses as 'baby-work' with pillow feathers. More pointedly, Catherine herself wishes to be a girl again, 'half savage, and hardy, and free' and imagines in her fevered state this is so. 'The whole last seven years of my life grew a blank! I did not recall that they had been at all. I was a child' (ch. 12). As she dies, her child self seems to return in full; Nelly describes Catherine in her last moments as a child stretching, 'reviving, and sinking again to sleep' (ch. 16).

With Heathcliff's return the pretence of adulthood has been stripped aside. Catherine, who had assumed, 'oddly enough, that she [could] maintain the two relationships, the social and the ungoverned, the married and the passionate',[9] now finds this impossible. Where Nelly had seen 'growing happiness' and relative stability for the new couple, Catherine now tells her of the 'very, very bitter misery' (ch. 10) she has endured. Her peace in marriage has been one of forgetting. She has denied her first and truest nature and become 'Mrs Linton, the lady of Thrushcross Grange, and the wife of a stranger; an exile, and outcast' (ch. 12). There is no return to the Eden of childhood and no further happiness where she is. To remain with Edgar is to yield to motherhood, lineage, and social position. To be again with Heathcliff is to remember (and long for) her lost independence and freedom and what Thomas Vogler calls 'the unself-conscious intensity of childlike emotions'.[10] One is no longer acceptable, the other no longer possible. Catherine is held by the Grange's soft restraints, trapped by the limitations of mortal life, by her nature, her society, and her physical body, by 'this shattered prison' which binds her to this world. Death is the only release. 'You and Edgar have broken my heart', Catherine tells Heathcliff; 'You have killed me' (ch. 15). She dies, more by willing it than by any certain illness, and the infant Cathy, like an afterthought, a by-product of her mother's death, is born. This generation too will seem under-parented.

The indifference Catherine bears toward her pregnancy is striking. 'On her existence depended that of another' (ch. 13), we are told, but we are

---

[9] Albert J. Guérard, 'Preface to *Wuthering Heights*', in Thomas A. Vogler, ed., *Twentieth Century Interpretations of Wuthering Heights* (Englewood Cliffs, New Jersey, Prentice-Hall, 1968), p. 63.
[10] Thomas A. Vogler, 'Introduction', in Vogler *Wuthering Heights*, p. 10.

not given much indication, beyond one rather stilted statement about 'half-a-dozen nephews' (ch. 10) to erase Isabella's title as heir, ('please Heaven!') to suggest any genuine concern on Catherine's part for the next generation. Illness is not the cause of her indifference. Compare the dying Frances's concern for the infant Hareton! What seems to be behind her indifference is a rejection of her role as an adult, the role demanded by both nature and society. Eve, in her fallen state is to be 'mother of all living'.[11] Catherine, once Heathcliff is back in her life, will have none of this.

In spite of his one comment about wishing to find Linton 'a worthy object of pride' (ch. 20), it is even more difficult to associate Heathcliff with parenthood than it is Catherine. Much of this comes from a consistent comparison of Heathcliff with winter and sterile elements in nature. He is the 'bleak, hilly, coal country' while Edgar is 'a beautiful fertile valley' (ch. 8), and even Catherine refers to him as 'an arid wilderness of furze and whinstone' (ch. 10). Yet, again following Catherine's lead, he produces a child, Linton, whom he values only as a means of enacting his revenge.

Neither Catherine nor Heathcliff wishes an existence beyond their own, beyond the one they shared together as children. To yield to parenthood is to yield the self, to yield autonomy. It is all part of the pattern of what splits apart the simple wholeness of the child, the innocence of boy and girl together, and splits them again into father or mother and offspring, into separate and opposing units. At some level, conflict is inevitable; the entrance of the new marks the end of the old. Like Heathcliff and Hindley contending throughout their lives for mastery of Wuthering Heights, the generations too must contend. They are, in a sense, in each other's way; and this in part seems to explain why so often in the novel the younger seem to bring death to the older; Heathcliff to the older Earnshaws, Catherine to the older Lintons, Cathy to Catherine, and perhaps even Linton to Isabella. This is the fate of generations, the trap of Genesis itself, Eve's curse, that 'in sorrow' she shall 'bring forth children' and that her disobedience brings death to her and Adam and to their unhappy race that follows.

'You loved me', cries Heathcliff, 'then what *right* had you to leave me? What right – answer me – for the poor fancy you felt for Linton? Because misery, and degradation, and death, and nothing that God or Satan could inflict would have parted us, *you*, of your own will, did it' (ch. 15). And yet what choice does Catherine have, and how can we blame her? Edgar Linton's attention flatters a part of Catherine that must inevitably appear; that is, she must grow up; and this may explain why Catherine can move so quickly from rough girl to apparent lady. One bite of the apple is enough, and all is changed. 'Who is to separate us?' (ch. 9) Catherine asks before Heathcliff leaves Wuthering Heights. But there is no stopping the biological clock that insists on childhood's end. And something more is at work. Catherine realizes a power in her ability to attract Edgar. Marriage

11Genesis, 3:20.

being part of the inevitable requirements of life, why not marry into the comforts that Hindley and Frances hoard to themselves, into even more than Hindley and Frances have? Catherine is not insulting Heathcliff when she says 'It would degrade me to marry Heathcliff now'. This is a fact. She is becoming an adult, and degradation is an adult's concern. As two dirty, half-savage children such degradation had no effect on them, but the fall into adulthood (into sexuality and social system) wedges in between the two, and the children who lay in each other's arms 'in a union which was prior to sexual differentiation'[12] are propelled into otherness, into class and sex roles, into inhibition and deceit.

Who is the villain now that enters paradise and shatters its peace? Is it so much the Linton element, Edgar's visits to the Heights tempting an Eve away from her natural and innocent state? Or is it perhaps simply the way life is in this world, caught up as we are with cycles and seasons and social standards that thrust us out of innocence into awareness, an apple of knowledge forced through our teeth, whether we choose to eat or not? The cycle of generations is a fact; social systems, hierarchies, inherited rights and all the artificialities that accompany these systems are unavoidable facts.

'Childhood's flower must waste its bloom', Emily Brontë writes in her poetry. Innocence disintegrates into awareness, experience, and – finally – adulthood. The 'iron man' of Emily Brontë's Gondal poems is no longer 'an ardent boy'.[13] He has lost the child's sense of hope, love and harmony with nature. The young Catherine who ran wild and free and hardy over the moors is tamed, encumbered and bound. Once she is married, we never again see Catherine outdoors but only in rooms. Her plea for open windows and her wish not to be buried 'under the chapel roof; but in the open air' (ch. 12) indicate how aware she has become of her separation from the outside and how much her girlhood freedom is lost to her. Emily Brontë is in full sympathy.

'My sister Emily loved the moors', Mrs Gaskell reports Charlotte as saying.

> Flowers brighter than the rose bloomed in in the blackest of the heath for her; – out of a sullen hollow in a livid hill-side, her mind could make an Eden. She found in the bleak solitude many and dear delights; and not the least and best-loved was liberty. Liberty was the breath of Emily's nostrils; without it she perished.[14]

Liberty and freedom were essentials for Emily Brontë as they are for her heroine Catherine; and when freedom is the ideal, imprisonment and restriction are the greatest terror, the greatest deprivation. This explains the recurring imagery of freedom threatened and lost in Emily Brontë's writing – the 'fetters', 'chains', and 'dungeon bars' in her poetry and the enclosures and barriers and the series of characters who are exiled or

[12]J. Hillis Miller, *Fiction and Repetition*: *Seven English Novels* (Cambridge, Mass., Harvard University Press, 1982), p. 61.
[13]Brontë, *Poems*, p. 40 and p. 105.
[14]Elizabeth C. Gaskell, *The Life of Charlotte Brontë* (East Kilbride, Oxford, 1919), p. 109.

imprisoned in *Wuthering Heights*. The mortal body, Catherine's 'shattered prison', is itself a form of bondage that separates her from the world of nature and unhampered spirit. 'I'm tired, tired of being enclosed here. I'm wearying to escape into that glorious world, and to be always there; not seeing it dimly through tears, and yearning for it through the walls of an aching heart; but really with it' (ch. 15). Even the enclosing wall of the churchyard is seen as a barrier to resist, so that Catherine, at her request, is buried 'neither in the chapel, under the carved monument of the Lintons, nor yet by the tombs of her own relations' but 'on a green slope, in a corner of the kirkyard, where the wall is so low that heath and bilberry plants have climbed over it from the moor' (ch. 16).

This sense of entrapment is most severe at the Heights. Gates are barred; doors are locked; Isabella, Cathy, Linton, and even Nelly all have their period of captivity there; Lockwood can neither enter the Heights nor leave it without considerable difficulty; and – most poignantly – the ghost child cannot make her way back. Yet the Grange has its own barriers and restrictions, as all limited realms must have. Catherine is the one who chafes most at the Grange's walls and closed windows, but young Cathy too recognizes the Grange's restrictions. Like a type of Sleeping Beauty, Cathy reaches the age of thirteen without once having been 'beyond the range of the park by herself' (ch. 18). Nelly tells the inquisitive girl to be content, that Penistone Crags 'are not worth the trouble of visiting' and that 'Thrushcross park is the finest place in the world'. But, says Cathy, 'I know the park, and I don't know those'. The outcome is inevitable. In a reversal of her mother and Heathcliff's earlier escape from the Heights into the Grange, she scales the walls of the Park, (her 'walled Eden',[15] J. Frank Goodridge calls it), escaping outward to the moors and from there, urged by our Satan figure, Heathcliff, goes on to Wuthering Heights and a further enactment of the Fall.

Traditional accounts of Eden admit only to the desirability of paradise and the bitterness of its loss: driven into the wilderness, Adam and Eve lament their lot; Cherubim and sword stand at the gate; you can't go home again. This is the fate of the ghost child lost on the moors, a 'waif for twenty years' (ch. 3). But what is not spoken of directly is that other human urge, the urge to defy restriction. What, after all, is the Forbidden Tree but the urge outward, the desire to reach beyond prescribed limits, to choose for oneself, to *know*? Sooner or later Pandora will open the box; sooner or later Adam and Eve will pluck and taste the forbidden fruit; sooner or later Cathy will scale the wall.

And yet the difference between what is restriction and what is security is all a matter of perspective. One character's heaven/paradise/Eden is another's hell; one character's prison is another's longed for and likely inaccessible haven. For Catherine and Heathcliff, the freedom they knew on the moors with one another is their Eden; separation from one another is their hell. Isabella flees from Wuthering Heights 'blest as a soul escaped

[15]J. Frank Goodridge, 'The Circumambient Universe', in Vogler, *Wuthering Heights*, p. 70.

from purgatory' (ch. 17). For Cathy, who shows a good share of her mother's free spirit, heaven is 'the whole world awake and wild with joy', while the passive and spiritless Linton, prefers 'a hot July day' spent 'lying from morning till evening on a bank of heath'. There is no reconciling the two viewpoints. 'I said his heaven would be only half alive, and he said mine would be drunk' (ch. 24). But the most significant comment on heaven, in this book full of conflicting heavens, comes in Catherine's account of her dream. 'I dreamt, once, that I was there', Catherine tells Nelly. 'Heaven did not seem to be my home; and I broke my heart with weeping to come back to earth; and the angels were so angry that they flung me out, into the middle of the heath on the top of Wuthering Heights; where I woke sobbing for joy' (ch. 9).

Catherine's rejection of a Christian heaven is not simply a matter of Satan's 'Evil, be thou my good', but rather a way of expressing the multiplicity of character and preference in *Wuthering Heights* and the resulting conflicts which come from such differences. Left to itself the stormy Wuthering Heights could carry on as before, charged with its own Blakeian energy. Left to itself Thrushcross Grange could dream on, static and secure. But the two meet, and opposites attract (if only temporarily), Catherine to Edgar, Isabella to Heathcliff; and Cathy to Linton. And these meetings and matings of opposites have their yieldings. As Goodridge writes:

> Brontë may lead us to question whether there is any one natural and social order, the same for all men and women. The conflicting individual heavens and hells confront one another at every turn: incompatible ways of life, coupled in grotesque ways sometimes lead to violence and hysteria, sometimes to lifeless neutrality and sometimes to new and fuller forms of life.[16]

When the storm of clashing extremes is cleared away, we have Cathy and Hareton, blendings of spirit and civilization, of Heights and Grange characteristics. These two, unlike Edgar and Catherine, can move toward one another, toward a union which brings closure to the book and which is best exemplified by the blending of the novel's two gardens.

Here again Emily Brontë brings us back to the underlying theme of Eden – plural Edens, Edens threatened, Edens lost, and (in this last account) an Eden regained. Cathy persuades Hareton 'to clear a large space of ground' at the Heights for 'an importation of plants' from Thrushcross Grange, and this 'importation' serves as more than a symbol of unity between the two young people and the two households they represent. Most telling is the devastation the transplanting of Grange flowers and Grange plants causes to 'the black current trees' described as 'the apple of Joseph's eye'. (A 'witty pun',[17] Stevie Davies calls this!) The long-standing order of the garden has been disrupted, and Joseph is outraged. Cathy is a witch, a trouble-causing woman, an Eve inciting her Adam to rebel. Like

16Goodridge, 'Circumambient', p. 77.
17Davies, p. 168.

an angry God, Heathcliff threatens expulsion. 'As to Hareton Earnshaw, if I see him listen to you, I'll send him seeking his bread where he can get it! Your love will make him an outcast, and a beggar' (ch. 33). The echoes of Genesis are evident.

But this is a threat that fails. Our new Cathy, our new Eve, reverses the Eden story, returning Hareton to the land and home he had lost and uniting what had previously been divided. These two, Nelly tells us, have escaped 'the sentiments of sober disenchanted maturity' (ch. 33), and the world seems renewed. When next we see the garden, it is April; and the transplanting has clearly succeeded; something of the Grange's orderly cultivation and milder climate has come to Wuthering Heights. 'The weather was sweet and warm, the grass as green as showers and sun could make it, and the two dwarf apple trees, near the southern wall, in full bloom' (ch. 34). At the barren and windy Heights a touch of the traditional Eden has taken hold, complete with apple trees (fittingly dwarf).

For a moment, Emily Brontë gives us a glimpse of peace regained, a sense of unity and continuity, as though – at last – matters have settled. But what we have is only a momentary pause in the recurring cycles and repetitions of life. It is true that an Eden – both new and rediscovered – has come to Wuthering Heights. The 'Hareton Earnshaw' of the 1500 carving over the entrance to the Heights lives again in the new Hareton Earnshaw restored to his lands; and, as well, something of Catherine Earnshaw continues in her daughter, in the similarity of their eyes, in something of their shared desire for freedom. But the particulars of any individual human spirit or any individual human form are never fully recovered; and even as we celebrate restoration and continuity in the characters and union of Cathy and Hareton, Emily Brontë requires us to feel the loss of Catherine and Heathcliff, her vivid and tempestuous rebels. With their departure, some great and wild force has gone from the earth. Wuthering Heights will be mostly 'shut up'; Cathy and Hareton will live at the Grange, and the world seems diminished.

There is only a hint or two that something of Catherine and Heathcliff's spirit still endures. Though Lockwood cannot imagine 'unquiet slumbers for the sleepers in that quiet earth', his description of the fluttering moths, the heath, the hare-bells and the 'soft wind breathing through the grass' (ch. 34) suggests a life that goes on, a slow stirring, a transmutation perhaps. And there is as well the boy who comes crying that he has seen the ghosts of 'Heathcliff and a woman, yonder, under t'Nab'. But again nothing is certain, and neither image is satisfactory. Emily Brontë chooses to leave the spirit its own mystery, and what is not offered to us, in any vision of ghost or grave, is a full return to innocence in the form we knew it first – not a transmutation into the natural world, not 'Heathcliff and a woman' (ghosts that *walk* and adult ghosts at that) but the children themselves, Catherine and Heathcliff, vivid and passionate, and running 'hardy, and free' over the moors.

Note

Few of the novels discussed in this article have been reprinted, although Virago have brought out Mary Braddon's *Aurora Floyd* and *Lady Audley's Secret*, and Rhoda Broughton's *Belinda*. As well as Braddon and Broughton's many works, other authors to look out for include Matilda Bentham-Edwards, Frances Browne, Rosa Nouchette Carey, Dinah Mulock Craik, Elizabeth Eiloart, Annie Edwardes, Elizabeth Caroline Grey, Frances Sarah Hoey, Matilda Charlotte Houston, Florence Marryat, Eliza Meteyard, Caroline Norton, Ouida (Marie Louise de la Ramée), Felicia Skene, Anna C. Steele, Anne Thackeray, Annie Thomas, Florence Wilford, Mrs Henry Wood and Charlotte Mary Yonge. Many of these wrote children's books, poetry, and religiously slanted works as well as novels with 'sensational' elements.

As yet, there exists no full account of women's reading patterns in the nineteenth century, and of the prescriptive attitudes which were held towards what she should, and should not read. The most helpful work so far published on the subject is Sally Mitchell's article, 'Sentiment and Suffering: Women's Recreational Reading in the 1860s', *Victorian Studies* 21 (1977), pp. 29–45. Questions of propriety in women's reading material are a central theme in Guinevere Griest, *Mudie's Circulating Library and the Victorian Novel* (Bloomington, Indiana University Press, 1970). The social context in which much of the reading took place is described in Patricia Branca, *Silent Sisterhood: Middle Class Women in the Victorian Home* (London, Croom Helm, 1975). J.N. Burstyn, *Victorian Education and the Ideal of Womanhood* (London, Croom Helm, 1982) is useful for the understanding of how psychological and physiological theories informed beliefs about women's mental capacities and aptitudes, as are Sara Delamont and Lorna Duffin (eds.), *The Nineteenth Century Woman: Her Physical and Cultural World* (London, Croom Helm, 1978) and Janet Sayers, *Biological Politics: Feminist And Anti-Feminist Perspectives* (London, Tavistock, 1982). Chapter 6 of Elaine Showalter's *A Literature of Their Own: British Women Novelists from Brontë to Lessing*, 'Subverting the Feminine Novel: Sensationalism and Feminine Protest', is a full discussion of a range of women 'sensation' novelists. Robert Wolff's *Sensational Victorian: the Life and Fiction of Mary Elizabeth Braddon* is a meticulous biography of one of these novelists, setting her firmly in the publishing conditions of her time.

4

The Woman Reader and the Opiate of Fiction: 1855–1870

Kate Flint

In 1859, W.R. Greg published an article in the *National Review* entitled 'False Morality of Lady Novelists'. It opens with the assertion 'It is not easy to over-estimate the importance of novels',[1] and goes on to give various reasons why one should take this form of literature so seriously. Firstly, novels are primarily read by those who are wealthy enough to enjoy leisure time. By extension, they are thus especially likely to influence those who, in their turn, have the most influence within the country. Secondly, since they are invariably read in leisure time, when the brain is comparatively passive, the critical faculties are asleep, and material is ingested without being judged or sifted. Thirdly, novels form, in Greg's view, an unfortunately large part of the habitual reading of the young, at a time when the memory is fresh; when what he calls 'the moral standard' is largely fluctuating and unformed, and experience has not yet been great enough to afford a 'criterion whereby to separate the true from the false in the delineations of life'. Finally, Greg speaks with the voice of patriarchal authority:

> Novels constitute a principal part of the reading of women, who are always impressionable, in whom at all times the emotional element is more awake and more powerful than the critical, whose feelings are more easily influenced than ours, while at the same time the correctness of their feelings and the justice of their sentiments are matters of the most special and pre-eminent concern.[2]

In the mid nineteenth century, the debate about women's reading largely centred around the novel: the opiate of leisure hours, the potential corruptor of young girls. What was it advisable for woman to read; how much should she read; what would be the effect, for better or worse, of certain reading materials upon her? Throughout the period, countless complaints are voiced against the habit, the addictive drug of fiction. 'Nobody will care to deny – what is indeed self-evident – that novels may be, and are,

[1] Unsigned article [W.R. Greg], 'False Morality of Lady Novelists', *National Review* VIII (1859), p. 144.
[2] 'False Morality' pp. 145–6.

the medium through which moral poison is frequently administered',[3] protested the *Saturday Review* in 1867. The anxiety about the effects of compulsive, indiscriminate novel-reading was based upon the belief that people are, whether wishing it or not, affected by what they read. Particularly at risk was the young, unprepared, inexperienced girl, who quickly learnt from novels, it was thought, that she must 'fall' in love. Hence, in her own life, she would quickly become apt to magnify any slight attentions paid to her; to mistake flutterings of vanity in her own breast for emotions of real love. As W.H. Davenport Adams put it: 'This fictitious sentiment she nourishes by novel-reading, idleness and indulgence in daydreaming.'[4] It was not just the moralizing critics, or those pundits who tried to lay down the terms of a woman's 'proper' role who helped to sustain this commonplace of the pernicious effect of fiction. The strongly feminist Rhoda Nunn, in Gissing's *The Odd Women*, comments bitterly on a past pupil of her clerical and secretarial school, now abandoned, penniless, by her lover. Nunn maintains that her belief in 'love', and her lack of discrimination between this and sexual passion, could very probably be attributed to a readily identifiable source:

> If every novelist could be strangled and thrown into the sea we should have some chance of reforming women. The girl's nature was corrupted by sentimentality, like that of . . . every woman who is intelligent enough to read what is called the best fiction, but not intelligent enough to understand its vice. . . . This Miss Royston – when she rushed off to perdition, ten to one she had in mind some idiotic heroine of a book.[5]

This fear of influence crept as far as Beatrice Webb, who, when she 'came out' in London society, was worried that novel-reading might have conditioned her expectations. Despite her knowledge of the probable reality of things, she is apprehensive that she goes to all dances expecting to meet the man of her dreams. In her journal, she writes that she is afraid that she is as bad a case of the poisonous conditioning of fiction as Rosamond Vincy had been.[6]

Much of the discussion about women's reading centred, as one might expect, on middle-class reading habits: the practices of a class where, whatever domestic responsibilities they were also required to take on board, young women were far more likely to have time on their hands which could be filled with reading than their less usually highly educated, wage earning and/or home running counterparts had at their disposal. The relative isolation, in the growing number of suburban homes, of commuters' wives who found escapist solace in the box of books from Mudie's Circulating Library, or in the fiction contained in the shilling-monthly family

[3]Unsigned article, 'Novel-Reading', *Saturday Review* XXIII (16 February 1867), p. 196.
[4]W.H. Davenport Adams, *Woman's Work and Worth* (London, John Hogg, 1880), p. 97.
[5]George Gissing, *The Odd Women* (1893: London, Virago, 1980), p. 58.
[6]Beatrice Webb, *The Diary of Beatrice Webb*, ed. Norman and Jeanne Mackenzie (London, Virago, 1982), I, p. 17.

magazines like the *Cornhill*, *Temple Bar*, and *Macmillan*'s, was, it has been suggested, an important factor in the increasing consumption of fiction.[7] Despite the shielding censorship of the circulating libraries, against which the novelists complained so bitterly in the later years of the century, and which was summed up by Mudie's stated belief that he had erected 'a barrier of some kind' between his subscribers 'and the lower floods of literature',[8] there remained considerable anxiety that a standard of modest decorum in both incidents and language should prevail in women's reading. It would be misleading, however, to regard such anxiety as exclusively directed towards the middle class. It is reflected in the lists of books to be found on the shelves of those public libraries which had separate 'ladies reading rooms', where, in these still largely working-class, metropolitan institutions, women were often segregated from the gazes and attentions of the rougher male elements of society, from tramps keeping warm and from the exchange of betting slips and racing news. Although religious considerations and economic paternalism were operative alongside more clear-cut issues of gender-suitability, the concern is also present in the catalogues of YWCA libraries, and in the private libraries run by some firms for their employees. Charlotte M. Yonge, in *What Books to Lend and What to Give*, is emphatic about the type of fiction which should be included in privately run village libraries. Whilst men, she says, 'must have manly books. Real solid literature alone will arrest their attention', their wives:

> like to lose their cares for a little while in some tale that excites either tears or laughter. It is all very well to say that they ought to have no time for reading. An industrious thrifty woman has little or none, but the cottager's wife who does as little needlework, washing, or tidying as possible, has a good many hours to spend in gossip or in reading. She may get cheap sensation novels, and the effects on a weak and narrow mind are often very serious. The only thing to be done is to take care that she has access to a full supply of what can do her no harm, and may by reiteration do her good.

Since, she believes, 'this class of woman must have incident, pathos, and sentiment to attract them',[9] Yonge goes on to give lists of works which would be suitable for library shelves, or for reading aloud at mothers' meetings, including improving tales by E.M. Sewell, Emma Marshall, Mrs. Marsh, Hesba Stretton, and herself.

Those periodicals which were aimed at the better-off members of the working class also contained dire warnings against the potentially pernicious effects of fiction. Thus *The Christian's Penny Magazine and*

[7] See Sally Mitchell, 'Sentiment and Suffering: Women's Recreational Reading in the 1860s', *Victorian Studies* 21 (1977), pp. 29–45.

[8] Charles Edward Mudie, quoted in an unsigned article, 'Mr. Mudie's Library', *Athenaeum* (6 October 1860), p. 451.

[9] Charlotte M. Yonge, *What Books to Lend and What to Give* (London, National Society's Depository, 1887), pp. 6–8.

Friend of the People, in 1859, addressed an imaginary young lady, and asked her to consider a particularly 'deplorable' and 'revolting' picture:

> A whole family, brought to destitution, has lately had all its misfortunes clearly traced by the authorities to an ungovernable passion for novel-reading entertained by the wife and mother. The husband was sober and industrious, but his wife was indolent, and addicted to reading everything procurable in the shape of a romance. This led her to utterly neglect her husband, herself and her eight children. One daughter, in despair, fled the parental home and threw herself into the haunts of vice. Another was found by the police chained by the legs, to protect her from following her sister's example. The house exhibited the most offensive appearance of filth and indigence. In the midst of this pollution, privation and poverty, the cause of it sat reading the latest 'sensation work' of the season, and refused to allow herself to be disturbed in her entertainment.[10]

Why should reading, especially the reading of novels, be assumed to have such a potentially damaging effect on women in particular? The answer partly lies in the circumstances of their home life, which have already been touched on, and partly in the physiological and psychological ways in which women were held to differ from men. The two factors coalesce in the *Church of England Quarterly Review* (1842):

> The great bulk of novel readers are females; and to them such impressions are peculiarly mischievous: for, first, they are naturally more sensitive, more impressable, than the other sex; and secondly, their engagements are of a less engrossing character – they have more time as well as more inclination to indulge in reveries of fiction.[11]

This belief that there was something about a woman's given nature and constitution which made her more vulnerable than a man would be was widespread. As Mrs Ellis put it, 'the female perceptions' are 'more quick, and the female character altogether more easy of adaptation, more sympathizing, and therefore more capable of identifying itself with the thoughts and feelings of others'.[12] Faith in the naturalness of these characteristics was continually reiterated throughout the mid years of the century, ostensibly with reference to the woman's overall role within the home, but in such a way that it is easy to apply the generalization to other more specific activities. Thus, to take a random but typical example, the *National Review* in 1858 spoke of the power of woman's intuitive, rather than deductive faculties, with 'the more instinctive nature of the woman finding its life among personal relations . . . her gracious prerogative and happiest attribute – the power to live in others'.[13] It was women's

(margin note: More sensitive to mischievous situations)

---

[10] T.C., 'Novel Reading. A Letter to a Young Lady', *Christian's Penny Magazine and Friend of the People* XIV (1859), p. 155.
[11] Unsigned review article, 'Morality and Political Tendency of the Modern Novels', *Church of England Quarterly Review* XI (1842), pp. 287–8.
[12] Mrs Ellis, ed., *The Young Ladies' Reader* (London, Fisher, Son & Co., 1845), p. 4.
[13] Unsigned review article, 'Woman', *National Review* 7 (1858), p. 342.

'imagination, memory and quickness of perception' as distinct from 'power of sustained thought, judgement, and creativeness'[14] – to quote *The Lancet's* classification of male/female attributes in 1868 – which could be assumed to make the genre of the novel so appealing to her in the first place.

There appears to be no attempt in mid-nineteenth-century scientific writing to describe or to analyse the physiology of reading, largely because the knowledge of brain processes was not yet sufficiently advanced. The localization of language use as a specific function of a particular part of the brain only began to be hypothesized about in the 1860s, largely by the French physiologist Paul Broca, and was not generally accepted as an idea until 1881. Even then, the issue was hotly contested. But if no functional description of the reading process was yet available, the moral–philosophical tradition which uneasily co-existed with the new physiological investigations of the mind's workings provided quasi-authoritative statements which seemed to bear out the popularly held beliefs about the differences between the male and the female minds.

Early in the Victorian period, Alexander Walker, in *Woman Physiologically Considered* . . . , argued that in the female, the organs of sense are larger than in the man. He based this assumption on the notion that such organs are contained in the frontal part of the brain, and the measurements he recorded revealed women as having habitually larger foreheads than men. It thus followed that there was correspondingly less room for the reasoning faculties, contained further back in the skull. A consequence of this anatomical difference is that 'the *sensibility* of woman is excessive; she is strongly affected by many sensations, which in men are so feeble as scarcely to excite attention'.[15] Later, Henry Maudsley wrote in the *Fortnightly Review* of 1874 about the relation of the brain to the other organs of the body. It is in the closest physiological sympathy with the other organs, having 'special correspondence with them by internuncial nerve-fibres; so that its functions habitually feel and declare the influence of the different organs. There is an intimate consensus of functions.' Alteration, or disorder, in one part of the body, will automatically lead to alteration within the mind. The most striking illustration of the kind of organic action which he is trying to describe 'is yielded', Maudsley said, 'by the influence of the reproductive organs upon the mind; a complete mental revolution being made when they come into activity'. This belief is here used to argue that men and women should have different types of education, which in each case should aim at the 'drawing out of the internal qualities of the individual into their highest perfection',[16] but it can have its place, also, in an implicit theory of reading. If woman's

[14]Unsigned article, 'Miss Becker on the Mental Characteristics of the Sexes', *Lancet* 2 (1868), 321.

[15]Alexander Walker, *Woman Physiologically Considered as to Mind, Morals, Matrimonial Slavery, Infidelity and Divorce* (London, A.H. Baily & Co 1839), p. 12.

[16]Henry Maudsley, 'Sex in Mind and in Education', *Fortnightly Review* n.s. 15 (1874), pp. 469–71.

'natural', physiological function is that of child-bearing and rearing, of the inculcation of moral beliefs along with physical nurturing, it must necessarily follow that such instincts as sympathetic imagination, and an identification with the experience of others, are unalterable facts about her mental operations, and hence about her methods of reading.

Further factors might render women particularly susceptible to certain types of writing. George Henry Lewes wrote in the *Fortnightly Review*, in 1865, not only about the indissolubly interwoven threads of Nutrition and Sensation in the human body, and about the intimate connections between Heart and Brain, but of the effect of the reactions of 'sensibility' on the circulation, and vice-versa. In certain 'feminine natures of both sexes' – the male/female dichotomy is less clear than usual, even if traditional vocabulary proved useful for Lewes – 'excessive sensitiveness does not lie in an unusual development of the nervous centres, but in an unusual development of the direct connection between brain and heart'.[17] Thus 'sensation' – of whatever kind, and such stimulus could certainly be provided by reading matter – would invariably transmit its shock, its agitating influence to the heart. Hence, since the heart is the central organ of the circulation, this sensation would, in a 'feminine nature', be the more readily passed along the pneumogastric nerves: the filaments which connect the heart with the spinal cord and hence to the cerebral masses. Thus, it could be argued in physiological terms that a typical feminine nature would be especially liable to the perturbing effects of the type of writing which was calculated to shock and surprise.

Of course, the vast amount of nineteenth-century anxiety about the damaging effects of reading should not blind one to the belief, also prevalent but never so anxiously stated, that if reading could influence for the bad it must also, if of the right kind, be able to influence for the good. Trollope, for one, believed in the morally educative power of fiction. In a lecture given in 1868, he advised his female listeners that if they:

> will take some little trouble in the choice of your novels, the lessons which you will find taught in them are good lessons. Honour and honesty, modesty and self-denial, are as strongly insisted on in our English novels as they are in our English sermons.[18]

As Davenport Adams put it in *Woman's Work and Worth*:

> The fancy of many a youth has been worthily kindled by contemplation of the heroic as presented in poem and romance; and there is no reason, we repeat, why our girls, our maidens, should not profit by a similar inspiration. There is much virtue in a good poem or a good novel. Why should not a girl strive to model herself by the fine patterns set before her? All depends upon the choice of model.[19]

[17]Editor [George Henry Lewes], 'The Heart and the Brain', *Fortnightly Review* I (1865), p. 74.
[18]Anthony Trollope, 'The Higher Education of Women' (1868), reprinted in Morris L. Parrish, ed., Trollope, *Four Lectures* (London, Constable, 1938), p. 85.
[19]Adams, *Woman's Work*, p. 142.

Adams is not short of possible examples. From Shakespeare, there are Juliet, Cordelia, Rosalind; Miranda, with her 'virgin openness of heart', or 'the lofty maidenhood of Isabella'. More up to date, he offers Tennyson's Dora, and, as one might wearily expect, what Adams calls 'Mr Coventry Patmore's fine panegyric of the domestic affections, that beautiful poem of "The Angel in the House".' Rather than swallowing the theory that a reader will habitually and uncritically identify herself with the central character in a work, he suggests that she should continually be matching herself up against protagonists, asking if she has the heroism of Charlotte Brontë's Shirley, or the 'glowing piety' of Dinah, in *Adam Bede*, or the 'amiability' of Evelina. Dorothea Brooke provides a particularly useful object lesson. Adams suffers no disappointment at her eventual fate as Will Ladislaw's helpmate; ignores the nascent critical implications of Eliot's remark that 'no one stated exactly what else that was in her power she ought rather to have done', and proclaims himself fully satisfied with the ending, with its emphasis on fulfilling the ideal that lies in front of one, in not spending oneself on vain dreams, hoping to become a new Theresa or Antigone.[20] The *Eclectic and Congregational Review*, in 1868, also turned in approval to what it saw as George Eliot's sympathetic knowledge of human nature, valuable since, it claimed, 'Women instinctively resort to fiction as a source of consolation and help.'[21] With *Middlemarch* not yet published, Romola was advanced as Eliot's 'sublimest creation of female character', and, more controversially, Maggie Tulliver was praised. Other critics had condemned Eliot: since she had her heroine drown in the Floss, this was 'not likely to point out the right path to others who may be drawn by a similar impulsive love into circumstances as difficult.' But this critic believed that now temptation had been overcome, error atoned by suffering, duty had usurped the place of love; so 'no more was left to be accomplished, and death was the natural crown to it all, that a fresh life might be commenced under newer and happier auspices'.[22] Nor were fiction and Shakespearean drama the only literary forms which could be beneficial. In 1842, Mrs Ellis, in her popular manual *The Daughters of England* claimed, unsurprisingly, that the Bible was the most important didactic reading, but she also made out a strong case for poetry. This case was linked in with popular conceptions of a woman's psyche and duty. A woman's whole life, as Ellis puts it, 'from the cradle to the grave, is one of feeling, rather than of action'; her 'highest duty is so often to suffer, and be still'; woman, 'in her inexhaustible sympathies, can only live in the existence of another'.[23] Poetry is the literary form which can most surely take a woman out of herself – something which, in any case, she naturally has no difficulty in accomplishing – and can only lead to beneficial effects. It can open up the reader to that which lies beyond the 'dull realities of common life', and it feeds a desirable type of idealism, since it offers us

[20]*Op. cit.*, pp. 123–36; p. 150.
[21]Unsigned article, 'Lady Novelists', *Eclectic and Congregational Review* XV (1868), p. 302.
[22]*Op. cit.*, p. 309.
[23]Mrs. Ellis, *The Daughters of England* (London, Fisher, Son & Co., 1842), p. 126.

sentiments of sublimity, tenderness and love. Hence 'for woman to cast away the love of poetry, is to pervert from their natural course the sweetest and loveliest tendencies of a truly feminine mind'.[24] Moreover, at a less abstract level, it would be a good idea if women, through their familiarity with the genre, came to accustom their husbands to poetry when they returned home in the evenings, since this would teach them that something lay beyond the world of their office, counter, or daily newspaper.

Defences were even offered for the types of writing which elsewhere were most strongly condemned. Some critics were determined to find laudably didactic qualities in 'sensation novels'. Thus the *Medical Critic's* correspondent wrote of Mary Braddon's *Aurora Floyd* that 'the whole novel may be regarded as an admonition to young ladies not to let their early fancies run away with them'. With a realism which tempers much of the contemporary hysteria on the subject of such fiction, he continues:

> although a sensation novelist must step a little over the bounds of probability, although clandestine marriages with grooms are unfrequent, and although, when contracted, they usually involve a totally different chain of consequences from those imagined by Miss Braddon – still, young ladies who read newspapers will not, on the whole, learn much previously unknown evil from the romance.[25]

But the measured tones of this contrast considerably with the far more frequently antagonistic criticism which was levelled against Mary Braddon, or Rhoda Broughton, or Florence Marryat, or many other names which are now even less well known. These sensation novels were a conspicuous commercial success. First serialized in popular magazines, they were snapped up by the customers of circulating libraries. They were characterized not just by their melodramatic domestic mysteries, but often by a sense of female anger, of frustration against the tedium of being trapped in a loveless marriage, against the marriage market itself. The heroine of Rhoda Broughton's *Cometh Up as a Flower* complains:

> His arm is round my waist, and he is brushing my eyes and cheeks and brow with his somewhat bristly moustache as often as he feels inclined – for am I not his property? Has not he every right to kiss my face if he chooses, to clasp me and hold me, and drag me about in whatever manner he wills, for has he not bought me?[26]

In this way, a wide readership came face to face, in dramatized form, with ideas which were being voiced in more traditionally serious quarters, as in a *Westminster Review* article of 1857, which condemned:

> those marriages which form the opprobrium of our social system, in which a portionless girl sells herself, or is sold by her parents, to the

[24]*Op. cit.* pp. 126–27.
[25]Unsigned article, 'Sensation Novels', *Medical Critic and Psychological Journal* III (1863), p. 519.
[26]Rhoda Broughton, *Cometh Up as a Flower* (2 vols., London, Richard Bentley, 1867), II, pp. 150–1.

highest bidder; for this is the plain English of marriages where beauty on the one side purchases wealth on the other – marriages which can be viewed in no other light than that of a legalised prostitution.[27]

Yet it was not such ideas which were most readily singled out for criticism, but rather the presence of sexual desire, sexual energy. Thus the Christian–moralistic Mrs Oliphant overstated the case, in *Blackwood's* of 1867, when she claimed, in shocked tones, that these novels feature women who 'marry their grooms in fits of sensual passion; women who pray their lovers to carry them off from husbands and homes they hate; women, at the very least of it, who give and receive burning kisses and frantic embraces, and live in a voluptuous dream'.[28] The *Christian Remembrancer* of 1863, speaking with a different conception of the physiological and psychological organization of the body from that held by Lewes, complained that the sensation novel played on the nerves, rather than on the heart; that it drugged thought and reason, preferring instead to trust to the power of intuition – something which, in this case, was *not* considered a particularly desirable attribute of Woman. The attention was, in such instances, stimulated 'through the lower and more animal instincts'. Chief among the dangers of this fiction was the fact that, for its young woman readers, it could 'open out a picture of life free from all the perhaps irksome checks that confine their own existence'. The novels were seen by this reviewer as a sign of the times, 'of impatience of old restraints, and a craving for some fundamental change in the working of society'.[29] Whilst there was certainly some truth in this theory, it was of course anathema for those who liked their society as it was, or as how they wished to believe it to be. The *Medical Critic* was right to point out, however, that it was not just in the novel alone that standards were changing: 'the popular craving for excitement' was pandered to in the columns of the daily papers, fast 'becoming formidable rivals to quiet novels'.[30] It also mentioned, although it did not support, a further fashionable theory: that what it itself put forward as a new direction in the present generation, the 'interest excited by sexual immorality', was due to the fashion for the crinoline, which led to the habitual display of women's legs, whether walking up or down hill, turning round quickly, getting over a stile or into a railway carriage:

> The rising generation of young women and girls have been trained to this display from their infancy. The result, it is argued, is the utter destruction of that modesty which is one of the strongest outposts of virtue. Modesty being destroyed, chastity becomes a mere matter of

[27]Unsigned review article, 'Capabilities and Disabilities of Women', *Westminster Review* 67 (1857), pp. 65–6.

[28]Unsigned review article [Mrs Oliphant], 'Novels', *Blackwood's Edinburgh Magazine* 12 (1867), p. 259.

[29]Unsigned article, 'Our Female Sensation Novelists', *Christian Remembrancer* n.s. XLVI (1863), p. 210.

[30]'Sensation Novels', *Medical Critic*, p. 514.

prudence and caution; and girls and women who are restrained by the fear of consequences from giving the rein to their own passions, still find a fictitious excitement in reading about, and also imagining, the gratified passions of others.[31]

But is this escapism necessarily a bad thing? This is a question which has been raised in several places recently, in relation to contemporary romantic and Gothic fiction, for example, by Tania Modleski in *Loving With a Vengeance*, or, in a wider context of women's reading habits and patterns of identification, by Rachel Brownstein in *Becoming a Heroine*. For reading fiction does allow women – and men, for that matter – temporarily to disappear from their daily life into a world where they can identify with a central character, share in the position of being at the centre of a world, a person to whom things happen, around whom events revolve. The process is akin to directed day-dreaming, often along the lines of what Freud termed the 'family romance'. Although he was talking about the common fantasy, as he saw it, of imagining oneself a son or daughter of royalty, the term can be applied to a pattern of reading, of identifying either with those in a higher social class than oneself, or, indeed, with those who appear in one way or another to have greater freedom than the reader. It is notable, as contemporary critics were often pointing out, how many orphans, how many motherless girls there were in mid-Victorian fiction: circumstances simultaneously conducive to reduced restrictions and increased danger. Protagonists were thus frequently presented as being forced into forms of self-assertion, coerced into taking charge of their own lives. They could often, therefore, be placed in positions where it was appropriate for them to articulate the social limitations and frustrations which they came across. Thus, as with Jane Eyre's famous lament that women 'suffer from too rigid a restraint, too absolute a stagnation',[32] they were potentially speaking not just to, but for, their readers. Although plenty of modern readers have felt cheated by Jane, it would seem, abdicating her hard-won sense of independence and self-responsibility to marry Rochester – albeit suitably mutilated and chastened – Brownstein has pointed out that, however pernicious its lasting effects, the marriage plot on which most nineteenth-century novels depend 'is about finding validation of one's uniqueness and importance by being singled out among all other women by a man. The man's love is proof of the girl's value, and payment for it.'[33] Day-dreaming of this particular validation, in a society which put such a heavy premium on marriage, must have been a rather sad, but perhaps necessary form of wistfulness among many of the half-million so-called 'surplus' or 'redundant' women of the mid century. The popularity of the governess fiction, as one could call the genre, can be gauged by the sulky reactions of some men, who found that *they* were

---

[31]*Op. cit.*, p. 517.
[32]Charlotte Brontë, *Jane Eyre* (1847: Oxford, Clarendon Press 1969), p. 153.
[33]Rachel M. Brownstein, *Becoming a Heroine* (1982: Harmondsworth, Penguin, 1984), p. xv.

deprived of a point of day-dreaming entry into such novels. A writer in the *Saturday Review*, in 1887, asked:

> Who can follow with attention the adventures of a heroine whose personal appearance he objects to? or who can enter with rapture into the aspirations and ambitions of a young man whom he would studiously avoid if he came across him at his club?[34]

It should not be thought that success on the marriage market was the only type of vicarious satisfaction which could be experienced through the reading of fiction. It did not, after all, have to be other women with whom the reader identified herself. Charlotte Yonge, writing of fiction for the working classes, noted that 'girls will often greatly prefer a book about the other sex', though 'boys almost universally disdain books about girls'.[35] Largely, of course, this represents a desire for escape into a more active and adventurous world. At a more complex level of argument, Elaine Showalter, in *A Literature of Their Own*, has drawn attention to the number of crippled or weakened male heroes populating mid-century fiction, such as the hero of Dinah Mulock Craik's *John Halifax, Gentleman*, and many of Charlotte Yonge's central male characters. These model heroes, as she puts it, 'are the product of female fantasies that are much more concerned with power and authority that with romance'.[36] Despite their physical condition, such men are extremely aggressive in bourgeois economic terms. Their defectiveness, argues Showalter, allows a means by which a woman, ill at ease with her own disadvantaged position within society, can enter into these fictional lives of people who achieve success despite the odds being stacked against them.

Showalter finds another type of writer's and reader's fantasy lurking within sensation novels: that of the woman, trapped in marriage, who can vicariously wreak her revenge on men. Thus, as she sees it, *Lady Audley's Secret*:

> presents one with a carefully controlled female fantasy, which Braddon understands and manipulates with minute exactitude. Braddon's bigamous heroine deserts her child, pushes husband number one down a well, thinks about poisoning husband number two, and sets fire to a hotel in which her other male acquaintances are residing.[37]

This is too absolute an explanation: in some ways, *Lady Audley's Secret* is itself fiction for the governess market, since the villainess, portrayed as ruthlessly selfish, silly and unsympathetic, throws into serious doubt the invariable goodness of the story-book heroine, the enviably pretty, golden-ringletted girl with whom everyone, from verger to porter, falls in love at

---

[34]Unsigned article, 'To Those About to Write a Novel', *Saturday Review* LXIII (27 January 1887), p. 122.

[35]Yonge, *Books to Lend*, p. 30.

[36]Elaine Showalter, *A Literature of Their Own: British Women Novelists from Brontë to Lessing* (1977: London, Virago, 1978), p. 136.

[37]*Op. cit.*, p. 163.

sight. Yet, within the novel, she is largely viewed from the perspective of the hero, and can thus also be seen as representative of a masculinist tradition, despite the sex of the author: a tradition of fear of sirens, like Margaret in Wilkie Collins's *Basil*, whose beauty allures the hero on an omnibus, leads him blindly into a strange, secret marriage with her, leaving him to discover at painful and melodramatic length that her physical charms mask innate deceit and shallow self-regard. Despite the fact that *Lady Audley's Secret* and its counterparts can readily be termed 'popular fiction', they are still resistant to a monolinear interpretation.

Nonetheless, Showalter's overall contention would seem, in many cases, to hold true: 'The enormous popularity of the woman sensationalists reflects the skill with which they articulated the fantasies of their readers, fantasies that they themselves fervently shared.'[38] Moreover, as the mid-nineteenth-century woman read, usually within the privacy, the loneliness even, of her own home, she could feel that she was not alone after all; that she shared needs, and fantasies, not just with the book's characters, and the book's author, but with an assumed community of other readers. It is this hypothesis, of links existing within and serving to maintain a type of literary community, which the rest of this article seeks to develop. My argument is that the very existence of literature of many types formed a shared bond between these individual reading centres, gave them a sense of knowledge, of a world in which they had their own competence; in which they could exchange, to use Pierre Bourdieu's term, 'cultural capital'.[39] Using three of the best known sensation novels as a starting point – Mary Braddon's *Lady Audley's Secret* and *Aurora Floyd*, and Rhoda Broughton's *Cometh Up as a Flower* – it is possible to distinguish three separate ways in which these novels make use of an assumed knowledge of further written contexts.

In the first place, a common grounding in general reading seems taken for granted. This allows an author to drop quotations into the voice of her autobiographical heroine–narrator, as in the case of Rhoda Broughton, or into her own authorial commentary. *Cometh Up as a Flower* is as studded with apposite poetic references as a Victorian girl's album. After Nell's handsome but penniless army suitor, Richard, bids her farewell in the lane at evening: 'Then, like a blast away I passed / And no man saw me more.'[40] When she muses on her family's declined financial fortunes, and on the absence of an heir, it is an apt moment to comment: 'The old order changeth; giving place to new, / And God fulfils himself in many ways.'[41] Nell is someone who, as dawn approaches, remarks with apparent spontaneity: 'The stars die and "O'er night's brim day boils at last".'[42] The frequency of poetic references, and of the enjoyable, deliberately self-

[38]*Op. cit.*, p. 159.
[39]Pierre Bourdieu, 'Cultural Reproduction and Social Reproduction', *Knowledge, Education and Cultural Change*, ed. Richard Brown (London, Tavistock Publications, 1973), p. 73.
[40]Broughton, *Cometh Up* I, p. 124.
[41]*Op. cit.*, p. 201.
[42]*Op. cit.*, p. 322.

conscious employment of 'literary' vocabulary; the occasional insertion of a *recherché* French phrase, all create a conspiracy of shared culture between the narrator and reader which serves to emphasize, among other factors, quite how wrong Sir Hugh is for her as a husband. As she drives back with him, reluctantly, from a picnic, he exclaims:

> "Jolly and big the moon looks, doesn't it? like a Cheshire cheese!"
> The moon, the sacred moon, the be-songed, be-sonneted moon, the moon that Romeo sware by, and that Milton saw
>
> "Stooping thro' a fleecy cloud,"
>
> like a *Cheshire cheese!*
>
> "How poetical," I said, sardonically.
>
> "No, it isn't poetical, I know. I'm not up to the dodge of poetry. I don't go in for these kinds of things."[43]

In *Aurora Floyd*, too, the text is underpinned by paraquotation, from Thackeray, Dickens, Macaulay, a variety of Shakespeare plays, *Frankenstein*, Victor Hugo, Tennyson, George Eliot, Charlotte M. Yonge. There are some references, however, which make one wonder quite what degree of literary competence Braddon expects from her readers, or whether, on occasion, she is anticipating references to be picked up within a relatively small circle of cognoscenti. Chapter 16, for example, ends with Mrs Powell, the sinister housekeeper companion, sneaking a look at a letter which her mistress had written to the stable manager – the man who was, of course, Aurora's legal husband.

> It was this second page which Mrs Powell saw. The words written at the top of the leaf were these: – "Above all, express no surprise. – A."
> There was no ordinary conclusion to the letter; no other signature than this big capital A.[44]

This is surely an employment of the badge of adultery in Hawthorne's *The Scarlet Letter*: a novel which, even if quite widely noted in England – *Blackwood*'s, for example, had spoken of 'the unwholesome fascination of this romance'[45] – could hardly be relied upon to feature in a repertoire of texts widely known among young women readers.

The second type of literary cross-referencing which takes place is between different types of contemporary fiction. In almost every case, the desire is to suggest a truth to nature, rather than to fictional convention, in the novel in which such a reference occurs. Thus Nell, married to the dull middle-aged sportsman Sir Hugh, is horrified when the suitor she had abandoned as faithless and uncaring reappears. She contemplates running off with him, but Richard, in his nobility, refuses to allow her to take such a course which would blacken her name. Waiting for her perfidious sister Dolly to pay a visit, she sits reading a novel which can only be *East Lynne*.

[43]*Op. cit.*, pp. 302-3.
[44]Mary E. Braddon, *Aurora Floyd* (1863: London, Virago, 1984), p. 155.
[45]Unsigned review article [Margaret Oliphant], 'Modern Novelists – Great and Small', *Blackwood's Edinburgh Magazine* LXXVII (1855), p. 563.

It interests me rather, for it is all about a married woman, who ran away from her husband and suffered the extremity of human ills in consequence . . . but even now, I can hardly imagine that I should have been very miserable if Dick had taken me away with him.[46]

She goes on to lament that in real life, no 'story book code of morality'[47] exists: her sister, forger of the fateful letter which has kept Richard away from Nell, is to be rewarded by marrying a cotton lord worth £80,000 a year. In *Lady Audley's Secret*, the male hero, Robert Audley, is used to receiving his stimulation from yellow-backed French novels: a highly familiar signifier of literary immorality. But once he gets embroiled with the facts of his close friend's disappearance, and presumed murder, at the hands of his bigamous wife, not only is he haunted by the implications of the situation, which seems the more sinister viewed in the recollection, he says, of Alexandre Dumas and Wilkie Collins, but 'the yellow papered fictions on the shelves above his head seemed stale and profitless'.[48] *Aurora Floyd* contains plenty of side-sweeps at the dullness of High Church novels, and of conventional romances, especially those where the pattern is for the curtain to drop on the heroine's marriage. But, asks Braddon:

is it necessary that the novelist, after devoting three volumes to the description of a courtship of six weeks' duration, should reserve for himself only half a page in which to tell us the events of two-thirds of a life time? Aurora is married, and settled, and happy; sheltered, one would imagine, from all dangers, safe under the wing of her stalwart adorer; but it does not therefore follow, [adds Braddon ominously, promisingly] that the story of her life is done.[49]

This form of allusion-making is one which is dependent on a quiet glow, rather than shock of recognition taking place in reading. It fosters a sense of security: that this is a highly familiar environment, in which fiction plays an important part in determining terms of reference, and yet the hint is also offered that this particular work is a little bit different, a little bit more true to the actual world, the world which the reader herself inhabits. It does not demand the alertness which is needed to respond to the third, less common type of cross-referencing. This also relies on the reader picking up references to the familiar – and then undermines her expectations. For example, in *Aurora Floyd*, Aurora is frequently compared to Cleopatra, called 'that Egyptian goddess, that Assyrian queen, with the flashing eyes and the serpentine coils of purple black hair'.[50] But she is hardly the sexual temptress, leading a noble man to his ruined doom, as she was presented on the Victorian stage of the time. Nor does she herself meet a tragic, if dignified death, but is last seen, happily married, on her husband's

[46]Broughton, *Cometh Up* II, p. 250.
[47]*Op. cit.*, p. 253.
[48]Mary E. Braddon, *Lady Audley's Secret* (3 vols., London, Tinsley Brothers, 1862) II, p. 5.
[49]Braddon, *Aurora Floyd*, p. 137.
[50]*Op. cit.*, p. 182.

comfortable Yorkshire estate. Similarly, the novel is full of references to *Othello*. Both Aurora's first and second husbands feel agonizing pangs of jealousy and bitterness, and Braddon makes the parallel with Shakespeare in both cases. Yet unlike Othello, Mellish refused to think 'ill of his wife. He resolutely shut his eyes to all damning evidence. He clung with a desperate tenacity to his belief in her purity.'[51] The first husband envies the satisfaction of revenge that 'the chap in the play' got 'for his trouble when the blackamoor smothers his wife',[52] but is murdered himself. Mrs Powell also harbours Iago-like resentment, but only, unlike Iago, meets defeat. This parallel has been noted by Robert Wolff in his biography of Braddon, *Sensational Victorian*, where he comments that 'most important, Desdemona is innocent and yet is killed; Aurora is guilty but gets away scot-free.'[53] Literary allusions, in other words, need not necessarily lead in the direction which they would seem to anticipate. The attention which is demanded on the part of the reader, not to mention the command which she is implicitly expected to uphold over a wide range of literary references, goes some way to giving the lie to the mindlessness which so many critics believed was induced by the opiate of sensation fiction.

Retrospective knowledge of the Victorian period; sympathy for the relatively restrictive conditioning to which many middle-class women were subject; an acknowledgement of the existence of a community of readers; a greater understanding of the necessary relief which can be provided through escapist reading: all of these can allow us, today, to recognize the injustice behind some of the attacks on the reading habits of Victorian women. But, at the time, public anxiety over what women read was too deeply entrenched as a fashion, the belief in the affective power of literature far too strong, for more than a few to query whether there might really be all that much danger in reading the more sensational type of fiction. To ensure that what prevailed were works which maintained suitable ideas of duty and Christian forebearance, couched in moderate language:

> Husbands and fathers, [as the *Christian Remembrancer* put it in 1863] may begin to look around them and scrutinize the parcel that arrives from Mudies, when young ladies are led to contrast the actual with the ideal we see worked out in popular romance; the mutual duties, the reciprocal forbearance, the inevitable trials of every relation in real life, with the triumph of mere female fascination, before which man falls prostrate and helpless.[54]

The thought that readers might legitimately enjoy a temporary escape from the trials of real life, imagining themselves into just such a position of power, exacting revenge for the paternalistic authority being exercised so unquestioningly over them, does not seem to have occurred.

[51]*Op. cit.*, p. 265.
[52]*Op. cit.*, p. 174.
[53]Robert Wolff, *Sensational Victorian: The Life and Fiction of Mary Elizabeth Braddon* (New York and London, Garland Publishing Inc., 1979), p. 151.
[54]'Our Female Sensation Novelists', *Christian Remembrancer*, p. 234.

Note

As a sample of the new historicism in literary scholarship one might mention David Norbrook, *Poetry and Politics in the English Renaissance* (London, Routledge, 1985) and Jerome McGann, *The Beauty of Inflections: Literary Investigations in Historical Method and Theory* (London, Oxford University Press, 1985). The historicism can also be coupled with an interest in those interpersonal features of the language of literary works which enable them to participate in real social discourse. See Roger Fowler, *Literature as Social Discourse: the Practice of Linguistic Criticism* (London, Batsford Academic and Educational, 1981); Roger D. Sell, 'The Unstable Discourse of Henry Vaughan: a Literary-Pragmatic Account', in Alan Rudrum, ed., *Essential Articles for the Study of Henry Vaughan* (Hamden, Archon Books, 1986). The present article does not go in for detailed linguistic analysis, but it should introduce some of the thinking behind accounts of the pragmatics of politeness and modality in Dickens which I hope to present elsewhere.

Authoritative texts of Dickens's novels are being established in the Clarendon Edition (Oxford) of his works. The Clarendon texts are also being reproduced in the paperback World's Classics series (Oxford, OUP). Good paperback editions are also available in the Penguin English Library series (Harmondsworth). Other Dickens texts: *The Speeches of Charles Dickens*, ed. K.J. Fielding (Oxford, Clarendon Press, 1960); *The Letters of Charles Dickens* (The Pilgrim Edition), ed. M. House and G. Storey (Oxford, Clarendon Press, 1965 – [in progress]).

The footnotes to the present article refer to several of the standard works of scholarship and criticism, and to some of the critical anthologies. Also noteworthy: Philip Collins, *Charles Dickens: the Critical Heritage* (London, Routledge and Kegan Paul, 1971); Stephen Wall, *Charles Dickens: a Critical Anthology* (Harmondsworth, Penguin Books, 1970); Edgar Johnson, *Charles Dickens: His Tragedy and Triumph*, two vols (London, Victor Gollancz, 1953) – the standard modern life; Philip Collins, *Dickens and Crime* (London, Macmillan, 1962) and *Dickens and Education* (London, Macmillan, 1963); H.P. Sucksmith, *The Narrative Art of Charles Dickens: the Rhetoric of Sympathy and Irony in his Novels* (Oxford, Clarendon Press, 1970); James R. Kincaid, *Dickens and the Rhetoric of Laughter* (Oxford, Clarendon Press, 1971); John Carey, *The Violent Effigy: a Study of Dickens's Imagination* (London, Faber, 1973); Angus Wilson, *The World of Charles Dickens* (London, Secker and Warburg, 1970); D. Walder, *Dickens and Religion* (London, Allen and Unwin, 1981).

Detailed bibliographies: Joseph Gold, *The Stature of Dickens: a Centenary Bibliography* (University of Manitoba Press and University of Toronto Press, 1971); R.C. Churchill, *A Bibliography of Dickensian Criticism 1836-1975* (London, Macmillan, 1975); John J. Fenstermaker, *Charles Dickens, 1940-1975: an Analytical Subject Index to Periodical Criticism of the Novels and Christmas Books* (London, George Prior, 1979); Alan M. Cohn and K.K. Collins, *The Cumulated Dickens Checklist 1970-1979* (Troy, Whitston Publishing Company, 1982). Dickens journals: *The Dickensian: a Magazine for Dickens Lovers*; *Dickens Studies: a Journal of Modern Research and Criticism* (1965–70); *Dickens Studies Annual*; *Dickens Studies Newsletter*.

5

Dickens and the New Historicism: the Polyvocal Audience and Discourse of *Dombey and Son*

Roger D. Sell

Dickens is often described as having belonged to, and as having written for, a middle class whose traits can be totted up readily enough: class pedantry; prudishness; a taste for domestic comfort, and for novels such as *David Copperfield*; and so on.[1] Middle-class readers of this stamp are said to have admired Dickens as an ordinary man of good humour, a benevolent friend of the family, and to have been faithful to him throughout his career.[2]

On the other hand, he is just as often described as having stopped short of full solidarity with such a grouping. His central characters may huddle round their middle-class hearth, but he always intimated, whether through strange characters glimpsed only once or through 'irrelevant' circumstances narrated 'parenthetically', peripheral worlds of misery and squalor.[3] He may have been a practical man of the world, who adopted the standards of taste and decorum of the middle-class audience on which he was financially dependent, but he could be unmerciful towards middle-class hypocrisy.[4] And especially from *Dombey and Son* onwards, it was from the grotesque contortions of the middle class that much of his comedy sprang.[5] The impression one gets here, then, is that while the public was relatively stable Dickens himself was ambiguous, undecided or subversive.

The trouble with all such discussion is that it tends to freeze the middle class in a single narrow stereotype and ignore the phenomenon which

---

[1] See Richard D. Altick, 'Varieties of Readers' Response: the Case of *Dombey and Son*', *Yearbook of English Studies* X (1980), pp. 70–94; Humphrey House, *The Dickens World* (London, Oxford University Press, second edn 1942), pp. 133–69; J.D. Jump, 'Dickens and his Readers', *Bulletin of the John Rylands Library* LIV (1971–2), pp. 384–97.

[2] See Philip Collins, 'The Popularity of Dickens', *The Dickensian* LXX (1974), pp. 5–20; George H. Ford, *Dickens and his Readers: Aspects of Novel Criticism since 1836* (New York, W.W. Norton, second edn 1965), pp. 3–155.

[3] See Susan R. Horton, *The Reader in the Dickens World: Style and Response* (London, Macmillan, 1981).

[4] See James M. Brown, *Dickens: Novelist in the Market-Place: a Sociological Reading of the Later Novels of Dickens* (London, Macmillan, 1982).

[5] See Roger B. Henkle, *Comedy and Culture: England 1820–1900* (Princeton, Princeton University Press, 1980).

Bakhtin has called heteroglossia: in any given culture at any given time there is not just one language, one voice, but many. True, some middle-class attitudes and speech habits were sometimes more dominant than others, and there are very long passages of Dickens for which we shall have to acknowledge that the clichés about Victorian mental and cultural life certainly do apply, not only to the public which enjoyed them but to Dickens himself as their author. But for all that, both the public and Dickens, like audiences and writers of all periods, were involved in a volatile process of self-discovery and self-creation.

Hence the range of response to Dickens himself, which was wider than we sometimes think, and which became still wider as time went on.[6] Partly this was because the Brontës, Thackeray and George Eliot started to suggest different forms of novelistic achievement. But it was also a readerly corre-lative to Dickens's increasing explicitness of social comment. Both public and author were evolving. So Arnold found in Dickens an ally against the Philistines, while Trollope thought of him as a radical with no true under-standing of political process.

Acceptance and rejection of criticism were always middle-class poten-tials, but acceptance/rejection is in any case too crude an antithesis to capture the manifold self-contradictions of early readers' responses, not only to Dickens's novels but also in major questions of morality and socio-economics. Dickens, too, was as self-contradictory as any reader. On matters of sexual morality, for instance, the middle class certainly did come to embrace the 'Victorian' clichés about domestic bliss. These doubtless seemed to represent the deeper wisdom, an ideal always to be held in view even if never wholly attained, or at any rate held in view of the countless children in the Victorian audience. Dickens himself held very strong views about his authorial responsibilities here.[7] Equally, however, nobody with Dickens's own experience, marital and extramarital, could adopt the clichés without some inner doubt, and the potentiality for such unsettling experience was of course ever-present in the lives of Dickens and his readers alike, sometimes casting a shadow of darker knowledge. Again, the clichés could also be undermined by an awareness of the role marriage could play in schemes of social betterment, power and prestige.

Similarly, on issues such as industrial and economic growth, analysis can distinguish at least three main strands in the middle-class response which in the day-to-day give-and-take of social discourse were sometimes inter-woven in no very logical fashion. First, there was the traditional bourgeois spirit of entrepreneurial keenness for new technology and new markets. This took a positive view of the growth of cities and factories, and of the engineering achievements represented by the railways and by the many British inventions which won prizes at the 1851 Exhibition. Sometimes

---

[6]See Ford, *Dickens and his Readers*, pp. 75–155.
[7]See David Paroissien, 'Literature's "Eternal Duties": Dickens's Professional Creed', in Robert Giddings, ed., *The Changing World of Charles Dickens* (London, Barnes and Noble, 1983), pp. 21–50.

such enthusiasm readily embraced the age's 'new' men, the ironmasters and captains of industry who, energetically combining four roles until then quite separate – engineer, manager, capitalist, merchant – were making Britain the leading industrial and trading nation. That Ruskin should have felt that Dickens himself had the ironmaster as his hero, was a 'leader of the steam-whistle party *par excellence*', reminds us of the favourable characterization of Doyce in *Little Dorrit* and Rouncewell in *Bleak House*.[8] To admire the new men, moreover, was not necessarily to set store by economic success at the expense of social justice. The middle class sometimes showed itself capable of implementing the hedonistic calculus of the utilitarians and working from practical reforms. Dickens himself was involved in ventures such as Urania Cottage, sewer improvement and Nova Scotia Gardens, and he continued his efforts in his fiction. *Little Dorrit* campaigned for sanitary engineering, and against bureaucratic red tape.

Secondly, however, the utilitarian stress on economic and material criteria was challenged throughout the age by the view that the truly important life of man and society was spiritual and emotional, a view which drew support from traditional Christian and moral teachings, and from poets and sages such as Wordsworth, Carlyle and Ruskin.[9] Even John Stuart Mill, as a young man, had a period of disaffection with utilitarianism, a crisis which ended only with his discovery of Wordsworth. As for Dickens, this is one of the points at which *Hard Times* is of interest: dedicated to Carlyle, it denounced utilitarian 'facts' and included a condemnation of a captain of industry – Bounderby – which might seem odd coming from the creator of Doyce and Rouncewell. In *The Old Curiosity Shop*, again, there are nightmare industrial landscapes which reflect a strong anti-urban tendency in this tradition.

Thirdly, the middle class increasingly distanced itself still further from industrialization and the city, in its aspirations to the life-style of the next class up. Science, technology, industry, commerce, on which middle-class prosperity – and the future of the country – depended, were sometimes among the great unmentionables. Sons were sent to private schools where, far from dirtying their hands with the practical subjects taught at Owen's College or the Mechanics' Institutes, they acquired a veneer of Latin and Greek.[10] Dickens, of course, laughed heartily at the foibles of the would-be genteel, created Doyce and Rouncewell, and was associated with the adult education movement. Yet much of the force of *Great Expectations* sprang from his ability not only to criticize the parvenu hero's pride of place but

[8]See Philip Collins, 'Dickens and Industrialism', *Studies in English Literature, 1500–1900* XX (1980), pp. 651–73; John Mac Veagh, *Tradeful Merchants: the Portrayal of the Capitalist in English Literature* (London, Routledge and Kegan Paul, 1981); Ivan Melada, *The Captain of Industry in English Fiction, 1821–1871* (Albuquerque, University of New Mexico Press, 1970).
[9]See John Colmer, *Coleridge to Catch-22: Images of Society* (London, Macmillan, 1978).
[10]See Eric Ashby, *Technology and the Academics: an Essay on the Universities and the Scientific Revolution* (London, Macmillan, 1958); Martin J. Wiener, *English Culture and the Decline of the Industrial Spirit, 1850–1980* (Cambridge, CUP, 1981).

also to render it understandable. His other heroes' tendency to end up in a condition of feather-bed respectability and radiant idleness was commented on by George Orwell, and some of his reflexes were clearly those of the middle-class territorial instinct.[11] Not that *Dombey and Son* and *David Copperfield* didn't satirize the ideological repression of the lower orders by charity schools. But the revelation of Uriah Heep's crimes only confirmed David and Dickens's own deep prejudice against him: some people were not really welcome in the meritocracy of hard work.[12] A similar class defensiveness gave a certain edge to descriptions of crowds and riots in *A Tale of Two Cities* and *Barnaby Rudge*.[13]

What, then, are the implications of this diversity of middle-class ideology for the novel? Bakhtin, although his account of the novel makes heteroglossia the master concept, explains that 'the novel can be defined as a diversity of social speech types . . . and a diversity of individual voices, *artistically organized*' (my italics).[14] When he goes on to speak of the novel 'orchestrating' its themes and 'dialogizing' the various social voices present we may even begin to wonder whether the process he has in mind is broadly analogous to the imagination's reconciliation of opposites as conceived by Coleridge or by Coleridge's modern descendants, the New Critical proponents of tension, ambiguity, paradox, irony. If so, and if Dickens's novels do have such a unity, it might be that the self-contradictions are synthesized in some ideologically higher structure.

What Bakhtin is thinking of in his account of 'hybridization' in *Little Dorrit* is certainly a kind of irony. Hybridization is the mixing, within a single utterance, of at least two linguistic consciousnesses, often widely separated in social space.

> That illustrious man and great national ornament, Mr Merdle, continued his shining course. It began to be widely understood that one who had done society the admirable service *of making so much money out of it*, could not be suffered to remain a commoner. A baronetcy was spoken of with confidence; a peerage was frequently mentioned.[15]

The italics are Bakhtin's, drawing attention to what we should normally describe as the ironical solidarity of all the other language in this passage with the hypocritically ceremonial general opinion of Merdle. 'Making so much money out of it' is a different, undercutting, outsider's voice, which we tend to attribute here to Dickens himself, and which points up the irony of the rest.

---

[11]See Ivanka Kovačević, *Fact into Fiction: English Literature and the Industrial Scene*, (Leicester, Leicester University Press, 1975).
[12]See Roger D. Sell, 'Projection Characters in *David Copperfield*', *Studia Neophilologica* LV (1983), pp. 19–30.
[13]See David Craig, 'The Crowd in Dickens' and Thomas J. Rice, 'The Politics of *Barnaby Rudge*', in Giddings, *Changing World*, pp. 75–90 and 51–74.
[14]M.M. Bakhtin, *The Dialogic Imagination: Four Essays*, (Austin, University of Texas Press, 1981), pp. 262–3.
[15]*Op. cit.*, p. 306.

Yet the irony in such cases seems to be rather a means of inventing copy than a principle in accordance with which the copy is organized into a book: the clash of voices generates a certain texture rather than a structure. As far as Dickens is concerned, Bakhtin's 'organization', 'orchestration', 'dialogization' do *not* seem to amount to a larger unity – not even an ironical or paradoxical unity – of the kind to satisfy critics in the Romantic–Symbolist tradition. And certainly it now seems far less easy to attribute such unity to Dickens's novels than twenty or thirty years ago. In drawing attention to images and symbols, to mythical elements and atmospheric details, critics of that period performed a valuable service. These things are really present in Dickens, and Dickens himself, in his later works especially, saw them as a means of drawing some of his materials closer together. But in declaring the result a total imaginative unity the critics were perhaps a little too eager. Their criteria of relevance were too generously elastic, and they were so far from the Aristotelian tradition in critical thought that they never really asked whether Dickens's novels had an artistic wholeness as mimesis – whether their actions have satisfying beginnings, middles and ends based on genuine necessities and probabilities. Even more to the point here, literary scholarship of the late 1980s is showing signs of a new historicism. This compels a recognition that the texts which have come to be designated as literary, far from being special heterocosms on their own, have functioned and can still function as interactive social discourse. We are now far more alert to the risk, in other words, that arguments for artistic unity in Dickens will tend to subvert Dickens's own voices, which were by no means monotonous or unchallenging. Heteroglossia in Dickens had a full expressive and affective charge which such art as he had did not shortcircuit.

Some scholars still try to wrench a *concordia discors* from him by allotting one voice to a 'real' Dickens and another voice to an anonymous 'narrative personality'. According to Richard J. Watts, the real Dickens deliberately implies that the narrative personality of *Hard Times* does not sufficiently practise the human sympathy he preaches, is unhealthily fascinated by the aristocracy, and can see no justification in the cause of the trade unions. This personality, Watts argues, may have been specially designed to appeal the prejudices of the first readers of the novel in *Household Words*, but the real Dickens, because his implications are so clear, can further address a wider and more enlightened audience such as our good selves.[16] So the novel would be a unity by having two messages at every point: a sustained and controlled ambiguity. But from such an interpretation Dickens emerges as a monster of calculation. Six or seven years ago, post-structuralist critics were of course going to the opposite extreme: Dickens had an infinite number of meanings which proliferated beyond

[16]Richard J. Watts, *The Pragmalinguistic Analysis of Narrative Texts: Narrative Co-operation in Charles Dickens's 'Hard Times'* (Tübingen, Gunter Nar Verlag, 1981). For a discussion of Watts's pragmalinguistic approach in a wider context of theory see Roger D. Sell, 'The Drama of Fictionalized Author and Reader: a Formalist Obstacle to Literary Pragmatics', *REAL: The Yearbook of Research in English and American Literature* IV (1986).

either his own control or a reader's power of determinate interpretation.[17] What is coming to seem much more natural today is, as I say, an account of Dickens's novels as social discourse. Roger Fowler, for instance, acknowledging his debt to Bakhtin, deals with *Hard Times* by analysing something of the clash of idiolects and sociolects. His argument is that we can speak only of 'polyphony' and 'problematic', of ideological tensions that remained unresolved.[18] Dickens, within the context of his own culture, meant several things at once, discretely interpretable and self-contradictory.

This applies in interesting ways to *Dombey and Son*, which was more representative of Dickens in being a long serial novel published in independent monthly numbers, and which was also the first novel on which he himself attempted to impose some sort of unity. William Axton, in an article typical of the early 1960s, argues that the novel's imagery does give it an all-embracing unity of tone.[19] Most other critics have spoken of an artistry which, aspiring to completeness, still falls short. For some, the book simply splits in two: a finely controlled part which ends with the death of Paul, and 'the rest', which is hardly controlled at all.[20] For a very different group of critics, the control goes all too far, encroaching on free creative play on the part of its author or its readers – so that, as Roland Barthes might have said, it is too *lisible*, too little *scriptible*.[21] Perhaps Steven Connor comes closest to the truth. He suggests that, both in every monthly number of every Dickens novel and in every Dickens novel as a completely published entity, there is a tension between what my earlier paragraph called texture and structure, or between what Connor himself, in structuralist terminology, calls the syntagmatic and the paradigmatic: between randomly 'metonymic' drift and a 'metaphorical' urge towards closure, shape, significance.[22]

Dickens's earliest critics were certainly right: the publication of a long novel in serial parts entailed real problems of organization. Among the first to try and refute the charge that Dickens had succumbed to these was Forster, in his account of *Dombey and Son* in his *Life of Dickens*; Dickens had a clear idea of the novel's main line from an early stage, one piece of evidence being a letter he wrote to Forster on 25 July 1846.[23] In modern

[17]See Susan R. Horton, *Interpreting Interpreting: Interpreting Dickens's Dombey* (Baltimore, Johns Hopkins University Press, 1979).

[18]Roger Fowler, 'Polyphony and Problematic in *Hard Times*', in Giddings, *Changing World*, pp. 91–108.

[19]William Axton, 'Tonal Unity in *Dombey and Son*', *PMLA* LXXVIII (1963), pp. 341–8.

[20]See George Gissing, *The Immortal Dickens* (London, Cecil Palmer, 1925), pp. 140–63; F.R. Leavis and Q.D. Leavis, *Dickens the Novelist* (Harmondsworth, Penguin, 1972), pp. 21–56.

[21]See G.K. Chesterton, Introduction to the Everyman edition of *Dombey and Son* (London, Dent, 1907); Gabriel Pearson, 'Towards a Reading of *Dombey and Son*', in Gabriel Josipovici, *The Modern English Novel: the Reader, the Writer and the Work* (London, Open Books, 1976), pp. 54–76.

[22]Steven Connor, *Charles Dickens* (Oxford, Basil Blackwell, 1985), e.g. p. 54.

[23]Reprinted in Alan Shelston, ed., *Charles Dickens: Dombey and Son and Little Dorrit: a Casebook* (London, Macmillan, 1985), pp. 38–42.

times further weight to the argument for planning and aesthetic unity has been given by John Butt and Kathleen Tillotson, who discuss, not only this letter, but other letters, the title, the cover design, the manuscripts (including the plans for each number), and the proof sheets.[24] Dickens himself, of course, though he might acknowledge the problems of serial publication from the point of view of the reader, implied that as novelist he stood quite above them:

> It would be very unreasonable to expect that many readers, pursuing a story in portions from month to month through nineteen months, will, until they have it before them complete, perceive the relations of its finer threads to the whole pattern which is always before the eyes of the story-weaver at his loom.[25]

Even from Forster's account, however, and even from Butt and Tillotson's, it is perfectly clear that important ideas for *Dombey and Son* came to Dickens as he went along. Sometimes he was actually uncertain which course to follow, and asked Forster's advice. Sometimes a particular emphasis, or lack of emphasis, resulted simply from his having to adjust his materials to the 31-page limit of the monthly number.

On reflection, some degree of randomness will not seem all that surprising. Much more astonishing, in something taking so long to create and so long to perceive, would be an unfailing homogeneity at every cross-section. In order either to write or to read such a book, a human being would lay himself open to Morfin's censure of all creatures of fossilized habit. Indeed, the most obvious resistance to change-through-time that we confront in Dickens is in his caricatures, whose mainspring of absurdity it is. Serial publication increased the chances that any self-contradictions or instabilities, in either the author or the readers, would actually come into the open. Small wonder that one modern critic describes Dickens's complexity as beginning in a 'series of separately assertive intents, passions, statements'.[26]

Other novelists published serial novels of course. Yet perhaps because Dickens was so sensitive about his own class position, and because of a strong hunch that his own instabilities were those of large sections of his reading public, his participation in the heteroglossia of the day came to be especially marked. To say this is not to take sides in one of those endless chicken-or-the-egg controversies between traditional liberal humanists and Marxian structuralists, for such controversy would quite miss the essential reciprocity of Dickens and his first readers, the circularity of their conditioning influence upon each other, the mutuality of heteroglossia. Dicken's own sense of the manifold options of attitude and tone available,

[24]John Butt and Kathleen Tillotson, *Dickens at Work* (London, Methuen, 1957), pp. 90–113.
[25]Postscript to *Our Mutual Friend*, ed. Stephen Gill (Harmondsworth, Penguin, 1971), p. 893.
[26]Barbara Hardy, 'The Complexity of Dickens', in Michael Slater, ed., *Dickens 1970: Centennial Essays* (London, Chapman and Hall, 1970), esp. p. 51.

and of a writer's opportunities for highlighting and extending them, was so sharp that, at least when he was reading novels by other people, he found a standardized version of English speech quite insipid. Some novels were 'so infernally conversational, that I forget who the people are before they have done talking, and don't in the least remember what they talked about before when they begin talking again'.[27]

In *Dombey and Son*, by contrast, not a single line of Cousin Feenix would let us forget who he is, and Cousin Feenix could never be mistaken for Major Bagstock, or Captain Cuttle for Mrs Skewton. In each Dickens caricature, one option from heteroglossia is refined, is mimetically frozen in time, so as to be always sharply, absurdly recognizable. When Dickens claimed that his fictional people were based on real people he was not exactly being untruthful. But the lady on whom he based Mrs Nickleby was quite correct when she suggested to Dickens that nobody like Mrs Nickleby had ever existed. By the same token, we cannot imagine Mrs Nickleby or any other Dickens caricature sitting down and reading a novel by Charles Dickens. In order to empathize with a Dickens text, a reader had (and has) to be normally unstable within heteroglossia, normally capable of sounding different options, in a way that Dickens's caricatures are not. Each caricature was a triumph of the compulsion to form over the tendency to drift – a 'momentary stay against confusion' in Robert Frost's phrase.

Moreover, if the caricatures momentarily simplified the perception of contemporary social reality, they also assigned to Dickens and his readers themselves a simplified position within that reality. An account of Dickens's characterization focusing exclusively on his ventriloquistic powers of theatrical empathy would overlook this essential psychological complement.[28] Each caricature was constantly freezing Dickens and his readers in a single response: that of the caricature's opposite number and judge within heteroglossia. The caricature's distinctiveness activated within them a pleasing but illusory superiority of unconfused opposition that worked as a principle of temporary self-definition. As long as they were empathizing with Major Bagstock, they were also defining themselves in purest contradistinction from the name-dropping, self-dramatizing parasitism of which Bagstock was the quintessentialization. For the time being their nearest class equal was perhaps even Dombey himself, whose blindness to Bagstock's insincerity, impositions and exploitiveness they could pity as a brother's. Something rather similar happened in the case of Cousin Feenix. Chesterton said that Dickens, despite much adverse criticism to the contrary, certainly could portray the gentry and aristocracy, but not as they themselves liked to be portrayed.[29] Precisely: Feenix was

[27]John Forster, *The Life of Charles Dickens*, ed. J.W.T. Ley (London, Doubleday Doran, 1928), p. 744.
[28]For all that, Robert Garis, *The Dickens Theatre: a Reassessment of the Novels* (Oxford, Clarendon Press, 1965) is in my view one of the very finest accounts of Dickens.
[29]Chesterton, Introduction to *Dombey and Son*.

consistently seen through the eyes of an intelligent member of the same class as Dombey, with an amusedly cynical attitude towards an old-boy network which was being rapidly outpaced or infiltrated, and with a large recognition of Feenix's genuine decency of feeling. Feenix represented an antiquated power factor with which, for the moment, Dickens and his readers, like Dombey but with more self-awareness, could unhesitatingly strike an alliance, gently bending it to their own purposes.

Yet the frozen posture of response *was* only temporary. Captain Cuttle's socially unaspiring naturalness was constantly inviting judgement from a genteel sophistication worthy of Mrs Skewton, but Mrs Skewton's artificiality and ambition constantly roused a Wordsworthian naturalness not unlike Captain Cuttle's. Exactly because the book contained not only Captain Cuttle but also Mrs Skewton, plus a great many other caricatures as well, and because throughout the nineteen months of serialization the different caricatures were all constantly coming and going and coming back, each single frozen posture of response was also constantly thawing out into some other no less distinctive posture. Dickens's novels, not only as mimesis but also as expressive and affective discourse, are remarkable for a steady flux within heteroglossia.

Or at least this is so where the caricatures are concerned. The 'main' characters form a group that is in some ways much less complex. For one thing, the English spoken by Edith, Carker, Walter and Florence is much less liable to fragment into as many separate idiolects.[30] Correspondingly, these characters must have set up less sharply particularized responses in Dickens and his readers, cushioning them, rather, in an ideological embrace that was altogether more standardizing. Here Dickens's offering was tinged with melodrama, pantomime comedy, fairy-tale pathos, genres whose basic assumptions were close to the 'Victorian' clichés about marriage, and to cheapened forms of the 'Wordsworthian' truth that the important life of man and society was spiritual and emotional – e.g. that those whose lives were spiritual and emotional in the right way would be rewarded with material comforts. This is where we shall have to acknowledge, and at considerable length, that something of the stereotyped account of the Victorian middle-class mentality certainly does apply, and apply to Dickens no less than to his readers. Attempts to whitewash these popular elements, for instance as the mythical archetypes so fashionable twenty years ago,[31] must be firmly rejected.

The melodrama centred on Edith. All flashing eye and curling lip, all heaving bosom and fustian language, she is, in Kathleen Tillotson's words, 'not a tragic heroine, but a tragedy queen.'[32] This was the role in which Edith could be reassuring to those who wished to remain complacent about

[30]See Johannes Söderlind, 'En språklig analys av en Dickensroman', *Annales Societatis Litterarum Humaniorum Regiae Upsaliensis* (1973–4), pp. 20–33.
[31]See William Axton, '*Dombey and Son*: from Stereotype to Archetype', *ELH* XXXI (1964), pp. 301–17.
[32]Kathleen Tillotson, *Novels of the Eighteen-Forties* (London, Oxford University Press, 1961), p. 179.

the clichés of marital bliss, for in this role she explicitly resisted, and not without a certain stagey nobility, not only the sexual threat ostensibly embodied in Carker, but also Dombey's own exploitation of her pedigree and beauty in his course of social self-aggrandizement.

Sometimes, it's true, the treatment of Edith is lighter, less a matter of direct speech, more a matter of acutely observed behaviour. There is the way she twists a bracelet on her arm, 'not winding it about with a light, womanly touch, but pressing and dragging it over the smooth skin, until the white limb showed a bar of red'.[33] There is also the way in which, on three significant nights of her bridal life – the eve of the wedding, the night of the homecoming from the honeymoon, the night of the house-warming party – she is drawn away from thoughts of Dombey and, on the last two occasions from the marriage bed as well, finding and giving more comfort with Florence, something which makes Dombey himself blush and blanch in physiological consciousness. Alan Horseman asks whether, in his second marriage, Dombey was denied all opportunity to father a son,[34] but given the spirit of these three episodes of chapter-final emphasis we hardly need a literal answer. Here at least, the decorum required for the family audience did not wipe out shadows of darker knowledge.

But Dickens allowed himself no more than this. He sensed, he communicated, the crushing despair of Edith's frustration. And then he showed her shedding harmless tears with little Florence. Rather than exploring a more fully 'feminist' reaction, and even though, in Alice, Edith dimly recognizes a sister in mortification at the hand of men, Dickens made her sublimate her drives in those Wordsworthian emotions with whose aid he brings about his gratifying reversal of the cruel-step-mother motif. Similarly, the sexual opening represented by Carker is, as I say, merely ostensible. The surprising thing is not that the manuscript notes suggest that Dickens suddenly decided to make Edith '*not* his mistress', but that he could ever have imagined that his treatment of Carker raised consummated adultery as even the remotest possibility. The notes only register the way his inbuilt censor had been operating through-out, and to gain a firmer sense of this we need only make the comparison with Galsworthy. The portrayal of Soames and Irene drew on *Dombey and Son* perhaps, but in the matter of sexual likelihoods Galsworthy, in some ways cruder than Dickens, was arguably more honest: Dickens, as we've seen, did not need to show Dombey attempting to take possession of Edith by rape, but Galsworthy was not afraid to make Bossiney attractive. Carker, apart from some of his speeches of hypocritical adulation addressed to Dombey, remained unreal throughout. Dickens had him meditatively eyeing Edith, and gave a notion of his voluptuary tastes in the refinement of his home and his connoisseurship of painting, yet such coding was at a

[33]Charles Dickens, *Dombey and Son*, ed. Alan Horseman (Oxford, OUP, The World's Classics, 1974), p. 473. Later page references to this edition are given parenthetically within the text.
[34]*Op. cit.*, p. x.

level of cliché to which no reader's blood would ever thrill. Even Carker's business abilities were defused of any living interest. Instead of sexual and socio-economic insight, Dickens consistently gave his readers Carker the cat, Carker the card-player, or simply Carker's teeth. He is a pantomime villain, Edith does not fall, and Gissing was right: 'The "realist" in fiction says to himself: Given such and such circumstances, what would be the probable issue? Dickens, on the other hand, was wont to ask: What would be the pleasant issue?'[35]

Another case in point is Walter, who is pure pantomime hero: all standardized diction, no angles, no humour, no change. Dickens himself rebelled against this cheap conception, as we know from his query to Forster. Would it be possible, he wondered, to show Walter 'gradually and naturally trailing away . . . into negligence, idleness, dissipation, dishonesty, and ruin. To show, in short, that common, every-day, miserable declension of which we know so much in our ordinary life.' Could it be done 'without making people angry'?[36] After he accepted Forster's warning against such a development, whole sections of the novel had to proceed at a level of benign simplicity worthy of Cuttle, whose fantasies follow the same Whittingtonian legend. That Dickens finally made Cuttle so much a presiding spirit, instead of developing him as a foil to a more tragic socio-economic vision,[37] correlated with a refusal to articulate more hard-nosed counterpoints naturally existing within heteroglossia.

Florence is unreal in the same ways as Walter, and because of her more central role the thinness of socio-economic notation is even more apparent. She always has just enough money to give to the poor, or to take a hackney to Old Sol's, or to buy a few clothes, and it would have been easy enough for Dickens to have said that Dombey was too proud to begrudge even a daughter the allowance decorum required, but he remained silent. Her money consequently comes to seem almost like a personal attribute, something she inalienably has, as if by magic. The same is true of her breeding. Walter, contemplating her sufferings, exclaims, 'To think that she, so young, so good, and beautiful, . . . *so delicately brought up*, and born to such a different fortune, should strive with the rough world!' (p. 588). The phrase I have italicized is just the problem: nobody has done much about making a lady of Florence at all, as Susan Nipper, the main adult companion of her youth – we are never told of a governess – is too aware of her own social status not to recognize: 'I've seen her, with no encouragement and no help, grow up to be a lady, thank God! that is the grace and pride of every company she goes in' (p. 514). Florence's maturation is depicted entirely as an initiation in unrequited daughterly love, a process in which normal educational pursuits, on the single occasion when they are

[35]Gissing, *Immortal Dickens*, pp. 160–1.
[36]Reprinted in Shelston, *Charles Dickens*, p. 40.
[37]See also Julian Moynaham, 'Dealings with the Firm of Dombey and Son: Dryness versus Wetness', in John Gross and Gabriel Pearson, eds., *Dickens and the Twentieth Century* (London, Routledge and Kegan Paul, 1962), pp. 121–31.

mentioned at all – 'her books, her music, and her work' – , are entirely secondary to her engrossing efforts 'to learn the road to a hard parent's heart' (p. 269). Some scholarship she had acquired, of course, like Maggie Tulliver, from helping her brother with his studies, yet the comparison only reminds us of the overall difference between George Eliot's finely judged observation and Dickens's fairytale here.

The abstract emotionality of her sufferings ensured that readers would not define themselves in contradistinction from her, just as no reader could entirely claim or disavow her standardized English. No less to the point, no reader could feel personally implicated in the responsibility for her misery. Especially after Dickens shifted the emphasis on to her after Paul's death, she was simply *nobody in particular*. The only exceptions were when she promoted a response in Dombey, Paul, Toots or Nipper, thus acquiring a vicarious reality that had to substitute for a more opaque form of her own. All too often, she was so unreservedly accessible, her soul so frontally presented, and in such adult language, that the writer and reader needed to make no effort at all, whether of self-judgement or imagination – for who could not endow her with a fantasy existence woven out of his own self-pity? Some readers respond to the gush of cheapened Wordsworthianism even today.[38]

The price exacted by the long serial novel was correspondingly high. Florence's existence through time is one of the most serious problems Dickens had to grapple with. Whereas the caricatures are each sharply fixed in a definite social attitude and intonation, Florence, for the entire length of the novel, has to be nothing in particular, nothing, that is, apart from the depersonalizing yearning for love. Dickens's own sense of the difficulty is reflected in the special 'mems' he had to make to remind himself of her precise age at various points. In the first chapter of Number Eight, describing 'Florence Solitary' while Dombey is in Leamington, he even tried to dodge the issue by noting the ravages of time upon the Dombey mansion with which Florence is still associated – the pace of dereliction is simply spanking. But a still greater strain is felt at those moments when Florence, by retaining her unwavering nonentity of loyal devotion, comes to seem either masochistic or downright stupid. When Edith, to protect Florence from Dombey's jealousy, becomes less familiar with her, Florence sometimes wonders what caused the change, but 'in the calm of its abandonment once more to silent grief and loneliness . . . [hers] was not a curious mind. Florence had only to remember that her star of promise was clouded in the general gloom that hung upon the house, and to weep and be resigned' (p. 544). No, not a curious mind. And because the mimetic and rhetorical conventions are not those of, say, Chaucer's *Clerk's Tale*, Dickens and some of his readers, relishing such passages, indulged in what

---

[38] See Nina Auerbach, 'Dickens and Dombey: a Daughter After All', *Dickens Studies Annual* V (1976), pp. 95–114; Denis Donoghue, 'The English Dickens and *Dombey and Son*', in Ada Nisbet and Blake Nevins, eds., *Dickens Centennial Essays* (Berkeley, University of California Press, 1971).

other readers would probably want to call bad taste. The invitation was to share the masochism and stupidity he did not refuse or qualify himself.

The criticisms I have made of Edith, Carker, Walter and Florence do not apply, however, to Paul and Dombey. Here the pressures of heteroglossia are once more very much in evidence, and the stereotyped view of Dickens and his middle-class audience again breaks down. Paul, admittedly, with all the echoes of the immortal sea that brought us hither, a Wordsworthian child on the shore who hears the mighty waters rolling evermore, offered a feast to moralizing sentimentalists. Yet he also offered resistance to such a response.

Most immediately, the difference from Florence was to be felt through the presentation. Paul was altogether more angled, with his own individual speech and core of mystery. Readers, like Mrs Pipchin, could never be sure what he was going to say next, and Dickens felt under no obligation to turn the first four numbers into a psychologically explicit *Bildungsroman*. Indeed, it was the Paul of Number Five who first acted as a catalyst to the development of that genre in *Jane Eyre* and *David Copperfield* in the following quinquennium. Paul in any case had an advantage over Florence, in not having to be authorially sustained beyond the novel's first quarter or his own childhood: if he had failed to cotton on to the full extent of his father's inhumanity this would have seemed not masochistic or stupid, but appropriate to his years. Dickens actually deals with his thoughts on such matters by means of a kind of suggestive concealment, and the risk, if there is one, is that Paul will seem prematurely wise. Even Number Five, for which the manuscript notes register Dickens's intention that 'his illness only [be] expressed in the child's own feelings', preserved Paul's strangeness. Readers could never be sure what he would feel next, and whereas Florence's later sufferings are, in Gérard Genette's terminology, focalized by Florence but vocalized by the adult, platitudinous author, much of Paul's illness is both focalized and most poignantly vocalized by Paul.

Such presentational distinctiveness helped to force a response more socially complex than mere sentimentality. As a matter of fact, this child's sufferings quietly controverted the fairytale plot of the Florence story, being caused not by parental neglect but by a particular type of parental concern. Even Blimber is not wilfully cruel to Paul. Indeed, in himself, Blimber is not actually evil. Yet Dickens's socio-economic observation, as fine, here, as anything in George Eliot, unfailingly registers the sheer failure of imagination within the class system on which Blimber thrives. Blimber's remunerative trade – that he would wince at the phrase not out of guilt but wounded pride is a sign of Dickens's exquisitely balanced judgement – , Blimber's veneering of middle-class boys with the classics, answers all too exactly to Dombey's own benighted conception of his son's needs, and Dombey, as we shall soon remark in more detail, is representative. So Dickens's readers, in shedding Wordsworthian tears for the disnaturing fate of Paul, found themselves also condemning their own – or at least the man next-door's! – aspirations to gentility. At this point, in other words, the novel is so alive with the counterpointings of heteroglossia that to think of it as 'only' a novel would be a mistake. A live novel is a microcosm of the forces at work in the culture within which it is written and read, and is charged with a social dynamism of its own. One of the essential points was again understood by Gissing: 'We may feel assured that many an English paterfamilias, who gave his opinion in favour of the modern against the ancient, and helped on the new spirit in matters educational was more or less consciously influenced by the reading of *Dombey and Son*.'[39]

Already I have begun to speak of Dombey himself, who, not only in his ambitions for Paul but also in his relations with his wives, must have triggered the same tension between moralization and gentility throughout. According to Philip Collins's stereotyping view of the book and its audience, the moralization had a free run. Combatting, not unreasonably, the notion that *Dombey and Son* appealed to its contemporaries as a symbolic structure or a wholesale critique of industrialization, Collins reduces it to a traditional lesson about pride and riches.[40] Obviously there was much in the novel that asked to be read this way, yet Dickens himself sometimes parodied such a reading, for instance in his supercilious reports from the servants' kitchen: ' "We are all brethren," says Mrs Perch, in a pause of her drink. "Except the sisters," says Mr Perch. "How are the mighty fallen!" remarks the Cook. "Pride shall have a fall, and it always was and will be so!" observes the Housemaid' (pp. 693–4). Here and at many other points, the class pride of Dickens and his readers would inevitably feel that, whatever Dombey's personal failings, there were certain things he stood for which should not be traduced by easy didacticism: dignity, style, keeping the lower orders in their place. The clear moral judgements invited by his behaviour would be attended with a reservation: 'I myself could occupy, *do* perhaps occupy, a similar position, without making similar mistakes.' Without some half-secret sense, in author and readers alike, of at least a rationale behind Dombey's attitudes, Dombey would have in any case evaporated into a cloud of sheer impossibility before the end of Number Two.

The moralizing option had to face another challenge as well. Perhaps I can suggest this by speaking of Dombey's attitude to time in one of the contexts of contemporary social reality. The nature of a man's time had been one of the main issues during the debates about the Factory Acts. Was time essentially a worker's own, given to him for his own life and enjoyment? Those who thought that it was can be credited with a Wordsworthian view of things: life is significant by its spiritual and emotional qualities. Or was time money? Should there be a direct correlation between

[39]Gissing, *Immortal Dickens*, p. 152. See also Philip Collins, 'Special Correspondent to Posterity: How Dickens's Contemporaries saw his Fictional World', in Samuel I. Mintz *et al.*, eds., *From Smollett to James: Studies in the Novel and Other Essays* (Charlottesville, University Press of Virginia, 1981), pp. 157–82.
[40]Philip Collins, '*Dombey and Son* – Then and Now'. *The Dickensian* LXIII (1967), pp. 82–94.

what a man did with his time and the amount of money he earned? If so, time had to do with the ethics of enterprise, and would lend itself to utilitarian measurement.[41] Now Dombey and Blimber, in trying to force Paul's development, in being associated with clocks or watches which tick off the seconds, were close to this second view and, through the dynamics of heteroglossia, were of course judged by the standards of the first. Yet when Dombey himself stayed away from his office, brooded over his emotional life in his private room at home, let the energetic Carker outwit him in business matters, he was clearly wasting commodity-time and the novel invited some reproof of him on the criteria of enterprise and utility. For many readers, the same would have applied to Dombey's courtship of Edith at Leamington. They would have had little sympathy for the scheme of a third-generation head of a family firm to link himself with the outdated oligarchy. He would have done better to have stayed in London and cultivated the acquaintance of a new man such as Joseph Paxton, the railway tycoon. Dombey's failure to respond to the economic potential of the railways, his defensively genteel attempts to force the Toodles into the paradigm of service, showed that the entrepreneurial spirit of his grandfather had atrophied in him.

Dombey's frontal exposure to the various types of ideological scrutiny was ensured by the presentation. He is usually seen quite from the outside,[42] and has the same firmness of outline, and often a similarly unmistakable speech, as the caricatures. He is static. He is absurd. And by refusing us, for the most part, all admission to Dombey's soul, Dickens astonishes us by what seems its awe-inspiring shallowness, blindness and predictability: we can almost guess what he will say in any situation, and he constantly flabbergasts us precisely by living up to our guess. In Edwin Muir's terms, the Dombey plot is not so much dramatic as choreographic. Dombey comes on and does his bit again and again, acquiring the same inflexible permanence as a Feenix or a Bagstock. However common the failings he typifies, he is thus rendered curious, alien. The readers were forced to meet him – and in him something of themselves – head-on.

But then at the end Dombey does change, or seems to change – 'becomes the best of fathers, and spoils a fine novel', to Taine's way of thinking[43] – and Dickens's technique of presentation changes as well. From as early as the letter of 25 July 1846 Dickens had planned a peripeteia here, and the letter made a convincing enough Wordsworthian tale of filial and paternal love out of it, a lyrical ballad in town clothes. In its exposition of this, however, the letter's discussion of Dombey was uniformly introspective, and the same was true of Dickens's attempt to meet criticism of Dombey's end in the preface to the cheap edition of 1858. Both the letter

[41]See N.N. Feltes, 'To Saunter, to Hurry: Dickens, Time, and Industrial Capitalism', *Victorian Studies* XX (1977), pp. 245–67.
[42]See Ian Milner, 'The Dickens Drama: Mr Dombey', in Nisbet and Nevins, *Centennial Essays*, pp. 155–65.
[43]Reprinted in Shelston, *Dickens*, p. 35.

and the preface could therefore make his change seem less psychologically radical than appeared in the novel: the idea is that he always had a shamed consciousness of the injustice of his treatment of Florence, which finally won expression. The novel, before the final section, did not probe such matters. If it had, it would have lost the force of Dombey's being so sheerly 'other' (while also so much 'the same' as the reader). At two or three points, certainly, it dropped its categorical language for linguistic forms that were modalized ('may do' and 'perhaps is' taking the place of 'does' and 'is'), actually formulating some questions about Dombey's inner life. But the return to categoricality was always very quick and assertive, and the temporary modalization only emphasized Dombey's opaqueness by acknowledging its impenetrability.[44] In changing his technique at the end, Dickens moved from the style of choreographic caricature to that of the standardizing emotionalism he used for Florence throughout, something readers can interpret in two ways. Either 'Dombey the man' was not really so fixed in attitude and tone as Dickens's earlier presentation made him appear; in which case the 1858 preface, though essentially right, is also a tacit admission of a tendency to falsification in the earlier caricature. Or there was now indeed a genuine personality change in Dombey; in Jungian terms, the persona Dombey had cultivated for many years was giving way to the shadow of his common spiritual humanity, as with other caricatures in later novels;[45] in which case the 1858 preface is essentially wrong, and the earlier caricature was not without all foundation in reality. Either way, however, Dombey's change or apparent change, and Dickens's change of technique, was bound to strike many readers as another lapse into the cheaper kind of Wordsworthianism, and a sad loss of individuality for Dombey. The contrast with Shakespeare is no less telling than the heavily intended parallel: Lear, reconciled to Cordelia though he becomes, is still not simply Everyman.

On the other hand, both here and in connection with all the main characters, easy pathos and moralization worthy of the cook and the house-maid were what large sections of the reading public were prepared to pay for. Nor need we be in any doubt that many of the same readers would have been among the first to admire the more external but more complex treatment of Dombey and the caricatures as well. Again and again we must remind ourselves not to expect more 'consistency' in Dickens's first audience than our own contemporaries are disposed to evince in their response to mass entertainment now – to television especially. Perhaps the last word on the matter should simply be that everybody has always appropriated Dickens for their own purposes. Dickens himself could clearly provide and use it all. His protean acting abilities could animate every area of his text, every voice of every character – distinct or standardized – and every response – oppositional or sympathetic – accordingly. Interestingly

---

[44]See also Patricia Ingham, 'Speech and Non-Communication in *Dombey and Son*', *Review of English Studies* XXX (1979), pp. 145–53.
[45]See Sell, 'Projection Characters'.

enough, much is now being written on the sociocultural uses that can still be made of Dickens today – in television, in film, in theatre, in translation, as intertext.[46] This is likely to enhance still further our understanding of the pragmatics of literature, our perception that, as a fact of human societies, and as a fact of Dickens's texts to at least as high a degree as most others, different readers will use different things in different contexts.

[46]Some of the essays in Giddings, *Changing World* are on these lines, for instance.

Note

Life. William Makepeace Thackeray was born in India in 1811 and lived there until 1817 when he was sent to England after the death of his father, a Collector with the East India Company. He was educated at Charterhouse and Trinity College, Cambridge, which he left in 1830 without taking a degree. As a young man he gambled freely, travelled in Europe, studied art, and dabbled in journalism. In 1830–1 he lived in Germany, mainly at Weimar, and in 1832 in Paris. In 1833 he lost most of his inherited fortune in the collapse of an Indian agency-house. From 1834 to 1837 he lived in Paris studying to become an artist and writing occasionally for journals. In 1836 he married Isabella Shawe, who bore him two surviving daughters before succumbing in 1840 to mental illness from which she never recovered. Thackeray began by writing, under different pseudonyms such as Michael Angelo Titmarsh, for various periodicals, including *Fraser's Magazine*, in which *The Luck of Barry Lyndon* (1844) appeared, and *Punch*, which published his parodies of leading contemporary writers as *Mr Punch's Prize Novelists* (1844–5). His first major novel *Vanity Fair* appeared in monthly parts in 1847–8. There followed *The History of Pendennis* (1848–50), *The History of Henry Esmond* (1852), *The Newcomes* (1853–5), and *The Virginians* (1857–9). He also gave lectures on his favourite eighteenth century which were later published as *The English Humourists* (1835) and *The Four Georges* (1860). He made two profitable lecture tours to the United States in 1852–3 and 1855–6. In 1859 he became the first editor of *The Cornhill Magazine* in which his last three novels appeared: *Lovel The Widower* (1860), *The Adventures of Philip* (1861–2), and the unfinished *Denis Duval* (1864). He died suddenly on Christmas Eve 1863. The standard biography, in two volumes, is by Gordon N. Ray, *Thackeray: the Uses of Adversity 1811–1846* (London, OUP, 1955), and *Thackeray: the Age of Wisdom 1847–1863* (London, OUP, 1958). The essential source is *The Letters and Private Papers of William Makepeace Thackeray*, ed. Gordon N. Ray (4 vols., London, OUP, 1945–6).

Texts and Criticism. There is no standard scholarly edition of the complete works. The fullest are the Centenary Biographical Edition, 26 vols. (1911) and the Oxford Edition, 17 vols. (1908). The Riverside edition of *Vanity Fair* (1963) is the most scholarly edition of a single work, and there are serviceable editions of *Vanity Fair* and *Barry Lyndon* in the Oxford World's Classics series, and of *Vanity Fair*, *Pendennis*, and *Henry Esmond* in the Penguin English Library.

Recommended general studies are Geoffrey Tillotson, *Thackerary the Novelist* (Cambridge, CUP, 1954) and Jack P. Rawlins, *Thackeray's Novels: a Fiction that is True* (Berkeley, University of California Press, 1974). John Carey, *Thackeray: Prodigal Genius* (London, Faber & Faber, 1977) is wittily clever but perverse in its determined reading of Thackeray's career as the history of a capitulation to conservatism and snobbery. J.A. Sutherland, *Thackeray at Work* (London, Athlone Press, 1974) is a valuable study of the genesis of the novels. J. Hillis Miller, *Fiction and Repetition* (Oxford, Blackwell, 1982) presents an ironic deconstructive reading of *Henry Esmond*, and Stephen Bann, *The Clothing of Clio* (Cambridge, CUP, 1984) an interpretation of it as an ironic historical novel, an anti-history. A more orthodox account of it as historical fiction is in Andrew Sanders, *The Victorian Historical Novel 1840–1880* (London, Macmillan, 1978). Two specific studies of Thackeray's handling of time are Jean Sudrann, ' "The Philosopher's Property": Thackeray and the use of Time', *Victorian Studies*, X(1966–7), pp. 359–88, and Henri-A. Talon, 'Time and Memory in Thackeray's *Henry Esmond*', *Review of English Studies*, XIII (1962), pp. 147–56.

6

Thackeray's *Henry Esmond* and the Struggle Against the Power of Time

J.M. Rignall

Thackeray's career as a novelist begins with parody, which prepares the ground for his serious fiction by mounting an attack on restricting conventions. In *Rebecca and Rowena*, his parodic continuation of Scott's *Ivanhoe*, it is the conventional ending that is exposed to mockery. Impatient with the practice of concluding a novel with the marriage of the youthful protagonists, he comically pursues the lives of Scott's characters further, showing Ivanhoe unhappily married to the frigidly proper Rowena and Robin Hood, grown into a fat conservative, handing out stiff sentences to poachers from the Magistrates' bench. The parody involves a sense of time's destructive passing, and this alliance of time and irony is to become a significant constituent of Thackeray's distinctive vision. Here, as later, time acts as the agent of irony, undermining the pattern of meaning which Scott had created, and which the novel conventionally creates. A similar procedure marks the notoriously problematic conclusion to *Vanity Fair*, where Dobbin finally wins Amelia but only after he has realized that she is not worthy of the love that for years he has devoted to her. The ending comes too late to be happy and to offer the comfortable certainties of a conventional resolution. Thackeray's practice of linking his novels genealogically has the same effect of stressing the melancholy erosion of time. *The Virginians*, for instance, follows on from *The History of Henry Esmond* in such a way as to present, in the apt words of a recent commentator, 'a world grown old, suffused with the sense of time past, greatness lost, and a present decay of the spirit'.[1] It is in the nature of Thackeray's ironic imagination thus to follow the passage of time beyond the moment of climax or significant achievement, and the effect is always disconcerting. Patterns dissolve, values become equivocal, and the 'spirit of process and inconclusiveness'[2] that characterizes the novel form may seem to turn against itself and become not energizing but destructive.

This ironic subversion of pattern and meaning through time is not

---

[1]Rawlins, *Thackeray's Novels*, p. 195.
[2]M.M. Bakhtin, *The Dialogic Imagination* (Austin and London, University of Texas Press, 1981), p. 7.

simply a manifestation of Thackeray's characteristic preoccupation with transience and 'vanitas', for it is related to the general orientation of the novel in the nineteenth century. There is, as Nietzsche suggests in the second of his *Untimely Meditations*, a latent nihilism in the developed historical sense of nineteenth-century culture,[3] in its understanding of life in terms of change and development. The realist novel, the literary form which most fully expresses that understanding, often brings that nihilism to the surface by pursuing the course of a life, or lives, to the point where time composed into the meaningful pattern of story or history collapses into meaningless sequence. Stendhal in *La Chartreuse de Parme*, for instance, shows meaningful history coming to an end at Waterloo and giving way to the drift of time, in which the promise of youth goes sadly unfulfilled. Dickens, in the double narrative of *Bleak House*, sets one view of time against the other. Esther's story, written in the light of its happy outcome, presents time as moving purposively towards a positive end, while in the lawless and menacing world of the third-person narrative time flows on, without order or purpose, in a perpetual present. That purposeless flux becomes the dominant feature of Flaubert's *L'Education Sentimentale* where history is emptied of significance and the central character's aimlessly drifting life achieves only ironic patterns of futility, ending with a backward glance that implies not development but empty circularity. No novel is more consistently nihilistic in its implications than Flaubert's, and although its radically subversive ironies have no direct parallel in English fiction, it indicates the direction in which other novels, including Thackeray's, appear to be moving.

Thackeray is, however, a less thoroughgoing and consistent ironist than Flaubert. He is, indeed, disposed to resist the nihilistic implications of his own ironic vision, so that his fiction bears the imprint of conflicting impulses. At its worst this appears as no more than a wavering between slack sentimentality and easy cynicism, but at its best it is a source of imaginative strength and vitality. *The History of Henry Esmond* is perhaps the best example of this productive inner conflict, for it is here that Thackeray engages most fully with the problematic nature of his characteristic sense of time and transience. Time in this novel is both the agent of irony, undermining conventional pieties and platitudes, and at the same time a destructive force whose tendency to lay everything waste has to be resisted. Not only does Thackeray create a character whose life is spent in search of an enduring love to anchor him amidst the flow of time and the turbulent currents of history, he also employs narrative devices that throw into relief the general problem of how to derive a pattern of meaning from the contingent stuff of life. Few novels correspond so closely to the definition of the novel form proposed by Lukács in *The Theory of the Novel*: 'in the novel meaning is separated from life, and hence the essential from the temporal; we might almost say that the entire inner action of the novel is

---

[3]Nietzsche, 'On the uses and disadvantages of history for life', *Untimely Meditations*, trans. R.J. Hollingdale (Cambridge, CUP, 1983), pp. 57–123.

nothing but a struggle against the power of time'.[4] This formula may not do justice to the full range and diversity of the genre, but it does serve to throw light on the particular nature and complicated ironic patterning of a work like *Henry Esmond*. It is as the site of just such a struggle that Thackeray's novel will be examined here.

The ironies of *Henry Esmond* have, of course, already received considerable critical attention, and the most vigorous and sustained ironic reading of the novel, a recent study by J. Hillis Miller,[5] sees it as a classic work of deconstruction which renders all meanings indeterminable and displays as the only certainty the negative, self-destructive power of irony. However penetrating the insights that such a deconstructive reading affords, its relentless emphasis on negation involves too ready an acquiescence in the very nihilism which in this novel Thackeray seems to be at pains to resist. Rather than negating meanings and certainties, his ironic procedures are better seen as interrogating them, creating a work that is open and questioning rather than negatively indeterminate. J.A. Sutherland's study of the genesis of the novel points in the same direction, showing that *Henry Esmond* was not as meticulously planned as was once believed, but took its final shape from the discoveries and adjustments Thackeray made in the process of writing.[6] Thus it is in the process of time that Thackeray, and his narrator Esmond, discover meanings and create order while at the same time revealing the way in which time destroys all order and meaning. The resulting pattern of ironic oppositions is one in which contrary views constantly call each other into question. And if, inevitably, time the destroyer always threatens to gain the upper hand, there is nevertheless a discernible movement in the novel away from a bitter and melancholy brooding on transience towards a calmer acknowledgement of the passage of time and the changes it brings.

The initial role of time in *Henry Esmond* is a subversive one, calling into question the conventions of historical writing. From the opening page of the novel it is pressed into service in a bid to strip history of its courtly pieties and cut heroes down to human size. It is 'old age and decrepitude' that rob Louis XIV of monarchical splendour and heroic stature, revealing him to Esmond's sceptical gaze as a 'little wrinkled old man' (p. 45).[7] 'Why', he asks, 'shall History go on kneeling to the end of time?' (p. 46). But his narrative shows the way in which time itself puts an end to the propensity to kneel by destroying the grounds for deference. The fate of the second Viscount Castlewood after the battle of Worcester, growing old in exile and succumbing to drink, provides a paradigm in the first chapter of how the lives of the great are to be seen in this novel:

What! does a stream rush out of a mountain free and pure, to roll

---

[4]Georg Lukács, *The Theory of the Novel* (London, Merlin Press, 1971), p. 122.
[5]Hillis Miller, '*Henry Esmond*: Repetition and Irony', *Fiction and Repetition*, pp. 73–115.
[6]Sutherland, *Thackeray at Work*, pp. 56–85.
[7]Page references are to the Penguin English Library edition of *The History of Henry Esmond*, ed. John Sutherland and Michael Greenfield (Harmondsworth, Penguin Books, 1970).

through fair pastures, to feed and throw out bright tributaries, and to end in a village gutter? Lives that have noble commencements have often no better endings; it is not without a kind of awe and reverence that an observer should speculate upon such careers as he traces the course of them. (p. 47)

The awe and reverence that Esmond urges here are not for the individual but for the workings of destiny, for the ironic pattern of decline, and it is this same pattern that emerges in the lives of the historically significant characters. The Pretender, 'heroic from misfortunes, and descended from a line of kings' (p. 447) turns out to be an irresponsible rake; and of 'the two greatest men of that age' (p. 420), Marlborough is seen to end in deserved disgrace and Swift as 'a lonely fallen Prometheus, groaning as the vulture tears him' (p. 420). Even the one historical figure to whom Esmond accords unequivocally heroic status, William of Orange, comes to an arbitrary and untimely end that belies the existence of a meaningful pattern in human affairs. And as with historical characters so with historical events: Thackeray's cunningly ironic handling of the battle of Blenheim, for instance, denies it the status of an heroic climax to the campaign of 1704. Announced as the 'great victory of Blenheim' (p. 278) before it is narrated, the victory is never finally seen since Esmond's account of the battle is broken off at the point where he is knocked unconscious. Instead of heroic triumph there is sobering emphasis on the bloody aftermath, on the dead and the wounded who represent the price and the consequence of military victory. Thackeray's characteristic practice of looking beyond the moment of climax to the long vista of time thus marks his treatment of both historical events and historical characters, and it is an essential instrument in his ironic reappraisal of history and its heroes.

The order traditionally dispensed by the 'stately Muse of History' (p. 277) is thoroughly undermined, but the levelling effect of this temporal perspective does not stop there. In Book One, where the gloomy insistence on transience is most marked, time is shown eating away at the Castlewoods' marriage and the domestic security that the orphan Henry Esmond has found in the Viscount's family. This erosion is more disturbing than the ironic demystification of history and its great men because it strikes at something whose value for Esmond, and by implication his creator, is deeply felt. This disintegration of the Castlewoods' marriage is the disintegration of an ordered world, even if that order is shown from the first to be sustained by precarious means, that is by Rachel's ominously excessive and adoring deference to her husband. It is also the death of love; and love and security are what the young Esmond needs and prizes from the moment he first encounters the Castlewood family and goes down on his knees before Rachel as before 'a superior being or angel' (p. 50). This kneeling is a recurrent motif in the novel and represents more than simply an attempt by Thackeray at lending period colour to a Jacobite tale. It expresses an emotional need for order which is ironically qualified but not mockingly dismissed. If History is mocked for being always on its knees, the characters of Esmond's personal history, including himself, are not. What time reveals, however is that the objects of such reverence are to a greater or lesser extent unworthy, mere mortals not gods or angels. The lesson is one of painful disillusionment.

The most dramatically disillusioning event, Esmond's private version of the Fall – into time and knowledge – is the smallpox episode which brings to an end the idyll of childhood, the happiest period of his life 'when the young mother, with her daughter and son, and the orphan lad whom she protected, read and worked and played, and were children together' (p. 109). The disease which the young Esmond contracts while paying court to the blacksmith's daughter Nancy Sievewright acts as an accelerated image of time, bringing an awareness of the body and its pains into this innocent, idealized nursery world. Stirrings of puberty and fears of mortality combine to disrupt the harmony as Rachel, fearful for her children's safety, turns on Esmond with a bitterness so extreme that it betrays her jealousy at his adolescent interest in another female. The experience marks Esmond's passage into adult life, and the passage of time is clearly imprinted on his and Rachel's features. The illness leaves him visibly aged and marked for life and transforms Rachel into a manifestly mortal being: 'the delicacy of her rosy colour and complexion were gone: her eyes had lost their brilliancy, her hair fell, and her face looked older. It was as if a coarse hand had rubbed off the delicate tints of that sweet picture, and brought it, as one has seen unskilful painting-cleaners do, to the dead colour' (p. 124). The coarse hand is that of time, but the metaphor of the picture and the simile of the painting-cleaner are already preparing the ground for the way in which the novel is to resist the destruction of time. Esmond's image of Rachel is a self-created one, a picture which, in the skilful hands of its painter, is susceptible to restoration.

The immediate consequence of the smallpox episode is the end of marital harmony in the Castlewood family and a series of melancholy reflections by the narrator on the transience of beauty and love. Beauty fades – 'Poor Nancy! her cheeks had shared the fate of roses and were withered now' (pp. 125–6) – and married couples inevitably awake from 'that absurd vision of conjugal felicity, which was to last for ever, and is over like any other dream' (p. 130). The corrosive melancholy even strikes at the very basis of social and domestic order in a meditation on the unlimited power, so easily and often abused, of the 'King of the Fireside' (p. 175). Less significant as expressions of Esmond's character than for their role in the ironic structure of the novel, these reflections serve as a form of ground bass in the narrative, calling into question, and at the same time being called into question by Esmond's eventual attainment of marital harmony with a Rachel who has been restored to her original beauty.

Melancholy begins to recede, and resistance to time's destruction to emerge, after Esmond embarks on a life of military action after his release from prison. The reflections or interjections of Esmond as narrator now become not variations on the same sad theme but a counterpoint of opposing attitudes. In giving an account of his months in prison after the death of Lord Castlewood in the duel with Mohun and his bitter experience of Rachel's unjust accusations, he dwells rhetorically on the permanence of suffering: 'O, dark months of grief and rage! of wrong and cruel endurance! He is old now who recalls you. Long ago he has forgiven and blest the soft hand that wounded him; but the mark is there, and the wound is cicatrized only – no time, tears, caresses, or repentance, can obliterate the scar' (p. 211). Shortly afterwards, in the account of his first military campaign, he observes sanguinely that 'wounds heal rapidly in the heart of two-and-twenty; hopes revive daily; and courage rallies in spite of a man' (p. 238). Instead of luxuriating in bitterness and melancholy, he now seeks the reassuring and consoling insight. When he later reflects on his feeling for Beatrix, he returns to the image of the scar but now gives it the value of a positive permanence:

> I invoke that beautiful spirit from the shades and love her still; or rather I should say such a past is always present to a man; such a passion once felt forms a part of his whole being, and cannot be separated from it; it becomes a portion of the man to-day, just as any great faith or conviction, the discovery of poetry, the awakening of religion, ever afterward influence him; just as the wound I had at Blenheim, and of which I wear the scar, hath become part of my frame and influenced my whole body, nay, spirit subsequently, though 'twas got and healed forty years ago. Parting and forgetting! What faithful heart can do these? Our great thoughts, our great affections, the Truths of our life, never leave us. Surely, they cannot separate from our consciousness; shall follow it whithersoever that shall go; and are of their nature divine and immortal. (p. 429)

What is displayed here is not so much a secure belief in something eternal as a will to believe in it, clearly discernible in the rhetorical effort of the 'surely' that introduces the final sentence. The struggle against the power of time is present in the very pattern of the meditation, which takes mortal scars and uses them as evidence for the immortality of human consciousness. The same procedure occurs again a few pages later where the lapse and renewal of memory are related to the resurrection and the final triumph of consciousness over time: 'We forget nothing. The memory sleeps, but wakes again; I often think how it shall be when, after the last sleep of death, the *réveillée* shall arouse us for ever, and the past in one flash of self-consciousness shall rush back, like the soul revivified' (p. 441). In the reconciliation scene with Rachel at Winchester even love itself, whose transience had earlier been so emphatically underlined in the same Rachel's relationship with her husband, is presented as the guarantee of immortality: 'But only true love lives after you – follows your memory with secret blessing – or precedes you, and intercedes for you. *Non omnis moriar* – if dying, I yet live in a tender heart or two; nor am lost and hopeless living, if a sainted departed soul still loves and prays for me' (p. 254).

These reflections are not to be read as ironic in themselves, for Esmond's attempts to secure some lasting truth from the flow of time are taken seriously.[8] Nevertheless the ironic structure of the novel juxtaposes such attempts with incidents and deliberations that challenge them. Thus the same chapter which opens with Esmond deriving the consolation of immortality from his unforgotten passion for Beatrix, closes after the death of Duke Hamilton with a celebrated elegiac meditation:

> As Esmond and the Dean walked away from Kensington discoursing of this tragedy, and how fatal it was to the cause which they both had at heart, the street-criers were already out with their broadsides, shouting through the town the full, true, and horrible account of the death of Lord Mohun and Duke Hamilton in a duel. A fellow had got to Kensington, and was crying it in the square there at very early morning, when Mr Esmond happened to pass by. He drove the man from under Beatrix's very window, whereof the casement had been set open. The sun was shining though 'twas November: he had seen the market-carts rolling into London, the guard relieved at the Palace, the labourers trudging to their work in the gardens between Kensington and the City – the wandering merchants and hawkers filling the air with their cries. The world was going to its business again, although dukes lay dead and ladies mourned for them; and kings, very likely, lost their chances. So night and day pass away, and to-morrow comes, and our place knows us not. Esmond thought of the courier, now galloping on the North road to inform him, who was Earl of Arran yesterday, that he was Duke of Hamilton to-day, and of a thousand great schemes, hopes, ambitions, that were alive in the gallant heart, beating a few hours since, and now in a little dust quiescent. (p. 434).

The quiet reflective tone of this passage contrasts with the somewhat strained assertiveness of Esmond's thoughts on immortality and seems to carry greater authority; yet its precise effect is difficult to define. In shifting attention from the doings of the great to the quotidian labours of the working world, it quietly cuts the former down to size. History, with its great men, dates and deeds, gives way to the anonymous life that continues unrecorded. However, the mere fact of life continuing carries here no particular power to console nor any intimations of immortality. The dominant note is that of a typically Thackerayan 'vanitas', though without the satirical scorn that so often accompanies it, and, what is more important, without the sense of bitter disillusionment to be found in the first part of the novel. This is elegiac but not anguished. Neither despairing nor consoling, the meditation remains calmly neutral, content for once to contemplate the passage of time without resistance. It marks a brief pause in the novel before the dramatic action of Esmond's plot to restore the Stewarts and anticipates in its calm the spirit of the conclusion, for it is towards this kind of peaceful contemplation of time and its changes that the novel moves.

---

[8] The passage corresponds closely in argument and phrasing to an emotional letter of Thackeray's to Jane Brookfield in Ray, *Letters and Private Papers*, vol. II, pp. 469–71.

The struggle against the power of time issues finally in a truce that is eloquently foreshadowed here.

The juxtaposition and alternation of conflicting and mutually qualifying senses of time is present not only in Esmond's general reflections on life but in the very texture of his narration. The notorious shifts of tense and person can, of course, be read in terms of Esmond's character as indicating an uneasy relationship to his own past. The predominant past tense and third person imply an attempt to distance himself from his own, often painful, experience in the act of recounting it. This then falters on occasions of strong emotion, such as in the recollection of Nancy Sievewright, when the first person and present tense break through. However, the significance of these grammatical changes is formal as well as psychological in that they throw light on the problem of narration itself, on the process of imposing order on the flux of experience. As has often been noted, Esmond alternates between writing as a man recollecting his past – 'Her heart melted I suppose (indeed she hath since owned as much)' (p. 49) – and writing about himself as if he were dead: 'To the very last hour of his life, Esmond remembered the lady as she then spoke and looked' (p. 50). Benjamin's observation that, in the novel, the meaning of a character's life is revealed only in his death,[9] provides a means of understanding this apparent discrepancy. In writing of himself as though he were dead, Esmond very obviously imposes on his life the finality that bestows meaning. Yet the figurative death represented by the end of the novel is also implied in the use of the first person and perfect tense, which point forward to the final tableau of the domestic idyll in Castlewood where Esmond is supposed to be writing. This, reached only 'after the drama of my own life was ended' (p. 511), presents life as fixed and finished, and involves a finality that is interchangeable with death. In both cases, the pattern of meaning which constitutes a fictional character is completed; and the alternation of tenses draws attention to the process by which meaning is conferred and form imposed.

The ending which is proposed by Esmond in the reconciliation scene at Winchester half-way through the novel proves, of course, to be premature precisely because the pattern of his life is manifestly incomplete. Rachel herself, in refusing his suggestion that they leave together for a new life in America, perceives him to have a life still before him, to be poised for a beginning rather than ripe for an ending: ' "Hush, boy!" she said . . . "The world is beginning for you" ' (p. 255). Their subsequent embrace, 'as a brother folds a sister to his heart; and as a mother cleaves to her son's breast' (p. 256), however equivocal it is about their age, clearly indicates what is absent not only from this relationship but from Esmond's experience up to that point. That absence is immediately made good by the appearance of Beatrix, now grown to be a woman with 'a dazzling completeness of beauty' (p. 257) and irresistible sexual attraction. Her role as the inspirer and object of Esmond's passionate longing needs no comment,

[9]Walter Benjamin, *Illuminations*, (London, Collins/Fontana Books, 1973), pp. 100–1.

but her significance is not confined to her beauty and her heartless egoism. Hillis Miller's reading of her as the embodiment of the negative principle of irony and its corrosive power comes close, in an abstract way, to explaining her subversive and melancholy function,[10] but what needs to be added is that her disturbing and ironic effect is closely related to the working of time. In her notorious fickleness Beatrix dramatically brings to life the changes wrought by time as Esmond's recourse to an analogy with Penelope makes clear: 'she was in so far like Penelope, that she had a crowd of suitors, and undid day after day and night after night the handiwork of fascination and the web of coquetry with which she was wont to allure them' (p. 394). Penelope's work, like that of time, is never done, and Beatrix's version of it, occupying days as well as nights, mimics even more closely the temporal process. And unlike Rachel who, in Esmond's eyes, seems finally to escape the ageing process, looking if anything younger at the end of the novel than she did after her illness, Beatrix is clearly subject to time. Refusing to reveal the number of years that have passed since her childhood, she makes an eloquent gesture: ' ". . . never mind how many years ago,'' and she flung back her curls and looked over her fair shoulder at the mirror superbly, as if she said, "Time, I defy you" ' (p. 402). The gesture of defiance only attests the power of what she is defying, and Esmond's reply ominously underlines the point: ' "You can afford to look in the glass still; and only be pleased by the truth it tells you" ' (p. 402). As yet the mirror only reflects the truth of her beauty, but it will not be long before it makes plain the truth of transience. Thus her bantering claim that ' "I intend to live to be a hundred" ' (p. 408) is to rebound ironically upon her. In the escapade with the Pretender she sleeps in the Viscountess Isabel's bed, and, in one of those repetitions so typical of Thackeray and which is foreshadowed in this incident, she is to repeat Isabel's fate in *The Virginians*. In that novel she is, indeed, to live on to a great age and to become like her aunt a form of living *memento mori*, beneath whose raddled and painted skin, the mocking ruin of former beauty, there lies clearly visible the mortal skull. The later novel makes explicit the melancholy irony of time intimated in her subversive effect on Esmond in this one. She not only speaks the truth to him about his own character but also conveys in her own person the truth of the transience of beauty and the disturbing possibility that love, too, may not endure. Her ironic function is thus finally to question the very basis of Esmond's hard-won security in the love of Rachel.

The kind of repetition hinted at when Beatrix sleeps in Isabel's bed characterizes the principal action of the latter part of the novel where Esmond devises and leads yet another Jacobite plot to retrieve the throne. He repeats the behaviour of his ancestors, although in a way which constantly threatens to descend into bathos. Marx's famous description of Napoleon III's *coup d'état*, which, by an historical conicidence, took place while Thackeray was writing this novel, is equally pertinent to this fictional

[10]Hillis Miller, *Fiction and Repetition*, pp. 113–14.

attempt at turning the clock back and repeating the past, for Thackeray's irony keeps Esmond's undertaking poised on the edge of farce. The struggle against the power of time takes on the aspect of comedy. The Quixotic parallels repeatedly drawn by other characters – ' "Well, honest Harry go and attack windmills"·' (p. 384) – point to the particular comic discrepancy between his actions and their context. True to the cavalier loyalties of his ancestors and seen by the admiring Rachel in an appropriately heroic light – 'never was such a glorious scheme to her partial mind, never such a devoted knight to execute it' (p. 441) – he attempts to foist a chivalric romance onto a world that will no longer accommodate it. Rachel and Beatrix, kneeling before the bed in which the intended king will sleep, play their part in this courtly charade, but the principal actor, the Pretender himself, is entirely miscast. Unable to take seriously Esmond's chivalric behaviour, he mocks him with names that hint again at the Quixotic analogy; ' "*le grand sérieux*", Don Bellianis of Greece' (p. 458). 'Constantly neglecting his part with an inconceivable levity' (p. 460), the Pretender casts a subversively ironic light on the plot and the feudal order which it intends to restore. As Frank remarks: ' "He seems to sneer at everything. He is not like a king: somehow, Harry, I fancy you are like a king. He does not stop to think what a stake we are all playing. He would have stopped at Canterbury to run after a barmaid there, had I not implored him to come on" ' (p. 458). Instead of living up to his claim of kingship by divine right, he is intent on exercising a 'droit de seigneur' with every attractive woman who crosses his path. Cast by Esmond for an heroic role in a chivalric romance he persists in acting like a figure in a French farce, and the conflict of roles and genres generates a wry Cervantic humour. Beatrix, too, plays her part in this parody of romance, refusing to play the part assigned to her. Seen by Esmond and Frank as a threatened innocent whose honour they ride desperately to preserve, she proves to be an ambitious, strong-willed woman perfectly capable of looking after herself. The romance intrigue which dominates the latter part of the novel has thus the double appeal of an ironic device; the simple entertainment of high drama is rendered even more entertaining by the sly strain of comic absurdity which keeps breaking through Esmond's earnest narration.

This comic version of the struggle against time casts further ironic light on history and men's power to make it. In involving his characters in a purely imaginary Jacobite plot and a parodic romance, Thackeray invites comparison with Scott's *Redgauntlet*; but where Scott uses Redgauntlet's anachronistic Stewart loyalties and headstrong heroics to throw into relief the historical progress of Britain since 1745, Thackeray implies no such clear historical development in exposing Esmond's enterprise as an anachronism. Although Esmond claims that if he were to have his life again he would be a Whig, his narrative does not present a Whig version of history. The Hanoverian succession is secured by default rather than superior fitteness and it represents no obvious advance over what has preceded it. Nor, conversely, is there in the 'weak and foolish young Pretender' (p. 511) any intimation of historical decline, for the earlier

Stewarts, like the 'wine-drabbled divinity' Charles II, are presented in no more flattering terms. History yields no pattern, whether of progress or of decline. It is ruled by contingency rather than by any laws of development. Thus Esmond's attempt to repeat the past is mocked not by historical progress but simply by time and chance; and as he watches the collapse of his plans in the applauding crowds that greet the accession of George I, he catches sight of 'one sad face' (p. 511) that ironically mirrors his own failure and its inevitability. Mr Holt, the tirelessly unsuccessful Jesuit conspirator, stands here as a comic reminder – for the reader if not for Esmond – of the futility of attempting to direct the course of history. 'Sure he was the most unlucky of men: he never played a game but he lost it; or engaged in a conspiracy but ''twas certain to end in defeat' (p. 511). His eventual end, like Esmond's in America, is a final illustration of the triumph of time over purposive effort and historical ambition: 'He lies buried in our neighbouring province of Maryland now, with a cross over him, and a mound of earth above him; under which that unquiet spirit is for ever at peace' (p. 511).

If Esmond is powerless to determine the course of history, he can nevertheless give shape and meaning to his own life, and after the anticlimax of the failed plot he swiftly brings his own life story to an end. The ending confers meaning, completes a pattern, and marks the climax of his struggle against the power of time – a climax that is qualified by irony but not threatened by comic absurdity. Turning aside from the muddle and chance of European history, he enters the idyllic new world of Virginia and domestic happiness. The rhetorical crescendo of the closing pages declares love to be permanent, America to be beyond trouble and conflict, and Rachel to be beyond the ravages of time. With the aid of an appropriate allusion to Milton's prelapsarian Eve, she is characterized in terms that deny the passage of time – 'the tender matron, as beautiful in her autumn, and as pure as virgins in their spring, with blushes of love and ''eyes of meek surrender'' ' (p. 513). Autumn merges with spring and the mature matron still enjoys the tenderness of youth. In this hard-won paradise history is banished and time suspended. To the extent that its passing is acknowledged at all, it is in a spirit of calm acceptance. The past is viewed with gratitude rather than a sense of loss – 'we have built a new Castlewood, and think with grateful hearts of our old home' (p. 513) – and the metaphors of autumn and Indian summer which Esmond uses to describe their serene transatlantic existence accommodate time and change to the inevitable but benign cycle of nature.

The presence of irony in this ending is signalled by the strained nature of its affirmations. The fulsome celebration of love and the idealization of Rachel proclaim themselves to be a rhetorical act of persuasion, and even self-persuasion, on Esmond's part. It is his conclusion rather than Thackeray's. Esmond concludes and Thackeray reveals that conclusion to be a rather desperate retrieval of happiness and security from the ruins of passion, although he does not mock the emotional need which it satisfies or the ideal of domestic happiness which it upholds. Irony distances the character from his creator but does not diminish or dismiss him.

Where Esmond is determined to conclude, Thackerary is inspired to continue. The final location of Castlewood, Virginia, turns our attention back to the preface which Thackeray appears to have written immediately after the ending,[11] and which serves more appropriately as an epilogue to this novel and a preface to *The Virginians*. It is in this preface that the qualifying irony implied in the ending is made explicit. Rachel Warrington's account of her parents' life brings a primarily temporal irony to bear on Esmond's concluding description of his idyllic American existence. In one respect nothing has changed, for Esmond remains proud and Rachel jealous; but in another everything is changing, for Castlewood in the new world is no more a haven from history than was Castlewood in the old. The Indian wars intervene to hasten Rachel's death, and 'the lamentable but glorious war of independence' (p. 38) later divides the family against itself. This is, in due course, to become the subject of *The Virginians*, so that what we witness in the preface to *Henry Esmond* is Thackeray's imagination, seized as ever by the long vistas of time, fanning the spark of a new novel out of the dying embers of the old.

This creative continuity is not, in this case, a positive one, since *The Virginians* sadly illustrates the dangers inherent in Thackeray's practice of continuing beyond the moment of climax. It capitulates to that nihilistic sense of transience which *Henry Esmond* both acknowledged and resisted, and effectively undoes the achievement of the earlier novel. The particular mode of undoing is the kind of ironic repetition that was at work in Esmond's plot to restore the Stewarts. Time continues and history repeats itself: Beatrix re-enacts the role of Countess Isabel, and Esmond's grandsons retrace their grandfather's movements and experiences, returning to the original Castlewood and making their different ways through London society, but only to appear as shadows of the former substance. Even Thackeray as narrator displays on occasions a marked contempt for, and boredom with, the tale that he is telling. Wearily declining to give the details of young Harry Warrington's courtship of his much older cousin Maria – herself a more scheming version of Esmond's mistress – he gives vent to a levelling cynicism: 'Is not one story as stale as the other? Are not they all alike? What is the use, I say, of telling them over and over? . . . The incidents of life, and love-making especially, I believe to resemble each other so much, that I am surprised, gentlemen and ladies, you read novels any more' (p. 186).[12] The surprise is not so much his at our reading but ours at his continuing to write: 'But *cui bono*? I say again. What is the good of telling the story' (p. 187). This kind of self-conscious intervention is not, of course, without irony: in one respect it is simply one of the poses that Thackeray playfully adopts in his role as narrator. Yet the weary impatience expressed here aptly defines the spirit, and the effect, of this

[11]Sutherland, *Thackeray at Work*, p. 67.
[12]Page references are to *The Virginians*, vol. I, in the Centenary Biographical Edition of *The Works of William Makepeace Thackeray* (London, Smith Elder & Co, 1911).

novel as a whole. Instead of the positive pattern of continuity and change that might have been expected, there is a combination of sameness and loss. The world of *Henry Esmond* and the character of its central figure haunt the action of *The Virginians* as objects of nostalgia, admired and lamented even by the once heartless Beatrix: ' "Henry Esmond was noble and good, and perhaps might have made me so" ' (p. 371). Repetition in this novel does not generate meaning so much as destroy it, hollowing out the significance of present experience. Thus life seems to be governed by a negative double law: nothing stands (even Castlewood House is altered and modernized), and everything repeats itself. The bleakness and monotony of this vision bring to the surface the nihilism that lurks in the nineteenth-century realist novel's concern with time and history and which Thackeray had so creatively confronted in the earlier work. The failure of *The Virginians* simply throws into relief the energy, vitality and ironic complexity of that struggle against the power of time that is presented in *The History of Henry Esmond*.

Note

Life. Wilkie Collins, son of Royal Academy painter William Collins, spent part of his childhood in London, part near Hampstead Heath. At 12, he accompanied his parents to Italy, where he garnered the Italian tales that, like a young David Copperfield, he is said to have told to an older boy at the English boarding school to which he returned. (Depending on his response, 'Steerforth' would remunerate Collins's narrative office with either pastry or a lashing.) Collins variously pursued trade, law, theatre and painting before, in response to his father's death, he wrote *The Life of William Collins* (1848), his first published work. While living in the new household he shared with his mother and younger brother – an arrangement he kept well into middle age – Collins began to bring out his fiction. *Antonina,* homage to the style and interests of Bulwer-Lytton, appeared in 1850, and *Basil*, his first sensation novel, in 1852. Many of Collins's works (including *The Dead Secret* in 1857, *The Woman in White* in 1860, *No Name* in 1862 and *The Moonstone* in 1868) appeared serially in Dickens's weeklies *Household Words* and *All the Year Round*. The popularity of *The Woman in White* sparked the successful promotion of 'woman in white' cloaks, dances and toiletries. Collins's lasting friendship with Dickens began in 1852. The two travelled abroad, hiking, visiting the Paris morgue and, as Dickens says, playing Don Giovannis. They collaborated on an account of their travels, *The Lazy Tour of Two Idle Apprentices* (1890), and they wrote and performed in plays for Dickens's theatrical group. Collins's didactic later works were significantly less popular for undertaking missions against marriage, vivisection, Jesuits and athleticism among young men. In his later years Collins suffered from rheumatic gout and painful eye problems, and took laudanum in large doses. He died on 23 September 1889, and was buried beneath an epitaph of his own composing, as the 'Author of *The Woman in White*'.

John Millais, in a biography of his father, tells an anecdote about Wilkie Collins that, as Collins himself might have thought, delineates character in being above all a good story. One evening in 'the 'fifties', as the Collins brothers walked John Everett Millais home from one of Mrs Collins's parties, they were approached by a white-cloaked woman, in apparent flight, and the young Millais reports Collins's thrilled response to her supplicant touch. She fled them, too, but Collins pursued her – the woman who would become, with intermittent lapses, his lifelong mistress; 'next day . . . he seemed indisposed to talk of his adventure': her name was Caroline Graves.

Lives. Biographies of Collins include Nuel Pharr Davis, *The Life of Wilkie Collins* (Urbana, University of Illinois Press, 1956), William Marshall, *Wilkie Collins* (New York, Twayne, 1970), and Kenneth Robinson, *Wilkie Collins* (London, Bodley Head, 1951). S.M. Ellis, *Wilkie Collins, Le Fanu and Others* (London, Constable, 1931); Dorothy Sayers, *Wilkie Collins: Critical and Biographical Study*, ed. E.R. Gregory (Toledo, OH, Friends of the University of Toledo Libraries, 1977); John G. Millais, *The Life and Letters of Sir John Everett Millais* (London, Methuen 1902); and *The Letters of Charles Dickens*, Madeline House and Graham Storey, eds. (Oxford, Clarendon Press, 1965–1981) also contain interesting biographical material on Collins.

Mary Ann O'Farrell

7

Cage aux Folles: Sensation and Gender in Wilkie Collins's *The Woman in White*

D.A. Miller

FOR E.K.S.

I

There is nothing 'boring' about the Victorian sensation novel: the excitement that seizes us here is as direct as the 'fight-or-flight' physiology that renders our reading bodies, neither fighting nor fleeing, theatres of neurasthenia. The genre offers us one of the first instances of modern literature to address itself primarily to the sympathetic nervous system, where it grounds its characteristic adrenalin effects: accelerated heart-rate and respiration, increased blood pressure, the pallor resulting from vasoconstriction, etc. It is not, of course, the last such instance, and no less current than the phenomenon is the contradictory manner in which, following in the Victorians' footsteps, we continue to acknowledge it.[1] On the one hand, a vulgar salesmanship unblinkingly identifies hyperventilation with aesthetic value, as though art now had no other aim or justification than its successful ability to rattle what the French would call, with anatomical precision, our *cage*. That the body is compelled to automatism, that the rhythm of reading is frankly addictive – such dreary evidence of involuntary servitude is routinely marshalled in ads and on backcovers to promote entertainments whose Pavlovian expertise has become more than sufficient recommendation. On the other hand, an over-nice literary criticism wishfully reassures us that these domineering texts, whose power is literally proved upon our pulses, are not worth a thought. By a kind of Cartesian censorship, in which pulp-as-flesh gets equated with pulp-as-trash, the emphatic physicality of thrills in such literature allows us to hold them cheap. Accordingly, the sensation novel is relegated to the margins of the canon of approved genres, and on the infrequent occasions when it is seriously discussed, 'sensation' – the modern nervousness that is as fundamental to this genre as its name – is the first thing to be dropped from the

[1] A valuable survey of Victorian responses to sensation fiction may be found in Elizabeth K. Helsinger, Robin Lauterbach Sheets, and William Veeder, *The Woman Question: Society and Literature in Britain and America, 1837–1883*, (3 vols., New York, Garland, 1983), vol 3; pp. 122–44.

discussion.[2] What neither view of sensation fiction questions – what both views, it might be argued, become strategies for not questioning – is the natural immediacy of sensation itself. The celebration of sensation (as a physical experience to be enjoyed for its own sake) merely *receives* it; the censure of sensation (granting it the obviousness of something about which there is nothing to say) refuses to *read* it. In either case, sensation is felt to occupy a natural site entirely outside of meaning, as though in the breathless body signification expired.

To be sure, the silence that falls over the question of sensation seems first enjoined by the sensation novel itself, which is obsessed with the project of finding meaning – of staging the suspense of its appearance – in everything except the sensations that the project excites in us. Yet in principle the sensation novel must always at least imply a reading of these sensations, for the simple reason that it can mobilize the sympathetic nervous system only by giving it something to sympathize with. In order to make us nervous, nervousness must first be represented: in situations of character and plot which, both in themselves and in the larger cultural allusions they carry, make the operation of our own nerves significant in particular ways. The fiction elaborates a fantasmatics of sensation in which our reading bodies take their place from the start, and of which our physiological responses thus become the hysterical acting out. To speak of hysteria here, of course, is also to recall the assumption that always camouflages it – that what the body suffers, the mind needn't think. 'So far as my own sensations were concerned, I can hardly say that I thought at all.'[3] The efficacy of psychosomatisms as 'defences' presupposes a rigorously enforced separation in the subject between *psyche* and *soma*, and hysteria successfully breaches the body's autonomy only on the condition that this autonomy will be felt to remain intact. Reading the sensation novel, our hystericized bodies 'naturalize' the meanings in which the narrative implicates them, but in doing so, they also nullify these meanings as such. Incarnate in the body, the latter no longer seem part of a cultural, historical process of signification, but instead dissolve into an inarticulable, merely palpable self-evidence. Thus, if every sensation novel necessarily provides an interpretation of the sensations to which it gives rise in its readers, the immediacy of these sensations can always be counted on to *disown* such an interpretation. It may even be that the non-recognition that thus obtains between our sensations and their narrative thematization allows the sensa-

[2]The omission is well exemplified in a recent article by Patrick Brantlinger entitled 'What is "Sensational" about the Sensation Novel?', *Nineteenth-Century Fiction* (June 1982), pp. 1–28. Having posed the crucial question, the author elides its most obvious answer – namely, the somatic experience of sensation itself – by at once proceeding to considerations of 'content' (murder, adultery, bigamy) and generic 'mixture' (domestic realism, Gothic romance, etc.).

[3]Wilkie Collins, *The Woman in White*, ed. Julian Symons (Harmondsworth, Penguin, 1974), p. 47. Subsequent references to the novel are to this edition and are cited parenthetically in the text by page number.

tion novel to 'say' certain things for which our culture – at least at its popular levels – has yet to develop another language.

Wilkie Collins's *The Woman in White* (1860) – of all sensation novels the best-known and considered the best – seems at any rate an exemplary text for making this case. For what 'happens' in this novel becomes fully clear and coherent only, I think, when one takes into account the novel's implicit reading of its own (still quite 'effective') performative dimension and thus restores sensation to its textual and cultural mediations. For the reason given above, the attempt to do so must be prepared to seem rather 'forced' – as unprovable as a connotation and as improbable as a latency – but it is worth undertaking for more than a better understanding of this particular text. The ideological valences with which sensation characteristically combines in the novel do not of course absolutely transcend the second half of the Victorian period in which they are elaborated – as though the social significance of nervousness (itself an historical construct) were fixed once and for all; but neither are they restricted to this period. Collins's novel continues to be not just thoroughly readable, but eminently 'writable' as well. If it is still capable of moving readers to the edge of their seats (and how sharp a sense of this edge may be is suggested when one character starts from his own seat 'as if a spike had grown up from the ground through the bottom of [his] chair', p. 41), this is because its particular staging of nervousness remains cognate with that of many of our own thrillers, printed or filmed. It thus offers a pertinent, if not exhaustive, demonstration of the value, meaning, and use that modern culture – which in this respect has by no means broken radically with Victorian culture – finds in the nervous state.

Without exception, such a state affects all the novel's principal characters, who are variously startled, affrighted, unsettled, chilled, agitated, flurried. All sooner or later inhabit the 'sensationalized' body where the blood curdles, the heart beats violently, the breath comes short and thick, the flesh creeps, the cheeks lose their colour. No one knows what is the matter with Mr Fairlie, but 'we all say it's on the nerves' (p. 61), and in widely different ways, his niece Laura is 'rather nervous and sensitive' (p. 63). The 'nervous sensitiveness' (p. 127) of her double and half-sister Anne Catherick, the 'woman in white', issues in the aneurism that causes her death. Characters who are not constitutionally nervous become circumstantially so, in the unnerving course of events. Unsettled by the mystery surrounding Anne, fearful that Laura may be implicated in it, suspecting that he is himself being watched, Walter Hartright develops a 'nervous contraction' about his lips and eyes (p. 178), which he appears to have caught from Laura herself, whose 'sweet, sensitive lips are subject to a slight nervous contraction' (p. 75). At first 'perfect self-possession' (p. 209), Sir Percival Glyde degenerates after his marriage to Laura into 'an unsettled, excitable manner . . . a kind of panic or frenzy of mind' (p. 417). And Marian Halcombe, Laura's other half-sister, has already lost the 'easy inborn confidence in herself and her position' (p. 60) that initially characterized her by the time of the first anxious and 'sadly distrustful' extract (p. 184) from her diary. In the course of keeping that diary, of gathering the increasingly less equivocal evidence of a 'plot' against Laura, she literally writes herself into a fever. It is a measure of Count Fosco's control over these characters that he is said to be 'born without nerves' (p. 376), though his 'eternal cigarettes' (p. 252) attest that even here nervousness is not so much missing as mastered, and mastered only in so far as its symptoms are masked in the banal practices of civilized society.

Nervousness seems the necessary 'condition' in the novel for perceiving its real plot and for participating in it as more than a pawn. The condition is not quite sufficient, as the case of the wilfully ignorant Mr Fairlie shows, but otherwise those without the capacity to become nervous also lack the capacity to interpret events, or even to see that events require interpreting. The servants, for instance, also called (more accurately) 'persons born without nerves' (p. 69), are uniformly oblivious to what is or might be going on: the 'unutterably tranquil' governess Mrs Vesey (p. 72), the maid who 'in a state of cheerful stupidity' grins at the sight of Mrs Catherick's wounded dog (p. 229), the housekeeper Mrs Michelson, whose Christian piety prevents her from advancing 'opinions' (p. 381). It is not exactly that the novel uses nervousness to mark middle-class status, since the trait fails to characterize the 'sanguine constitution' of Mr Gilmore, the family lawyer, who 'philosophically' walks off his 'uneasiness' about Laura's marriage (p. 159). Rather the novel makes nervousness a metonymy for reading, its cause or effect. No reader can identify with unruffled characters like Gilmore or Mrs Michelson, even when they narrate parts of the story, because every reader is by definition committed to a hermeneutic project that neither of these characters finds necessary or desirable. Instead we identify with nerve-racked figures like Walter and Marian who carry forward the activity of our own deciphering. We identify even with Anne Catherick in her 'nervous dread' (p. 134), though she is never capable of articulating its object, because that dread holds at least the promise of the story we will read. Nervousness is our justification in the novel, as Mrs Michelson's faith is hers, in so far as it validates the attempt to read, to uncover the grounds for *being* nervous.

The association of nervousness with reading is complicated – not to say troubled – by its concident, no less insistent or regular association with femininity. However general a phenomenon, nervousness is always gendered in the novel as, like Laura's headache symptom, an 'essentially feminine malady' (p. 59). Of the novel's three characters who seem 'born' nervous, two are women (Anne and Laura), and the third, Mr Fairlie, an effeminate. 'I am nothing', the latter pronounces himself, 'but a bundle of nerves dressed up to look like a man' (p. 370). No one, however, is much convinced by the drag, and Walter's first impression – 'he had a frail, languid-fretful, over-refined look – something singularly and unpleasantly delicate in its association with a man' (p. 66) – never stands in need of correction. Even in the less fey male characters, nervousness remains a signifier of femininity. At best it declares Walter still 'unformed', and Sir Percival's imposture – that he is not, so to speak, the man he is pretending to be – is already in a manner disclosed when Mrs Michelson observes that 'he seemed to be almost as nervous and fluttered . . . as his lady herself' (p. 403). Fosco himself, Marian informs us, 'is as nervously sensitive as the weakest of us [women]. He starts at chance noises as inveterately as Laura herself' (p. 242).

The novel's 'primal scene', which it obsessively repeats and remembers ('Anne Catherick again!') as though this were the trauma it needed to work through, rehearses the 'origins' of male nervousness in female contagion – strictly, in the woman's touch. When Anne Catherick, in flight from the asylum where she has been shut away, 'lightly and suddenly' lays her hand on Walter Hartright's shoulder, it brings 'every drop of blood in [his] body . . . to a stop' (p. 47). Released from – and with – the Woman, nervousness touches and enters the Man: Anne's nervous gesture is at once sympathetically 'caught' in Walter's nervous response to it. Attempting to recover himself, Walter tightens his fingers round 'the handle of [his] stick,' as though the touch – 'from behind [him]' (p. 47) – were a violation requiring violent counteraction, and what was violated were a gender-identification that needed to be reaffirmed. Yet Anne Catherick impinges on him again: 'the loneliness and helplessness of the woman touched me' (p. 49). His formulation hopefully denies what is happening to him – Anne's weak femininity is supposed to evince *a contrario* his strong masculinity – but the denial seems only to produce further evidence of the gender slippage it means to arrest. Even in his classic gallantry, Walter somehow feels insufficiently manly, 'immature': 'The natural impulse to assist her and spare her got the better of the judgement, the caution, the worldly tact, which an older, wiser, and colder man might have summoned to help him in this strange emergency' (p. 49). He is even 'distressed by an uneasy sense of having done wrong' (p. 54), of having betrayed his sex: 'What had I done? Assisted the victim of the most horrible of all false imprisonments to escape; or cast loose on the wide world of London an unfortunate creature, whose actions it was my duty, and every man's duty, mercifully to control?' (p. 55). Walter's protection has in fact suspended the control that is 'every man's duty' to exercise over the activity of the neuropathic woman. Thanks to his help, Anne eludes a manifold of male guardians: the turnpike man at the entry-gate of the city; the two men from the asylum including its director; the policeman who, significantly, is assumed to be at their disposal; and even Walter himself, who puts her into a cab, destination unknown. 'A dangerous woman to be at large' (p. 177): the female trouble first transmitted to Walter will extend throughout the thick ramifications of plot to excite sympathetic vibrations in Laura and Marian, and in Sir Percival and even Fosco as well. And not just in them. 'The reader's nerves are affected like the hero's', writes Mrs Oliphant in a contemporary review of the novel; in what I have called the novel's primal scene, this means that 'the silent woman lays her hand upon our shoulder as well as upon that of Mr Walter Hartright'.[4] As the first of the novel's sensation effects *on us*, the scene thus fictionalizes the beginning of our physiological experience of the sensation novel as such. Our first sensation concides with – is positively triggered by – the novel's originary account of sensation. Fantasmatically, then, we 'catch' sensation from the neuropathic body of the woman who, no longer confined or controlled in an asylum, is free to make our bodies resonate with – like – hers.

Every reader is consequently implied to be a version or extension of the woman in white, a fact which entails particularly interesting consequences when the reader is – as the text explicitly assumes he is – male.[5] This reader willy-nilly falls victim to an hysteria in which what is acted out (desired, repressed) is an essentially female 'sensation'. His excitements come from – become – her nervous excitability; his ribcage, arithmetically Adam's, houses a woman's quickened respiration and his heart beats to her skittish rhythm; even his pallor (which of course he cannot see) is mirrored back to him only as hers, the woman in white's. This reader thus lends himself to elaborating a fantasy of *anima muliebris in corpore virili inclusa* – or as we might appropriately translate here, 'a woman's breath caught in a man's body'. The usual translation, of course, is 'a woman's soul trapped . . .', and it will be recognized as nineteenth-century sexology's classic formulation (coined by Karl Ulrichs in the 1860s) for male homosexuality.[6] I cite it, not just to anticipate the homosexual component given to readerly sensation by the novel, but also, letting the

---

[4]Mrs [Margaret] Oliphant, 'Sensation Novels,' *Blackwood's Magazine* (May 1862, xci), reprinted in Norman Page, ed., *Wilkie Collins: the Critical Heritage*, (London, Routledge and Kegan Paul, 1974), pp. 119 and 118.

[5]For example, Walter, the master narrator who solicits the others' narratives and organizes them into a whole, speaks of Laura to the reader: 'Think of her as you thought of the first woman who quickened the pulses within you' (p. 76). The same identification is also sustained implicitly, as in the equation between the reader and a judge (p. 33).

[6]See Jeffrey Weeks, *Coming Out: Homosexual Politics in Britain, from the Nineteenth Century to the Present* (London, Quartet Books, 1977), pp. 26–7. It does not seem altogether an historical 'irony' that this intrinsically ambiguous notion – so useful to the apologists for homosexuality in the late nineteenth and early twentieth centuries – should popularly survive today as part of the mythological rationale for 'vulgar' homophobia, which draws on an equally vulgar misogyny to oppress gay men.

It may also be pertinent here to note that turn-of-the-century sexology is almost universally agreed on 'a marked tendency to nervous development in the [homosexual] subject, not infrequently associated with nervous maladies' (Edward Carpenter, *The Intermediate Sex*, 1908, in *Selected Writings*, Vol. 1, London, Gay Men's Press, 1984, p. 209). Criticizing Krafft-Ebing for continuing to link homosexuality with ' "an hereditary neuropathic or psychopathic tendency" – *neuro(psycho)-pathische Belastung*,' Carpenter remarks that 'there are few people in modern life, perhaps none, who could be pronounced absolutely free from such a *Belastung*!' (p. 210). His ostensible point – that nervous disorders are far too widespread in modern life to be the distinctive mark of homosexuals, whose 'neuropathic tendency' would bespeak rather a social than a metaphysical fatality – is still (*mutatis mutandis*) worth making. Yet in a discursive formation that insistently yokes male homosexuality and neuropathology together (in the femininity common to both), his observation might also be taken to conclude that this homosexuality *too* (if principally in its reactive, homophobic form) is a general modern phenomenon.

phrase resonate beyond Ulrichs's intentions, to situate this component among the others that determine its context. For if what essentially characterizes male homosexuality in this way of putting it is the woman-in-the-man, and if this 'woman' is *inclusa*, incarcerated or shut up, her freedoms abridged accordingly, then homosexuality would be by its very nature homophobic: imprisoned in a carceral problematic that does little more than channel into the homosexual's 'ontology' the social and legal sanctions that might otherwise be imposed on him. Meant to win a certain intermediate space for homosexuals, Ulrichs's formulation in fact ultimately colludes with the prison or closet drama – of keeping the 'woman' well put away – that it would relegate to the unenlightened past. And homosexuals' are not the only souls to be imprisoned in male bodies; Ulrichs's phrase does perhaps far better as a general description of the condition of nineteenth-century women, whose 'spirit' (whether understood as intellect, integrity, or sexuality) is massively interned in male corporations, constitutions, contexts. His metaphor thus may be seen to link or condense together (1) a particular fantasy about male homosexuality; (2) a homophobic defence against that fantasy; and (3) the male oppression of women that, among other things, extends that defence. All three meanings bear pointedly on Collins's novel, which is profoundly about enclosing and secluding the woman in male 'bodies', among them institutions like marriage and madhouses. And the sequestration of the woman takes for its object not just women, who need to be put away in safe places or asylums, but men as well, who must monitor and master what is fantasized as the 'woman inside' them.

II

Like *The Moonstone*, *The Woman in White* accords itself the status of a quasi-legal document.

> If the machinery of the Law could be depended on to fathom every case of suspicion, and to conduct every process of inquiry, with moderate assistance only from the lubricating influences of oil of gold, the events which fill these pages might have claimed their share of the public attention in a Court of Justice. But the Law is still, in certain inevitable cases, the pre-engaged servant of the long purse; and the story is left to be told, for the first time, in this place. As the Judge might once have heard it, so the Reader shall hear it now . . . Thus, the story here presented will be told by more than one pen, as the story of an offence against the laws is told in Court by more than one witness – with the same object, in both cases, to present the truth always in its most direct and most intelligible aspect. (p. 33).

The organizational device is a curious one, since nothing in the story ever appears to motivate it. Why and for whom does this story need to be thus told? At the end of the novel – after which Walter Hartright presumably gathers his narratives together – neither legal action nor even a para-legal hearing seems in the least required. And it is of course pure mystification to preface a mystery story with a claim to be presenting the truth 'always in its most direct and most intelligible aspect'. But the obvious gimmickiness of the device offers only the crudest evidence of the limited pertinence of the legal model that the text here invokes. On the face of it, despite its conventionally bitter references to oil of gold and the long purse, the text is eager to retain the law – the juridical model of an inquest – for its own narrative. It simply proposes to extend this model to a case that it wouldn't ordinarily cover. The explicit ideal thus served would be a law which fathomed every case of suspicion and conducted every process of inquiry. But what law has ever done this, or wanted to? Certainly not the English law, which like all non-totalitarian legal systems is on principle concerned to limit the matters that fall under its jurisdiction. The desire to extend the law as totally as the preamble utopically envisions – to *every* case of suspicion and *every* process of inquiry – would therefore supersede the legal model to which, the better not to alarm us, it nominally clings. For the project of such a desire makes sense only in a world where suspicion and inquiry have already become everyday practices, and whose affinities lie less with a given legal code or apparatus than with a vast multifaceted network of inquests-without-end. Under the guise of a pedantic, legalistic organization, the novel in fact aligns itself with extra-, infra- and supra-legal modern discipline.

Not, of course, that *The Woman in White* represents the world of discipline in the manner of either *Bleak House* or *Barchester Towers*. Its most important relationship to this world, at any rate, does not come at the level of an 'objective' portrayal, either of institutions (like the Court of Chancery and the Detective Police in Dickens) or of less formal means of social control (like 'moderate schism' and the norm in Trollope).[7] It would be quite difficult to educe a sociological understanding of Victorian asylums from Collins's novel, which, voiding a lively contemporary concern with the private madhouse, describes neither its structure nor the (medicinal? physical? psychological?) therapies that may or may not be practised within it.[8] Anne never says, and Laura finds it too painfully confusing to recall, what goes on there. The asylum remains a very black 'black box', the melodramatic site of 'the most horrible of false imprisonments', where the sane middle-class might mistakenly be sent. The asylum, in short, is available to representation mainly in so far as it has been *incorporated*: in Walter's 'unsettled state' when he first learns that Anne is a fugitive from there, in Anne's nervous panic at the very word, in the

[7]My understanding of the workings of discipline in Dickens and Trollope is elaborated in D.A. Miller, 'Discipline in Different Voices: Bureaucracy, Police, Family, and *Bleak House*,' *Representations* 1 (February 1983), pp. 59–89; and 'The Novel as Usual: Trollope's *Barchester Towers*,' in Ruth Bernard Yeazell, ed., *Sex, Politics, and Science in the Nineteenth-Century Novel* (Baltimore, Johns Hopkins University Press, 1985), pp. 1–38.
[8]See William Ll. Parry-Jones, *The Trade in Lunacy: a Study of Private Madhouses in England in the Eighteenth and Nineteenth Centuries* (Toronto, University of Toronto Press, 1972).

difference between Laura's body before she enters the place and after she leaves, in the way we are invited to fill in the blank horror of what she cannot remember with the stuff of our own nightmares. What the example may be broadened to suggest is that the novel represents discipline mainly in terms of certain general isolated effects on the disciplinary *subject*, whose sensationalized body both dramatizes and facilitates his functioning as *the subject/object of continual supervision*.

These effects, together with the juridical metaphor under which they are first inscribed, are best pursued in the contradiction between the Judge and the Reader who is supposed to take his place. 'As the Judge might once have heard [the story], so the Reader shall hear it now.' The pronouncement, of course, confers on the latter role all the connotations of sobriety and even serenity attached to the former. That 'wretches hang that jurymen may dine' will always give scandal to our Western mythology of justice, in which the judge – set above superstition, prejudice, 'interest' of any kind – weighs the evidence with long and patient scruple before pronouncing sentence. Nothing, however, could be less judicial, or judicious, than the actual hermeneutic practice of the reader of this novel, whose technology of nervous stimulation – in many ways still the state of the art – has him repeatedly jumping to unproven conclusions, often literally jumping at them. Far from encouraging reflective calm, the novel aims to deliver 'positive personal shocks of surprise and excitement' which so sensationalize the reader's body that he is scarcely able to reflect at all.[9] The novel's only character with strictly judicial habits of mind is the lawyer Gilmore, who judges only to misjudge. Hearing Sir Percival's explanation of his dealings with Anne Catherick, he says: 'my function was of the purely judicial kind. I was to weigh the explanation we had just heard . . . and to decide honestly whether the probabilities, on Sir Percival's own showing, were plainly with him, or plainly against him. My own conviction was that they were plainly with him' (p. 155). Characters who rely on utterly unlegal standards of evidence like intuition, coincidence, literary connotation, get closer to what will eventually be revealed as the truth. In her first conversation with Walter, Anne Catherick nervously inquires about an unnamed Baronet in Hampshire; Walter later learns that Laura is engaged to a Baronet in Hampshire named Sir Percival Glyde. 'Judging by the ordinary rules of evidence, I had not the shadow of a reason thus far, for connecting Sir Percival Glyde with the suspicious words of inquiry that had been spoken to me by the woman in white. And yet, I did connect them' (p. 101). Similarly, when after Sir Percival's explanation, Gilmore wonders what excuse Laura can possibly have for changing her mind about him, Marian answers: 'In the eyes of law and reason, Mr Gilmore, no excuse, I dare say. If she still hesitates, and if I still hesitate, you must attribute our strange conduct, if you like, to caprice in both cases' (p. 162). The competent reader, who does not weigh evidence so much as he simply assents to the ways in which it has been weighted, fully accepts the validity

[9]Mrs Oliphant, *Wilkie Collins: the Critical Heritage*, p. 112.

of such ungrounded connections and inexcusable hesitations: they validate, among other things, the sensations they make him feel. And this reader is capable of making what by the ordinary rules of evidence are comparably tenuous assumptions of his own. We can't know, just because Sir Percival's men are watching Somebody, and Walter may be being watched, that Walter is that Somebody; and yet, we are convinced that we do know this. Or again, the loose seal on the letter that Marian recovers from the postbag after she has seen Fosco hovering about it does not establish the fact that Fosco has opened and resealed her letter; but we take it firmly for granted nonetheless. Our judgements are often informed by no better than the silliest folk wisdom. Laura's pet greyhound shrinks from Sir Percival; 'a trifle' Gilmore considers it (p. 156) even though Nina later jumps eagerly enough into his own lap. In the strange court of justice over which we preside, we consider her evidence unimpeachable. Yet neither adhering to ordinary rules of evidence nor inhering in a decisive institutional context (except of course that provided by the conventions of this kind of novel), such 'acts of judgement' are in fact only entitled to the considerably less authoritative status of *suspicions*, whose 'uncertainty' in both these senses makes it easy to discredit them. Walter is the first to refer his hypotheses to their possible source in 'delusion' and 'monomania' (pp. 101, 105). Like the characters who figure him, the reader becomes – what a judge is never supposed to be – paranoid. From trifles and common coincidences, he suspiciously infers a complicated structure of persecution, an elaborately totalizing 'plot'.

What a judge is never supposed to be? Yet the most famous paranoid of modern times *was* a judge, and his paranoia was triggered precisely when, at Dresden, he entered on his duties as Senatspräsident. Schreber's case suggests that paranoia is 'born' at the moment when the judge, without ceasing to be judge, has also become the accused, when he is both one and the other. It was, of course, his homosexuality that put Schreber in this institutionally untenable position, since the law he was expected to administer would certainly include, as Hocquengham has pointed out, interdictions against homosexuality itself.[10] Schreber's delusion does nothing so much as elaborate the paradoxical aspect of his actual situation as a judge who might well have to judge (others like) himself. The Rays of God, having constituted his monstrosity (literally: by feminizing his constitution via the nerves), taunt him with it thus: 'So *this* sets up to have been a Senatspräsident, this person who lets himself be f——d!'[11] In *The Woman in White*, another case of feminization via the nerves, Mrs Michelson's article of unsuspecting faith – 'Judge not that ye be not judged'

[10]Guy Hocquengham, *Homosexual Desire*, trans. Daniella Dangoor (London, Allison & Busby, 1978), pp. 42–3.
[11]Quoted in Sigmund Freud, *Psycho-Analytic Notes on an Autobiographical Account of Paranoia*, in *The Standard Edition of the Complete Works of Sigmund Freud*, ed. James Strachey (24 vols, London, Hogarth Press and the Institute of Psycho-Analysis, 1953–74), vol 12, p. 20.

(p. 381) – postulates an inevitable slippage between subject and object whenever judgement is attempted. The slippage is in fact far more likely to occur when judgement, no longer governed by an institutional practice with established roles and rules of evidence, has devolved into mere suspicion. Unlike legal judgement, suspicion presupposes the reversibility of the direction in which it passes. The novel abounds with suspicious characters, in the telling ambiguity of the phrase, for what Anne, Walter, and Marian all suspect is that *they are themselves suspected*. Why else would Anne be pursued, Walter watched, Marian's correspondence opened? They are suspected, moreover, precisely, *for being suspicious*. For Walter to notice that Anne's manner is 'a little touched by suspicion' is already to suspect her, as she instantly recognizes ('Why do you suspect me?', p. 48). Hence the urgency, as well as the futility, of the suspicious character's obsessive desire *not to excite suspicion* (pp. 260, 275, 293, 311, 325), since the act of suspecting always already implies the state of being suspect. The whole vertiginous game (in which I suspect him of suspecting me of suspecting him) is meant to ward off – but only by passing along – the violation of privacy that it thus at once promotes and resists. In what Roland Barthes would call the novel's symbolic code, this violation connotes the sexual attack whose possibility 'haunts' the novel no less thoroughly than the virginal presence – insistent like a dare – of the woman in white. What stands behind the vague fears of Anne and Walter during their first encounter; what subtends Mr Fairlie's malicious greeting of the latter ('So glad to possess you at Limmeridge, Mr Hartright', p. 66); what Sir Percival sadistically fantasizes when he invites his wife to imagine her lover 'with the marks of my horsewhip on his shoulders' (p. 283); and what Fosco finally accomplishes when he reads Marian's *journal intime*, is virtual rape. We might consider what is implied or at stake in the fact that the head-game of suspicion is always implicitly transcoded by the novel into the body-game of rape.

Perhaps the most fundamental value that the novel as a cultural institution may be said to uphold is privacy, the determination of an integral, autonomous 'secret' self. Novel-reading takes for granted the existence of a space in which the reading subject remains safe from the surveillance, suspicion, reading, and rape of others. Yet this privacy is always specified as the freedom to read about characters who oversee, suspect, read, and rape one another. It is not just that, strictly private subjects, we read about violated, objectified subjects, but that, in the very act of reading about them, we contribute largely to constituting them as such. We enjoy our privacy in the act of watching privacy being violated, in the act of watching that is already itself a violation of privacy. Our most intense identification with characters never blinds us to our ontological privilege over them: they will never be reading about *us*. It is built into the structure of the novel that every reader must realize the definitive fantasy of the liberal subject, who imagines himself free from the surveillance that he nonetheless sees operating everywhere around him.

The sensation novel, however, submits this panoptic immunity to a crucial modification: it produces repeated and undeniable evidence – 'on the nerves' – that we are perturbed by what we are watching. We remain of course unseen, but not untouched: our bodies are rocked by the same 'positive personal shocks' as the characters are said to be. For us, these shocks have the ambivalent character of being both a kind of untroubled pleasure (with a certain 'male' adventurism we read the sensation novel to *have* them) and a kind of less tame and more painful *jouissance* (with a certain 'female' helplessness we often protest that we can't *bear* them, though they keep on coming). The specificity of the sensation novel in nineteenth-century fiction is that it renders the liberal subject the subject of a *body*, whose fear and desire of violation displaces, reworks, and exceeds his constitutive fantasy of intact privacy. The themes that the liberal subject ordinarily defines himself against – by reading *about* them – are here inscribed into his reading body. Moreover, in *The Woman in White* this body is gendered: not only has its gender been *decided*, but also its gender-identification is an active and determining *question*. The drama in which the novel writes its reader turns on the disjunction between his allegedly masculine gender and his effectively feminine gender-identification (as a creature of 'nerves'): with the result that his experience of sensation must include his panic at having the experience at all, of being in the position to have it. In this sense, the novel's initial assumption that its reader is male is precisely what cannot be assumed (or better, what stands most in need of proof), since his formal title – say, 'a man' – is not or not yet a substantial entity – say, 'a real man.'

By far the most shocking moment in the reader's drama comes almost in the exact middle of the novel, when the text of Marian's diary, lapsing into illegible fragments, abruptly yields to a postscript by the very character on whom its suspicions centre. Not only has Count Fosco read Marian's 'secret pages' (p. 240), he lets her know it, and even returns them to her. In a fever which soon turns to typhus, Marian is in no condition even to take cognizance of this revelation, whose only immediate register is the reader's own body. Peter Brooks articulates our state of shock thus: 'our readerly intimacy with Marian is violated, our act of reading adulterated by profane eyes, made secondary to the villain's reading and indeed dependent on his permission.'[12] It is not just, then, that Marian has been 'raped', as both the Count's amorous flourish ('Admirable woman!', p. 258) and her subsequent powerless rage against him are meant to suggest. We are 'taken' too, taken by surprise, which is itself an overtaking. We are taken, moreover, from behind: from a place where, in the wings of the ostensible drama, the novelist disposes of a whole plot machinery whose existence – so long as it didn't oblige us by making creaking sounds (and here it is as 'noiseless' as Fosco himself, p. 242) – we never suspected. (We never suspected, though the novel has trained us to be nothing if not suspicious. Surprise – the recognition of what one 'never suspected' – is precisely what the paranoid seeks to eliminate, but it is also what, in the

---

[12]Peter Brooks, *Reading for the Plot* (New York, Knopf, 1984), p. 169.

event, he survives by reading as a frightening incentive: he can never be paranoid enough.) To being the object of violation here, however, there is an equally disturbing alternative: to identify with Fosco, with the novelistic agency of violation. For the Count's postscript only puts him in the position we already occupy. Having just finished reading Marian's diary ourselves we are thus implicated in the sadism of his act, which, even as it violates our readerly intimacy with Marian, reveals that 'intimacy' to be itself a violation. The ambivalent structure of readerly identification here thus condenses together – as simultaneous, but opposite renderings of the same powerful shock – homosexual panic and heterosexual violence.

This is the shock, however, that, having administered, the novel (like any good administration) will work to absorb. The shock in fact proves the point of transition between what the narrative will soothingly render as a *succession*: on one side, a passive, paranoid, homosexual feminization; on the other, an active, corroborative, heterosexual masculine protest. Marian alerts us to this succession ('our endurance must end, and our resistance must begin', p. 321), but only towards the end of her narrative, since the moment of 'resistance' will need to be effectively sponsored not just by a male agent, but by an indefectibly composed male discourse as well. The master narrator and actor in the second half of the novel is therefore Walter: no longer the immature Walter whose nerve-ridden opening narrative seemed – tonally at any rate – merely continued in Marian's diary, but the Walter who has returned from his trials in Central America a changed man: 'In the stern school of extremity and danger my will had learnt to be strong, my heart to be resolute, my mind to rely on itself. I had gone out to fly from my own future. I came back to face it, as a man should' (p. 427). Concomitantly, the helpless paranoia of the first half of the novel now seeks *to prove itself*, as Walter aggressively attempts to 'force a confession' from Sir Percival and Fosco 'on [his] own terms' (p. 470). Shocks decline 'dramatically' in both frequency and intensity (our last sensation: its absence) as characters and readers alike come to get answers to the question that sensation could never do more than merely pose of the event occasioning it – namely, 'what did it mean?' (p. 99). Foremost on the novel's agenda in its second half is the dissolution of sensation in the achievement of decided meaning. What the narrative must most importantly get straight is, from this perspective, as much certain sexual and gender deviancies as the obscure tangles of plot in which they thrive. In short, the novel needs to realize the normative requirements of the heterosexual ménage whose happy picture concludes it.

This conclusion, of course, marks the most banal moment in the text, when the sensation novel becomes least distinguishable from any other kind of Victorian fiction. Herein, one might argue, lies the 'morality' of sensation fiction, in its ultimately fulfilled wish to abolish itself: to abandon the grotesque aberrations of character and situation that have typified its representation, which now coincides with the norm of the Victorian household. But the project, however successful, is nothing here if not drastic. In *Barchester Towers*, by contrast, the normative elements of heterosexual coupling – the manly husband, the feminine wife – are ready-to-hand early on, and the plot is mainly a question of overcoming various inhibitions and misunderstandings that temporarily prevent them from acknowledging their appropriateness for one another. In *The Woman in White*, however, these elements have to be 'engendered' in the course of the plot through the most extreme and violent expedients. The sufficiently manly husband needs to have survived plague, pygmy arrows, and shipwreck in Central America, and the suitably feminine wife must have been schooled in a lunatic asylum, where she is half-cretinized. Such desperate measures no doubt dramatize the supreme value of a norm for whose incarnation no price, including the most brutal aversion therapy, is considered too high to pay. But they do something else besides, something which Victorians, in thrall to this norm, suspected when they accused the sensation novel of immorality, and which we, more laxly oppressed than they, are perhaps in a better position to specify. This is simply that, recontextualized in a 'sensational' account of its genesis, such a norm risks appearing *monstrous*: as aberrant as any of the abnormal conditions that determine its realization.

III

'It ended, as you probably guess by this time, in his insisting on securing his own safety by shutting her up' (p. 557). Male security in *The Woman in White* seems always to depend on female claustration. Sir Percival not only shuts up Anne in the asylum, but successfully conspires with Fosco to shut up Laura there as well. In a double sense, he also shuts up Anne's mother, whose silence he purchases with a 'handsome' allowance and ensures by insisting she not leave the town where she has been shamed and therefore 'no virtuous female friends would tempt [her] into dangerous gossiping at the tea-table' (pp. 554–5). Thanks to 'the iron rod' that Fosco keeps 'private' (p. 224), Madame Fosco, who once 'advocated the Rights of Women' (p. 255), now lives in a 'state of suppression' that extends to 'stiff little rows of very short curls' on either side of her face and 'quiet black or grey gowns, made high round the throat' (pp. 238–9). She walks in a favourite circle, 'round and round the great fish pond' (p. 290) – the Blackwater estate is in any case already 'shut in – almost suffocated . . . by trees' (p. 220) – as though she were taking yard-exercise. The novel does not of course approve of these restraining orders, which originate in unambiguously criminal depravity, but as we shall see, it is not above exploiting them as the stick with which to contrast and complement the carrot of a far more ordinary and acceptable mode of sequestration.

Gilbert and Gubar have argued that 'dramatizations of imprisonment and escape are so all-pervasive in nineteenth-century literature by women that . . . they represent a uniquely female tradition in this period'. Male carceral representations, 'more consciously and objectively' elaborated, tend to be 'metaphysical and metaphorical', whereas female ones remain 'social and actual'.[13] Yet at least in the nineteenth-century novel, the representation of imprisonment is too pervasive to be exclusively or even chiefly a female property, and too consistent overall to be divided between male and female authors on the basis of the distinctions proposed. On the one hand it is a commonplace that Dickens's carceral fictions are grounded in actual social institutions, and there is little that is metaphysical in Trollope's rendering of social control: what little there is, in the form of 'religion' or 'providence', merely sanctions the social mechanisms concretely at work. On the other, Charlotte Brontë's 'dramatizations of imprisonment' do not deal with literal prisons at all, as Gilbert and Gubar themselves demonstrate. In so far as these critics endorse a familiar series of oppositions (masculine/feminine = abstract/concrete = conscious/unconscious = objective/subjective) that, even graphically, keeps women behind a lot of bars, their attempt to isolate the essential paradigm of female writing unwittingly risks recycling the feminine mystique. We are nonetheless indebted to them for posing the question of the specific historical configuration, in the nineteenth-century English novel, of what might be called the 'feminine carceral'. As they convincingly show, this configuration centres on the representation, in varying degrees of alienation, of the 'madwoman', and if this representation is not a uniquely female tradition, one readily grants that it is dominantly so. *The Woman in White*, however, with impressive ease incorporating the story of female 'imprisonment and escape' (again, *anima muliebris inclusa*), suggests that there is a radical ambiguity about the 'madwoman' that allows the feminist concerns she often voices to have already been appropriated in anti-feminist ways. To the extent that novelists (or critics) underwrite the validity of female 'madness', as virtually the only mode of its subject's authenticity, they inevitably slight the fact that it is also her socially given *role*, whose quasi-mandatory performance under certain conditions apotheosizes the familiar stereotypes of the woman as 'unconscious' and 'subjective' (read: irresponsible) that contribute largely to her oppression. The madwoman finds a considerable part of her truth – in the corpus of nineteenth-century fiction, at any rate – in being implicitly juxtaposed to the male *crimincl* she is never allowed to be. If, typically, *he* ends up in the prison or its metaphorical equivalents, *she* ends up in the asylum or *its* metaphorical equivalents. (As a child perusing the shelves of a public library, I thought *The Woman in White* must be the story of a nurse: it at least proves to be the story of various women's subservience to 'the doctor', to medical domination.) The distinction between criminal men (like Sir Percival and Fosco) and innocently sick women (like Anne and Laura) bespeaks a paternalism whose 'chivalry' merely sublimates a system of constraints. In this light, the best way to read the madwoman would be not to derive the diagnosis from her social psychology ('who wouldn't go crazy under such conditions?'), but rather to derive her social psychology from

---

[13]Sandra M. Gilbert and Susan Gubar, *The Madwoman in the Attic* (New Haven, Yale University Press, 1979), pp. 85–6.

the diagnosis: from the very category of madness that, like a fate, lies ever in wait to 'cover' – account for and occlude – whatever behaviours, desires, or tendencies might be considered socially deviant, undesirable, or dangerous.

The achievement of blowing this cover belongs to *Lady Audley's Secret* (1862), the novel where, writing under the ambiguous stimulus of *The Woman in White*, Mary Elizabeth Braddon demonstrates that the madwoman's primary 'alienation' lies in the rubric under which she is put down. Not unlike Anne Catherick, 'always weak in the head' (p. 554), Lady Audley appears to have been born with the 'taint' of madness in her blood. She inherits the taint from her mother, whose own madness was in turn 'an hereditary disease transmitted to her from her mother, who died mad'. Passed on like a curse through – and as – the woman, madness virtually belongs to the condition of being female. But the novel is not so much concerned to conjoin madness and femininity, each the 'truth' of the other, as to display how – under what assumptions and by what procedures – such a conjunction comes to be socially achieved. For in fact the text leaves ample room for doubt on the score of Lady Audley's 'madness'. Her acts, including bigamy, arson, and attempted murder, qualify as crimes in a strict legal sense; and they are motivated (like crime in English detective fiction generally) by impeccably rational considerations of self-interest. When her nephew Robert Audley at last detects her, however, he simply arranges for her to be pronounced 'mad' and imprisoned accordingly in a *maison de santé* abroad. The 'secret' let out at the end of the novel is not, therefore, that Lady Audley is a madwoman, but rather that, *whether she is one or not*, she must be treated as such. Robert feels no embarrassment at the incommensurability thus betrayed between the diagnosis and the data that are supposed to confirm it; if need be, these data can be dispensed with altogether, as in the findings of the doctor ('experienced in cases of mania') whom he calls in for an opinion:

> 'I have talked to the lady,' [the doctor] said quietly, 'and we understand each other very well. There is latent insanity! Insanity which might never appear; or which might appear only once or twice in a lifetime. It would be a *dementia* in its worst phase, perhaps; acute mania; but its duration would be very brief, and it would only arise under extreme mental pressure. The lady is not mad; but she has the hereditary taint in her blood. She has the cunning of madness, with the prudence of intelligence. I will tell you what she is, Mr. Audley. She is dangerous!'[14]

The doctor's double-talk ('the cunning of madness, with the prudence of intelligence') will be required to sanction two contradictory propositions: (1) Lady Audley is criminal – in the sense that her crimes must be punished; and (2) Lady Audley is not criminal – in the sense that neither her crimes nor her punishment must be made public in a male order of things. ('My greatest fear,' Robert tells the doctor, 'is the necessity of any

[14]Mary Elizabeth Braddon, *Lady Audley's Secret* (New York, Dover, 1974), p. 249.

exposure – any disgrace.') 'Latent insanity, an insanity which might never appear' nicely meets the requirements of the case. At the same time that it removes the necessity for evidence (do Lady Audley's crimes manifest her latent insanity? or has the latter, quite independently of them, yet to make its appearance?), it adduces the grounds for confining her to a madhouse. Lady Audley is mad, then, only because she must not be criminal. She must not, in other words, be supposed capable of acting on her own dia- bolical responsibility and hence of publicly spoiling her assigned role as the conduit of power transactions between men.[15] Whatever doubts the doctor entertains in pronouncing her mad do not affect his certainty that she is, at all events, dangerous, and this social judgement entirely suffices to dis- count the ambiguities which the properly medical one need not bother to resolve.

Lady Audley's Secret thus portrays the woman's carceral condition as her fundamental and final truth. The novel's power as a revision of *The Woman in White* consists in its refusal of the liberal dialectic whereby the latter thinks to surpass this truth. Up to a certain point – say, up to the success of the conspiracy to confine Laura – Collins's novel is willing to tell the same story as Braddon's: of an incarceration whose patriarchal expediency takes priority over whatever humane considerations may or may not be invoked to rationalize it. (Anne's mental disorder, though real enough, is only a plausible pretext for confining her on other grounds; and Laura's confinement has no medical justification whatsoever.) But unlike Lady Audley, Lady Glyde *escapes* from her asylum, and there fortunately proves somewhere else to go. The asylum has an 'alibi' in Limmeridge House (twice called an 'asylum' in the text, pp. 367, 368), where in the end Laura settles happily down with Walter. Whereas in the first move- ment of the novel, the woman is shut up, in the second, she is liberated, and it is rather the 'feminine carceral' that is put away instead. Laura thus follows a common itinerary of the liberal subject in nineteenth-century fiction: she takes a nightmarish detour through the carceral ghetto on her way *home*, to the domestic haven where she is always felt to belong. Yet while her history plainly dichotomizes carceral and liberal spaces, the asylum that keeps one inside and the 'asylum' that keeps others out, it also gives evidence of continuities and overlappings between them. If her situa- tion as Mrs Hartright throws domesticity into relief as relief indeed from the brutalities of the asylum, her state as Lady Glyde (at Sir Percival's 'stifling' house, p. 227) merely anticipates the asylum, which in turn only perfects Sir Percival's control over her. The difference between the

---

[15] A Victorian reviewer, W. Fraser Ray, criticizes the characterization of Lady Audley thus: 'In drawing her, the authoress may have intended to portray a female Mephistopheles; but if so, she should have known that a woman cannot fill such a part' ('Sensation Novelists: Miss Brad- don,' *North British Review* 43, 1865, quoted in *The Woman Question*, p. 127). Ray might have spared himself the trouble (not to mention, in our hindsight, the embarrassment of failing to read the text that nonetheless proves quite capable of reading him), since his objec- tion merely rehearses the same principle that, within the novel, Robert Audley victoriously carries in having Lady Audley confined.

asylum-as-confinement and the 'asylum'-as-refuge is sufficiently dramatic to make a properly enclosed domestic circle the object of both desire and, later, gratitude; but evidently, it is also sufficiently precarious to warrant – as the means of maintaining it – a domestic self-discipline that must have internalized the institutional control it thereby forestalls. The same internment that renders Laura's body docile, and her mind imbecile, also fits her to incarnate the norm of the submissive Victorian wife. (Sir Percival might well turn in his grave to see his successor effortlessly reaping what, with nothing to show but acute frustration, *he* had sown.) Collins makes Laura's second marriage so different from her first that he has no reason to conceal the considerable evidence of its resemblance to what can be counted upon to remain its 'opposite'.

   This evidence comes as early as when, virtually at first sight, Walter falls in love with Laura. 'Think of her', he invites the reader who would understand his feelings, 'as you thought of the first woman who quickened the pulses within you' (p. 76). As here, so everywhere else his passion declares itself in the language of sensation: of thrill and chill (p. 86), of pang and pain (p. 96), of 'sympathies' that, lying 'too deep for words, too deep almost for thoughts', have been 'touched' (p. 76). Concomitantly, in the associative pattern we have already established, his sensationalized body puts him in an essentially feminine position. His 'hardly-earned self-control' is as completely lost to him as if he had never possessed it (p. 90), and 'aggravated by the sense of [his] own miserable weakness' (p. 91), his situation becomes one of 'helplessness and humiliation' (p. 92) – the same hendiadys that Marian will apply to herself and Laura at Blackwater Park (p. 272). This is all to say that, notwithstanding Walter's implication, Laura Fairlie is *not* the first woman to quicken his pulses, but rather the object of a repetition compulsion whose origin lies in his (sensationalizing, feminizing) first encounter with the woman in white. Walter replays this primal trauma, however, with an important difference that in principle marks out the path to mastering it. He moves from an identification with the woman to a desire for her, heterosexual choice replacing homosexual surprise. The woman is once more (or for the first time) the other, and the man, who now at least 'knows what he wants', has to that extent taken himself in charge.

   Yet the sensational features of Walter's desire necessarily threaten to reabsorb it in the identification against which it erects itself as a first line of defence. Something more, therefore, is required to stabilize his male self-mastery, something that Walter does *not* know that he wants. 'Crush it', Marian counsels him: 'Don't shrink under it like a woman. Tear it out; trample it under foot like a man!' (p. 96). But the eventual recipient of this violence will be as much the object of Walter's passion as the passion itself. From the very beginning of his exposure to it, Laura's 'charm' has suggested to him 'the idea of something wanting':

   At one time it seemed like something wanting in *her*; at another, like something wanting in myself, which hindered me from understanding her as I ought. The impression was always strongest in the most contradictory manner, when she looked at me, or, in other words, when I was most conscious of the harmony and charm of her face, and yet, at the same time, most troubled by the sense of an incompleteness which it was impossible to discover. Something wanting, something wanting – and where it was, and what it was, I could not say. (pp. 76–7).

This is not (or not just) a Freudian riddle (Q. What does a woman want? A. What she is wanting), though even as such it attests the particular anxiety of the man responsible for posing it: who desires Laura 'because' (= so that) she, not he, is wanting. For shortly afterwards, with 'a thrill of the same feeling which ran through [him] when the touch was laid upon [his] shoulder on the lonely high-road', Walter comes to see that the 'something wanting' is '[his] own recognition of the ominous likeness between the fugitive from the asylum and [his] pupil at Limmeridge House' (p. 86). Laura's strange 'incompleteness' would thus consist in what has made this likeness imperfect – namely, that absence of 'pro-faning marks' of 'sorrow and suffering' which alone is said to differentiate her from her double (p. 120). Accordingly, the Laura Walter most deeply dreams of loving proves to be none other than the Anne who has been put away. It is as though, to be quite perfect, his pupil must be taught a lesson: what is wanting, what Laura obscurely lacks and Walter obscurely wishes for, is her sequestration in the asylum.

Courtesy of Sir Percival and Fosco, the want will of course be supplied, but long before her actual internment, Laura has been well prepared for it at Limmeridge House, where, on the grounds that her delicacy requires protection, men systematically keep their distance from her. Rather than deal with her directly, Sir Percival, Mr Gilmore, Mr Fairlie and Walter him-self all prefer to have recourse to the mannish Marian who serves as their intermediary. 'I shrank', says Walter at one point, 'I shrink still – from invading the innermost sanctuary of her heart, and laying it open to others, as I have laid open my own' (p. 90). His many such gallant pro-nouncements entail an unwillingness to *know* Laura, the better to affirm without interference the difference between him and her, man and woman. ('Me Tarzan, you Jane': notice how male solipsism overbears the very opposition that guarantees male difference. Laura is a closed sanctuary/Walter is an open book, but it is Walter here who empowers himself to decide, by his shrinking reticence, what Laura shall be.) More than anything else, this 'respect' is responsible in the text for rendering Laura – even in terms of a genre that does not specialize in complex char-acter studies – a psychological cipher. (An English translation of the French translation of the novel might be entitled, precisely, *The Woman as Blank*). From turbid motives of her own, Marian is more than willing to do her part in drawing round Laura this *cordon sanitaire*. Like an efficient secretary in love with her boss, she spares Laura all troublesome importuni-ties, and she is no less aggressive in forbidding an interview between Laura and Anne ('Not to be thought of for a moment', p. 13) than in dispatching Walter from Limmeridge House, 'before more harm is done' (p. 95). Laura's subsequent experience of the asylum only further justifies the imperative to isolate her. 'The wrong that had been inflicted on her . . . must be redressed without her knowledge and without her help' (p. 456). And now a self-evident opposition between parent and child is available to overdetermine what had been the all-too-doubtful difference between man and woman. 'Oh, don't, don't, don't treat me like a child!', Laura implores, but Walter immediately takes the plea for more evidence of her childishness and accordingly gives her some pretend-work to do. When she asks him 'as a child might have' whether he is as fond of her as he used to be, he reassures her that she is dearer to him now than she had ever been in the past times (p. 458). His profession carries conviction, and no wonder, since his passion for her, now become a part-parental, part-pedophilic condescension, no longer makes him feel like a woman. Though the text takes perfunctory notice of 'the healing influences of her new life' with Walter (p. 576), these have no power to produce a Laura who in any way exceeds men's (literal or 'liberal') incarcerating fantasies about her. It is not just, as the text puts it, that the mark of the asylum is 'too deep to be effaced', but that it has always already effaced everything else.

The same could not be said of Marian Halcombe, whose far more 'interesting' character represents the only significant variation on business-as-usual in the novel's gynaeceum. As the conspicuously curious case of a woman's body that gives all the signs of containing a man's soul, Marian figures the exact inversion of what we have taken to be the novel's governing fantasy. Yet we must not conceive of this inversion standing in opposition to what it inverts, as though it implied not just the existence of a rival set of matching *female* fears and fantasies, but also the consequent assurance that, in the love and war between the sexes, all at least was fair: *così fan tutte*, too. No less than that of the woman-in-the-man, the motif of the man-in-the-woman is a function of the novel's anxious male imperatives ('*cherchez, cachez, couchez la femme*') that, even as a configuration of resistance, it rationalizes, flatters, and positively encourages. Thus, however 'phallic', 'lesbian' and 'male-identified' Marian may be considered at the beginning of the novel, the implicit structuring of these attributes is precisely what is responsible for converting her – if with a certain violence, then also with a certain ease – into the castrated, hetero-sexualized 'good angel' (p. 646) of the Victorian household at the end.

Our memorable first view of her comes in the disappointed appraisal of Walter's idly cruising eye:

> The instant my eyes rested on her, I was struck by the rare beauty of her form, and by the unaffected grace of her attitude. Her figure was tall, yet not too tall; comely and well-developed, yet not fat; her head set on her shoulders with an easy, pliant firmness; her waist, perfection in the eyes of a man, for it occupied its natural place, it filled out its natural circle, it was visibly and delightfully undeformed by stays. She had not

heard my entrance into the room; and I allowed myself the luxury of admiring her for a moment, before I moved one of the chairs near me, as the least embarrassing means of attracting her attention. She turned towards me immediately. The easy elegance of every movement of her limbs and body as soon as she began to advance from the far end of the room, set me in a flutter of expectation to see her face clearly. She left the window – and I said to myself, The lady is dark. She moved forward a few steps – and I said to myself, The lady is young. She approached nearer – and I said to myself (with a sense of surprise which words fail me to express), The lady is ugly!

Never was the old conventional maxim, that Nature cannot err, more flatly contradicted – never was the fair promise of a lovely figure more strangely and startlingly belied by the face and head that crowned it. The lady's complexion was almost swarthy, and the dark down on her upper lip was almost a moustache. She had a large, firm, masculine mouth and jaw; prominent, piercing, resolute brown eyes; and thick, coal-black hair, growing unusually low down on her forehead. Her expression – bright, frank, and intelligent – appeared, while she was silent, to be altogether wanting in those feminine attractions of gentleness and pliability, without which the beauty of the handsomest woman alive is beauty incomplete. To see such a face as this set on shoulders that a sculptor would have longed to model – to be charmed by the modest graces of action through which the symmetrical limbs betrayed their beauty when they moved, and then to be almost repelled by the masculine form and masculine look of the features in which the perfectly shaped figure ended – was to feel a sensation oddly akin to the helpless discomfort familiar to us all in sleep, when we recognize yet cannot reconcile the anomalies and contradictions of a dream. (pp. 58–9)

Though the passage develops all the rhetorical suspense of a strip-tease, in which, as Barthes has written, 'the entire excitation takes refuge in the hope of seeing the sexual organ', the place of the latter seems strangely occupied here by Marian's 'head and face'.[16] What Barthes calls the 'schoolboy's dream' turns into a far less euphoric 'sensation' of 'helpless discomfort' when, at the climactic moment of unveiling, the woman's head virtually proves her a man in drag. Banal as this kind of revelation has become in our culture (where it is ritualized in a variety of spectacles, jokes, and folkloric anecdotes), it never ceases to be consumed, as here, 'with a sense of surprise'. The surprise would perhaps better be understood as a stubborn refusal to recognize how unsurprising it is that an obsessively phallocentric system of sexual difference, always and everywhere on the lookout for its founding attribute (if only in the case of women to make sure it isn't there) should sometimes, as though overcome by eyestrain, find this attribute even in its absence. Yet Walter's sense of surprise

[16]Roland Barthes, *The Pleasure of the Text*, trans. Richard Miller (New York, Hill and Wang, 1975), p. 10.

exceeds the more or less conscious ruse that serves to divorce his quasi-heterosexual identity from its quasi-homosexual genealogy. Surprise is also the text's figure for the violence of that double metamorphosis which overtakes this identity and thus calls for such a ruse. Marian's sudden transformation from the object that Walter looks at into the subject whose 'piercing' eyes might look back at him – look at his back – simultaneously entails the reverse transformation in him. In a context, then, where the positions of subject and object are respectively gendered as male and female, and where the relation between them is eroticized accordingly, the nature of Walter's surprise, 'which words fail [him] to express', may go without saying. Necessarily, his recovery has recourse to the affect of *repulsion*, which will reinstate the distance that surprise has momentarily abolished between him and the amphibolous figure of the 'masculine woman'. Walter's recoil carries the 'instinctive' proof – more than welcome after his unnerving encounter with the woman in white – both of his competence in a male code of sexual signs (which Marian's monstrosity, far from compromising, offers the occasion for rehearsing and confirming) and of his own stable, unambiguous position in that code (as a man who judges with 'the eyes of a man'). On such a basis, he succeeds in containing his potentially disturbing vision within the assured comic effects ('The lady was ugly!') of a worldly raconteur to whom Marian's sexual anomalousness presents no threat of contagion.

For Marian's 'masculine look' may be seen in two ways, as not just what poses the problems she embodies, but also what resolves it. Precisely in her 'masculinity', she incarnates that wit which men familiarly direct against women who are 'altogether wanting in those feminine attractions of gentleness and pliability'. We notice, for a characteristic example of such wit, that someone – an erring Nature, if not the anxious drawing-master who faithfully copies Nature's work – *has drawn a moustache on her*. However perturbed Walter may be that Marian lacks the lack, he is also plainly gratified to take inventory of the numerous phallic signs on her person, as though these could finally only mock the absence of the penile referent. The well-known anxiety attaching to male jokes about the 'masculine woman' in no way extenuates the strategy that it energizes: which is to render the woman who is their target external to the system of sexual difference that gets along quite well without her. Unable to compete (when the chaps are down), she cannot be 'male'; unable to attract (as though the derisive signs remained persuasive after all), neither can she be 'female'. What is thereby neutralized, in the root as well as derived senses of the word, is any sexuality – female and/or male – which cannot be reduced to either term of a phallic binarism.

Yet Walter's aggressive indifference to Marian as a relevant sexual counter is eventually belied when Count Fosco – who is as helpful in acting out the implications of Walter's fantasy here as he is in the case of Laura – takes a pronounced, even violent erotic interest in her. How does this ugly, neutered woman come to be targeted for what, as we have seen, the novel encodes as 'rape'? We noticed that, though Walter's portrait of

Marian abounds in phallic *signs*, it nowhere offers a phallic *symbol*: only later, too late, will the novelist hand her 'the horrid heavy man's umbrella' (p. 235). Where, then, *is* the phallus so bountifully signified? If it isn't *on* Marian, whose unimpeachably curvilinear body (like the perfect waist that is its synecdoche) is 'visibly and delightfully undeformed by stays', then it must be *in* her, the iron in the soul that manifests itself only through the soul's traditional windows: those 'prominent, piercing, resolute brown eyes' with their 'masculine look'. (Even her moustache suggests that the masculine signs defacing her body have pushed through from within.) Psychoanalysis and the male adolescent alike are familiar with the castration fantasy in which – act one – the penis gets 'locked' in the vagina during intercourse and – act two – having broken off, remains inside the female body. *Anima virilis in corpore muliebri inclusa*: Marian is not just the 'dog' that no self-respecting male adolescent would be 'caught with'; she is also – the 'evidence' for act one of course being canine – the dog that he would not be caught *in*.[17] As the focus of fears of *male* incarceration, Marian's body becomes the operational theatre for the two tactics of 'men's liberation' that usually respond to these fears. She is firmly abandoned by Walter's erotic interest and forcibly seduced by Fosco's. Both tactics cohere in a single strategy, since perhaps the most important fantasy feature of rape is the reaffirmation of the rapist's unimpaired capacity to withdraw, the integrity of his body (if not his victim's) recovered intact. (Fosco, we recall, returns to Marian the journal he has indelibly signed, and she, evidently, is stuck with it.)[18] As its sexual variant, seduction-and-abandonment would thus in both senses of the word 'betray' the constitutive myth of the liberal (male) subject, whose human rights must include the freedom, as he pleases, to come and go.

The meaning of Marian's 'rape' if of course further determined by another, better known figure of the *anima virilis*: the lesbian. 'She will be *his* Laura instead of mine!' (p. 207), writes Marian of the bride of

[17]The novel's elaborate canine thematics more than justify this slang usage, which of course postdates it. Marian's first lesson at Blackwater Park, for instance, involves being instructed in the destiny of dogs there. A housemaid thus accounts to her for the wounded dog found in the boat-house: ' "Bless you, miss! Baxter's the keeper, and when he finds strange dogs hunting about, he takes and shoots 'em. It's keeper's dooty, miss. I think that dog will die. Here's where he's been shot, ain't it? That's Baxter's doings, that is. Baxter's doings, miss, and Baxter's dooty'' ' (p. 229). 'Baxter's' doings indeed: if the keeper is little more than a name in the novel, the name nonetheless contains almost all the elements in the novel's representation of female containment. For one thing, the suffix *-ster* originally designates a specifically feminine agency (in Old English, a 'baxter' means a female baker): whence perhaps Baxter's violence, as though he were protesting the femininity latently inscribed in his name. For another, in the context of the novel's insistence on 'the touch from behind', the name would also signify the person who handles (its gender-inflection keeps us from quite saying 'manhandles') the hinder part of the body.

[18]In this context one must read Fosco's dandiacal lament after the episode where – 'to the astonishment of all the men' who watch him – he successfully intimidates 'a chained bloodhound – a beast so savage that the very groom who feeds him keeps out of his reach': ' "Ah! my nice waistcoat! . . . Some of that brute's slobber has got on my pretty clean waistcoat!'' ' (pp. 243–4).

Limmeridge – having taken the precaution, however, of promoting rather this faint-hearted marriage to Sir Percival than the obvious love-match with Walter, as if already anticipating the consolation that an unhappy Lady Glyde will not fail to bring to her closet: 'Oh, Marian! . . . promise you will never marry, and leave me. It is selfish to say so, but you are so much better off as a single woman – unless – unless you are very fond of your husband – but you won't be very fond of anybody but me, will you?' (p. 235). Important as it is not to censor the existence of erotic feeling between women in the text (in any of the ways this can be done, including a certain way of acknowledging it),[19] it is perhaps more important to recognize that what would also get absorbed here under the name of lesbianism is a woman's unwillingness to lend her full co-operation to male appropriations of her, as though Marian's 'gayness' were the only conceivable key to passages like the following:

> 'Men! They are the enemies of our innocence and our peace – they drag us away from our parents' love and our sisters' friendship – they take us body and soul to themselves, and fasten our helpless lives to theirs as they chain up a dog to his kennel. And what does the best of them give us in return? Let me go, Laura – I'm mad when I think of it!' (p. 203)

In general, the 'lesbianism' contextualized in *The Woman in White* amounts mainly to a male charge, in which the accusation is hard to dissociate from the excitation. In particular, the novel most effectively renders Marian 'lesbian' in the sense that it makes her suffer the regular fate of the lesbian in male representations: who defiantly bides her time with women until the inevitable and irrevocable heterosexual initiation that she, if no one else, may not have known that she always wanted. One recalls this exchange from *Goldfinger*, after James Bond has seduced Pussy Galore: 'He said, "They told me you only liked women". She said, "I never met a man before" '.[20] Not dissimilarly, Marian's 'half-willing, half-unwilling liking for the Count' (p. 246) – what in a rape trial would be called her 'complicity' – provides the novel's compelling, compulsive proof of the male erotic power that operates even and especially where it is denied. 'I am almost afraid to confess it, even to these secret pages. The man has interested me, has attracted me, has forced me to like him' (p. 240). Fosco's eyes 'have at times a clear, cold, beautiful, irresistible glitter in

19For example: 'Does [Marian] . . . have Lesbian tendencies?' the editor of the Penguin edition boldly speculates, before prudently concluding that 'it is doubtful whether such thoughts were in Collins's mind' (p. 15). The response, which rationalizes its titillation as a sophisticated willingness to call things by their names, and then rationalizes its disavowal of that titillation (and of those names) as scholarly caution, typifies the only acknowledgment that homoeroticism, female or male, is accustomed to receive in the criticism of nineteenth-century fiction. Here it does little more than faithfully reproduce – 'Mind that dog, sir!' (p. 243) – the novel's own equivocal structuring of the evidence for Marian's lesbianism. One may observe in passing how a similar fidelity entails that the editor who can mention lesbianism must fall entirely silent on the *male* homoerotics of the novel (see p. 117 for why this should be so).

20Ian Fleming, *Goldfinger* (1959; New York, Berkley Books, 1982), p. 261.

them which forces me to look at him, and yet causes me sensations, when I do look, which I would rather not feel' (p. 241, repeated almost verbatim on p. 287). Like Pussy Bonded, Marian Foscoed (hearing the metathesis in the name of the 'wily Italian', p. 264, we need not even consider resorting to what Freud called Schreber's 'shamefaced' elision) is a changed woman. If it is not her ultimate destiny to roll up the Count's endless cigarettes 'with the look of mute submissive inquiry which we are all familiar with in the eyes of a faithful dog' (p. 239), as she abjectly fantasizes, he has nonetheless well trained her to be another man's best friend. 'What a woman's hands *are* fit for', she tells Walter, whom she entrusts with her avengement, 'early and late, these hands of mine shall do . . . It's my weakness that cries, not me. The house-work shall conquer it, if *I* can't' (pp. 453–4). The old signs of Marian's 'masculinity' – the hands that were 'as awkward as a man's' (p. 253), the tears that came 'almost like men's' (p. 187) – now realize what had always been their implied potential to attest a 'weakness' that (like the housework she takes on 'as her own right') refeminizes her. In the novel's last image, almost exactly according to the proper Freudian resolution of *Penisneid*, Marian is able to 'rise' only on condition that she 'hold up' Walter's son and heir 'kicking and crowing in her arms' (p. 646). Almost exactly, but not quite, since the child is not of course her own. It is as though the woman whom Fosco 'rapes' and the woman whom Walter 'neuters' prove finally one and the same odd thing – as though, in other words, a woman's heterosexuality ('hetero-' indeed) were no sexuality of hers.

Even as the victim of terrific male aggression, however, Marian is simultaneously the beneficiary of considerable male admiration. Walter aptly imagines that she 'would have secured the respect of the most audacious man breathing' (p. 60), and apart from Fosco, who eventually embodies that hypothetical man, apart even from Walter, who at once finds in the ugly lady an old friend (p. 59), the novelist himself unexceptionally portrays Marian as a 'positive', immensely likable character. Demonstrably, then, *The Woman in White* accords a far warmer welcome to the fantasy of the man-in-the-woman (which, fully personified, the novel works through to a narrative resolution) than to the apparently complementary fantasy of the woman-in-the-man (which, as we have seen, the novel only broaches obscurely, in the blind spot of 'non-recognition' between textual thematics and male reading bodies). This is doubtless because the *anima virilis* includes, in addition to the aspects aforementioned, a male identification. 'I don't think much of my own sex', Marian admits to Walter on their first meeting; 'no woman does think much of her own sex, though few of them confess it as freely as I do' (p. 60). As though misogyny were primarily a female phenomenon and as such justified the male phenomenon that ventriloquially might go without saying, Marian's voice becomes the novel's principal articulation of that traditional code according to which women are quarrelsome, chattering, capricious, superstitious, inaccurate, unable to draw or play billiards. For all the pluck that it inspires, Marian's male identification consistently vouches for her female dependency. Thus, determined 'on justifying the Count's opinion of [her] courage and sharpness' (p. 340), she bravely makes her night-crawl onto the eaves of the house at Blackwater to overhear Fosco's conversation with Sir Percival. But – perhaps because, as the male-identified woman necessarily comes to think, her 'courage was only a woman's courage after all' (pp. 341–2) – this determination obliges her to remove 'the white and cumbersome parts of [her] underclothing' (p. 342) and so to prepare herself for the violation that, on one way of looking at it, follows soon afterwards, but that, on another, has already succeeded. If the woman-in-the-man requires his *keeping her* inside him, the man-in-the-woman takes for granted her *letting him* inside her. The sexual difference that the former endangers, the latter reaffirms: by determining a single view of women – men's – to which women accede in the course of constructing a male-identified femininity. Fosco 'flatters' Marian's vanity 'by talking to [her] as seriously and sensibly as if [she were] a man' (p. 245), and she more than returns the favour by addressing Fosco, Walter, and the male reader on the same premise, reassuring all concerned that even the woman who speaks as 'freely' as a man remains the prolocutor of a masculist discourse that keeps her in place. Finally, therefore, Marian may be taken to suggest how the novel envisions that *female* reader whom, though it nominally ignores, it has always taken into practical account. For the same sensation effects that 'feminize' the male reading body also (the quotation marks are still indispensable) 'feminize' the female: with the difference that this feminization is construed in the one case to threaten sexual identity and in the other to confirm it. Implicitly, that is, the text glosses the female reader's sensationalized body in exactly the terms of Marian's erotic responsiveness to Fosco: as the corporal confession of a 'femininity' whose conception is all but exhausted in providing the unmarked term in opposition to a thus replenished 'masculinity'. If only on its own terms (though, when one is trembling, these terms may be hard to shake), the sensation novel constitutes proof of women's inability, as Marian puts it, to 'resist a man's tongue when he knows how to speak to them' (p. 278) and especially, we might add with Marian emblematically in mind, when he knows how to speak through them.

IV

Precisely in so far as it does not fail, the project of confining or containing the woman cannot succeed in achieving narrative quiescence or closure. Safely shut up in the various ways we have considered, women cease being active participants in the drama that nonetheless remains to be played out (for over a hundred pages) 'man to man'. For when the text produces the configuration of incarcerated femininity, it simultaneously cathects the congruent configuration of phobic male homoeroticism: thus, for instance, its 'paradoxical' rendering of Fosco, who is at once 'a man who could tame anything' (p. 239) and 'a fat St Cecilia masquerading in male attire' (p. 250). Accordingly, the novel needs to supplement its misogynistic plot with a misanthropic one, in which it will detail the frightening, even calamitous consequences of unmediated relations between men, thereby administering to its hero an aversion therapy calculated to issue in a renunciation of what Eve Kosofsky Sedgwick has called 'male homosocial desire', or in a liberation from what, with a more carceral but no less erotic shade of meaning, we might also call male bonds.[21] After Sedgwick's (here, actively) inspiring demonstration that men's desire for men is the very motor of patriarchally given social structures, it might seem implausible even to entertain the possibility of such a renunciation or liberation, which would amount to a withdrawal from the social *tout court*. Yet this is apparently what the endings of many nineteenth-century novels paradigmatically stage: the hero's thorough-going disenchantment with the (homo)social, from which he is resigned to isolate himself. By and large, nineteenth-century fiction is no less heavily invested than Sedgwick's analysis of it in luridly portraying the dysphoric effects – particularly on men – of homosocial desire, and this fact must raise the question of the status of such effects within the general rhetorical strategy of the fiction that cultivates them. If, for example, *The Woman in White* obligingly constitutes a 'pathology' of male homosocial desire, this is evidently not because the novel shares, say, Sedgwick's ambition to formulate a feminist/gay critique of homophobically patriarchal structure; but neither is it because the novel so naïvely embraces this structure that it recounts-without-counting the latter's psychological costs. Rather, as we will see, the novel puts its homosocial pathology in the service of promoting a familiar homosocial cure: a cure that has the effect of a renunciation of men's desire for men only because, in this treated form, and by contrast, such desire exists in a 'normal' or relatively silent state.

The novel's most obvious specimen of an abnormal male homosocial *Bund* – the one it adduces at the end, as though at last to consolidate the freely floating homoerotics of the text and thus to name and contain them – is that secret Italian political association which (Walter is quite correct in saying) is 'sufficiently individualized' for his purposes if he calls it, simply, 'The Brotherhood' (p. 595). The novel tolerates this exotic free-masonry on two ideological conditions, which, if they were not so inveter-ately combined in a policy of quarantine, might otherwise strike us as incompatible. On the one hand, The Brotherhood owes its existence to the political adolescence of Italy (pp. 595–6), to which, in case the point is lost, Pesca correlates his own immaturity when he became a member (p. 597). The advanced nation as well as the enlightened parent may rest assured imagining that The Brotherhood is only a phase that in the normal course of political or personal development will be superseded. Yet on the other hand, no possible course of development can retrieve someone once he has been admitted into this society of fellows and bears its 'secret mark',

---

[21]Readers of Sedgwick's *Between Men: English Literature and Male Homosocial Desire* (New York, Columbia University Press, 1985) will recognize how nearly its concerns touch on those of the present essay.

which, like his membership, lasts for life (p. 596). Strange as it may be for Walter to learn that one of his best friends belongs to the secret fraternity, the revelation occasions no alarm (lest, for instance, an attempt be made to initiate *him*), since the pathos of Pesca's case is well cultivated by Pesca himself, who admits to suffering still from those youthful impulses ('I try to forget them – and they will not forget *me*!' (p. 642) which forever condemn him to consort in such dubious company. (In the usual distribution of roles, Walter's mother, but not his sullenly nubile sister, has welcomed Pesca into the household.) A congenial point is borne in the activities of The Brotherhood itself, whose in-house purges are the 'outside' world's best protection against it. Walter's sword need never cross with Fosco's – a mercy given the impressive estimates we are invited to make of the 'length' of the latter (p. 611) – in the duel that 'other vengeance' has rendered unnecessary (p. 642). The Brotherhood has mortally called the Count to 'the day of reckoning' (p. 642) – not for his offences against Walter, but for his all-too-promiscuous fraternizing within and without its organization. The wound struck 'exactly over his heart' (p. 643) hints broadly at the 'passional' nature of the crime in which – for which – Fosco is murdered. Thus, at the exhibition of his naked and knifed corpse (the former 'Napoleon', p. 241, now, as it were, the dead Marat, and the rueful Parisian morgue, also as it were, the gayer continental baths), we hear the curator's familiarly excited double discourse, in which a flushed moralism never quite manages to pacify the sheer erotic fascination that hence remains available to incite it: 'There he lay, unowned, unknown, exposed to the flippant curiosity of a French mob! There was the dreadful end of that long life of degraded ability and heartless crime! Hushed in the sublime repose of death, the broad, firm, massive face and head fronted us so grandly that the chattering French-women about me lifted their hands in admiration, and cried in shrill chorus, "Ah, what a handsome man!"' (p.643).

'And all men kill the thing they love': what is often taken for Wilde's gay depressiveness (though in Reading Goal, what else is left to intelligence but to read its prison?) provides a not-so-oddly apt formula for the novel's pathology of male bonds, whose godforsaken expression coincides with its providential punishment in death. (Besides the murder of Fosco, we may cite the 'suicide' of his boon companion: it is no accident that, having locked himself in the vestry, Sir Percival accidentally sets it on fire.) A couple of reasons obtain for bringing out, as I have pseudo-anachronistically been doing, the continuities between the novel's representation of 'brotherhood' and our media's no less sensational staging of male homosexuality. One would be to begin measuring the extent to which nineteenth-century culture has contributed to the formation of the context in which an uncloseted gayness is popularly determined. (Thus, the homophobic virulence that dispreads in rivalrous response to homosexual immunodeficiency is 'only' the most recent, extreme, and potentially catastrophic figure of an interpretative framework that precedes AIDS by well over a century.) Another would be to recognize that if our culture can only 'think' male homosexual desire within a practice of aversion therapy, this is because – for a long while and with apparently greater efficacy – it has routinely subjected male homosocial desire to the same treatment.

Representationally, this treatment consists of a diptych, in which the baleful images of homosocial apocalypse on one panel confront a comparatively cheering family portrait on the other. The fact that Fosco and Sir Percival are both married is far from making them what *The Woman in White* understands by family men. For as the novel's final tableau makes abundantly clear, what is distinctively cheering about the family portrait is less the connection between husband and wife (Marian, not Laura, holds up his son to Walter's charmed gaze) than the bond between father and son. Thus, the aim of what we have called aversion therapy is not to redirect men's desire for men onto women, but, through women, onto boys: that is, to privatize homosocial desire within the middle-class nuclear family, where it takes the 'normal' shape of an Oedipal triangle. Yet the twinned projects whose achievement the novel makes *precede* the establishment of a family curiously correspond to what, at least since Freud's summation of nineteenth-century culture, we may recognize as the family's own defining features: (1) shut up the woman – or, in the rivalry between father and son of which she is the object, keep mother from becoming the subject of a desire of her own; and (2) turn from the man – or, in that same rivalry, develop an aversion therapy for home use. The foundation of the Hartright family, therefore, cannot put an end to the brutalities of its prehistory, nor will these brutalities have dialectically prepared the way for a civilizing familialism, since the violent workings of an Oedipal family organization (Sir Percival is a much older man than Walter, and so forth) have implicitly generated the narrative that this organization is explicitly constituted to conclude. At the end, then, the novel has merely discovered its beginning, in the family matrix where such violence has acquired its specific structure and whence it has made its fearful *entrée dans le monde*. 'And there is more where that came from', if only because where that came from is also where that eventually returns. As though refusing to cease shocking us, even where it least surprises us, *The Woman in White* 'ends' only by recurring to that family circle which will continue to relay – with no end in sight – a plot that still takes many people's breath away.[22]

[22]Like the woman's, or the homosexual's, or (for she has figured in both roles) Marian's: 'Let Marian end our Story' (p. 646), but – these are the text's last words, as well as Walter's – what follows is dead silence.

What also follows is my particular gratitude to those friends whom this essay did not leave speechless: Marston Anderson, Ann Bermingham, Mitchell Breitwieser, Carol T. Christ, Martin Cogan, Christopher Craft, Lizbeth Hasse, Mary Ann O'Farrell, Caroline Newman, Eve Kosofsky Sedgwick, and Alex Zwerdling.

V

Note on the author's body: shortly after I began writing this essay, the muscles on my shoulders and back went into spasm. Referring this thoracic pain to other matters (excessive working out, an affair of the heart) than the work on which it continually interrupted my progress, I consulted physical and psychological therapists. Only when the former at last pronounced that a rib was out of place (which may have been what the latter was getting at when he diagnosed, on the insurance form, a personality disorder), was I willing to entertain the possibility that I had become, in relation to my own writing, an improbably pat case of hysteria. Now that a practised hand has put the fugitive rib back into its cage, my spine tingles to have borne out my assumption of that 'non-recognition' which evidently also obtains between the somatics of writing and what is written about. I am less pleased (though still thrilled) to understand that, on the same assumption, what dumbfounds me also lays the foundation for my dumbness: too stupid to utter what has already been said in the interaction between body and text, and in the traces of that interaction within body or text; and too mute to do more than designate the crucial task of identifying in this writing the equivocal places where 'sensation' has gone, not to say love.

Note

Life and Work.   Marian Evans, born in the English Midlands in 1819, spent her early life caring for her family and educating herself with the support of her father and some excellent friends. In her thirties she moved to London as an assistant editor of the major Victorian publication *The Westminster Review*, where she rapidly made her mark as an editor, essayist, translator and, finally, under the pseudonym George Eliot, as one of England's greatest novelists. She translated epoch-making books by David Friedrich Strauss (*Das Leben Jesu*, 1835–6 – *The Life of Jesus*, 1846), by Ludwig Feuerbach (*Das Wesen des Christenthums*, 1841 – *The Essence of Christianity*, 1854), and Spinoza (*Tractatus Theologico-politicus*, 1670; *Ethica Ordine Geometrico Demonstrata*, 1677 – George Eliot's translation published, 1981). Her essays for the *Westminster* and other reviews have been most accessible in Thomas Pinney's excellent edition, *Essays of George Eliot* (New York, Columbia University Press, 1963). She published her first fiction (apart from juvenilia) when she was nearly forty, and these early stories in *Blackwood's Magazine* led to six major novels and a novella: *Adam Bede* (1859), *The Mill on the Floss* (1860), the short *Silas Marner* (1861), *Romola* (1863), *Felix Holt, the Radical* (1866), *Middlemarch* (1871–2), and *Daniel Deronda* (1876). From her mid thirties on she lived with the accomplished George Henry Lewes, artist, editor, biographer, historian, translator, playwright, and scientist of considerable achievement. Although they were prevented by English divorce laws from formally marrying, they lived together as man and wife for thirty productive years. Outfacing the partial social ostracism resulting from this domestic arrangement, George Eliot became a highly popular and successful novelist in England. Her letters are an essential source and are collected in the invaluable edition by Gordon S. Haight (nine vols, New Haven and London, Yale University Press, 1954, 1978).

Criticism.   A full bibliography would occupy too much space; the bibliography in my own *George Eliot* (Boston, G.K. Hall, 1985), can be consulted for fuller information. Two valuable collections including reviews by George Eliot's usually appreciative and well-informed contemporaries are: D.R. Carroll, ed., *George Eliot, the Critical Heritage* (New York, Barnes and Noble, 1971) and Gordon S. Haight, *A Century of George Eliot Criticism* (New York, Houghton Mifflin, 1965). Also strongly to be recommended are Barbara Hardy, *The Novels of George Eliot* (London, Athlone Press, 1959) and Jerome Thale, *The Novels of George Eliot* (New York, Columbia University Press, 1959).

All the novels are available in good Penguin editions, and Clarendon Press has published two volumes of the projected complete and definitive edition of the works.

8

'Th' Observed of All Observers': George Eliot's Narrator and Shakespeare's Audience

Elizabeth Deeds Ermarth

In the nineteenth century the literary narrator flourished fully for the first time. Although we know much about the historical situation of the novel form, the preconditions of that flowering are not yet understood. We know from Ian Watt, for example, that the rise of the novel had to do with particular conditions of social and domestic life; but what exactly do such conditions as the increase of privacy and leisure have to do with the narrator, that distinctive literary phenomenon that appeared so suddenly in the late eighteenth century? And what does that manifestation tell us about cultural discourse then or now? The omnipresent narrative voice of nineteenth-century fiction cannot adequately be explained with reference to the author or even to contemporaneous cultural 'influence'. The appearance of a new, even radically new literary format gestures toward the deepest organizing forces of a culture, forces whose 'causes' are widely distributed and impossible to canvas by ordinary quantitative methods of demonstration. My purpose in this essay is to inquire broadly into the preconditions for the appearance of the narrator as a primary value in literary representation.

The narrator of novels like *Vanity Fair*, *Little Dorrit*, *Middlemarch*, or *The Ambassadors* makes the power of presiding consciousness present continuously in the text. These narrators with their indiscreet powers of inclusiveness, their vantage point in the far future of the narrated events, their lack of individual identity or accessibility in the history narrated, all voice a common power, the power of interpretation. That power itself is more important than any specific interpretation; without it the story could not exist and neither could the reader, to the extent that the reader's consciousness is supplemented or supplanted by the narrator in the text. The main discourse of this fiction is that of an interpreting observer – engaged and distanced at the same time, performing a zig-zag between locale and generalization, between particular and meaning, between one impulse and its opposite. Characters come and go, but the narrator is a constant: a necessity for the text yet only invisibly present.

This description, with minor alterations, fits the audience of a Shakespearian drama: characters come and go, but the audience is a constant, and an interpreting necessity to the text at the same time that it is only invisibly present. Despite the many evident differences between Shakespearian drama and nineteenth-century narration, both may be instructively considered as versions of a single gesture, the gesture of distributing consciousness abroad in a large and social conception. The comparison is instructive because it helps us to recognize how unique and remarkable this gesture is among world cultural traditions. My hypothesis is this: that the power of consciousness institutionalized in literary form in the nineteenth-century narrator and with its attendant implications concerning interpretation and historicity, is a power with relatives and progenitors in the hypothesized audience of a Shakespearian playhouse, particularly at those moments when a stage character embarks upon soliloquy.

To say that Shakespeare's audience *is* the narrator for his plays would be an overextension of my hypothesis, though perhaps not an unhelpful one for those who can avoid totalizing the argument. The conditions of theatre-going and of novel-reading involve different structures and, most importantly, different distributions of power and authority; but the differences do not alter the common definitions of conscience or consciousness that can be found at the extremes of a particular cultural development, one that introduced the modern idea of the subject in its deeply social construction. The power of mutual self-consciousness, obliquely shared between character and audience in *Hamlet*, a dialogue institutionalized in the narrator of *Middlemarch*, declares in these differing degrees and circumstances a power beyond enactment. It is a power that is quintessentially and self-consciously 'human'.

Why do I take this to be an important demonstration? Partly because it begins to address the common properties between Shakespearian and Victorian realism: but mainly because the investigation brings into relief questions that the novel form helps to mask. Deeply historical itself, this seductive form does not encourage us to recognize its own historicity and that of its premises, especially those conceptions of individual and collective possibility that we take for granted so easily and that are inscribed in nineteenth-century narrative. In the novel of maximum historical and representational commitment, the historicity of the form itself, and therefore of its particular distribution of value, remains unexplored and unexplorable. To uncover this sequestered property is not to vitiate the form or its premises; neither is it to compromise them or to imply judgement for or against them. The fact remains that the nineteenth-century novel and its premises have been distanced and historicized by subsequent change and the more interesting question to me is, what is at stake in these changes? A partial answer to such questions will emerge from the following discussion of the narrator in *Middlemarch* and the soliloquy in *Hamlet*.

Before turning to texts some properties of the narrator are worth reiterating. The narrator is at once human and not personal or individual. Present at every transaction and limited to none, the narrative voice doubles the level of consciousness at every moment of the history. From the Prelude of *Middlemarch* to the last page a tension exists between individual consciousness and the collected consciousness represented by the narrator. The consciousness of an individual character is always under pressure to open itself to the wider circuit of mutual awareness that the narrator represents. But the narrator *qua* narrator has no individual or personal identity and is not accessible in the text except as a power of language and consciousness. The profound sense of audience in the nineteenth-century novel comes at least in part from the fullness with which authors deploy this narrative power. As a co-ordinated reflex of a multitude of minds, the narrator always involves readers on the boundary line between self and other.

The full discussion of this narrator – its transparency, its power – is one I have made elsewhere and it is crucial to full development of the points sketched here.[1] The present point about its amphibian nature, however, can be made with a passage from Feuerbach which defines *human* consciousness as necessarily a form of *species consciousness*. The difference between humankind and beasts, according to Feuerbach, is not consciousness (animals have that) but *self*-consciousness, and self-consciousness depends on *generic* identity:

> Consciousness in the strictest sense is present only in a being to whom his species, his essential nature, is an object of thought. The brute is indeed conscious of himself as an individual – and he has accordingly the feeling of self as the common centre of successive sensations – but not as a species: hence, he is without that consciousness which in its nature, as in its name, is akin to science. Where there is this higher consciousness there is a capability of science. Science is the cognisance of species. . . . Man is himself at once I and thou; he can put himself in the place of another, for this reason, that to him his species, his essential nature, and not merely his individuality, is an object of thought.[2]

Specifically *human* consciousness, that is, has a double valence; it always involves the double action of engagement and reflection. To be at once I and Thou, conscious of self *and* of other is to be individual only *as* a member of a universally collective entity, the species hypothesized as the basis for all specifically human definition. This power of engaged abstraction appears everywhere in the novel of the nineteenth century, including those by Walter Scott, Dickens, George Eliot, Meredith, Hardy, and Henry James to name a few, and among these none was more aware of this unique power of self-consciousness than George Eliot, translator of Feuerbach for English speaking readers and author of novels whose narrators have generated considerable discussion.

The tensional relation between self and other that defines narrative

---

[1]See the chapter on 'The Narrator as Nobody', in Elizabeth Ermarth, *Realism and Consensus in the English Novel* (Princeton, Princeton University Press, 1983).
[2]Ludwig Feuerbach, *The Essence of Christianity*, trans. Marian Evans [George Eliot], 1854 (New York, Harper and Row, 1957), vol. I, p. i. *Das Wesen Des Christentums* was originally published in 1841.

action is consistently in evidence in *Middlemarch*; three occasions from that novel will serve as instances of that narrative dynamic: first, the Prelude to the novel where the tension between individual and other is introduced so as to involve readers; second, the widely discussed scene where Dorothea endures her dark night of the soul, in solitude but still accessible to the power of narrative consciousness; and third, a scene where Lydgate, in his socially complex isolation, refuses a helping hand. Each passage demonstrates how the narrative consciousness enacts the reflex of human consciousness between self and other, a reflex thematized in the central plots of the novel.

The Prelude to *Middlemarch* begins as follows:

> Who that cares much to know the history of man, and how the mysterious mixture behaves under the varying experiments of Time, has not dwelt, at least briefly, on the life of Saint Theresa, has not smiled with some gentleness at the thought of the little girl walking forth one morning hand-in-hand with her still smaller brother, to go and seek martyrdom in the country of the Moors?[3]

Who, indeed? I must confess that until I read *Middlemarch* the subject had never entered my mind. Nevertheless I fancy that I care about the history in question. Why should Saint Theresa be a credential for caring about human history? I resent it slightly, although I comfort myself with the silent thought that this speaker, whoever it is, doesn't understand much if he or she thinks that caring necessarily entails this saint. It seems parochial. I can dismiss the opinion as an eccentricity because the language of the passage betrays a capacity rather larger than the opinion contained in it. The sentence periods might agreeably and competently enough come to an end after the first mention of Saint Theresa; but instead another extended period introduces a parallel that devolves into a charming particular, one quite at odds with the biblical reversals of the first phrase and the scientific metaphors of the second, and one that gathers them all to a point of incarnate life that draws a reader irresistibly from initial querulousness to final warmth.

The agent of this demonstrably flexible power is not well defined. We cannot assume that the voice is George Eliot's own; yet it seems reasonable to ask, whose voice is it? I am both uncomfortable and comfortable with it as I move from initial skirmish to final agreement in my mental negotiations with the text. And by the end of the brief, telling Prelude I am fully engaged in a general human problem of which Saint Theresa is one representative among many others, and of which the development of cygnet to swan is a final metaphor. The transition involves a complex negotiation: the translation of invisible and potential life into concrete, particular, mature form.

This summary only begins to touch the complex sonorities of reader-

---

[3]*Middlemarch* (1872), ed. Gordon S. Haight (Boston, Houghton Mifflin, 1956). All references will be to this text and will be included parenthetically in the text.

consciousness in the Prelude but it provides a model for much of what goes on between George Eliot's readers and the text. The invisible power of the narrative voice, activated in readers but never accessible in the novel as a single point of view, has a relation to events that defies description. It does not merely preside over them, because it is also engaged, even eccentric. Its human limitations are demonstrable yet its human lineaments invisible. It observes all other observers and is a manifestly potent agency in the text, yet it remains itself unobserved or observable only as a process of interpretation within which the reader must function in order to grasp the text at all. The constant demands of this narrator might be taken as distracting if one ignored the fact that this activity – the continuous shuttle of interpretive observation negotiated by the power of consciousness – *is* the text's primary representation.

This narrative consciousness is present in all Victorian fiction but nowhere with fuller range than in George Eliot. In *Middlemarch* it is at its subtlest and most flexible, accompanying the nuanced exchanges that import social life even into the most private moments. The death watches and funerals, the engagement or holiday parties, the tête-à-têtes and the crises of conscience all belong to the common stream maintained and largely constituted by the narrative voice – not through any particular statements so much as through its invisible but palpable presence.

Dorothea's dark night of the soul (ch. 80), a classic locus of discussion, is a case in point. The chapter begins matter-of-factly ('When Dorothea had seen Mr. Farebrother in the morning') with a confirmed event of the recent past being brought up to date later in the day, after Dorothea has had her shock at finding Ladislaw bending over a weeping Rosamond and has returned home only to remember her next appointment with Farebrother ('When she reached home and remembered her engagement, she was glad of it'). A page of details follows – details about Farebrother's gardening seeds, about being on time, about Aunt Henrietta's tortoiseshell lozenge box – the whole sequence sustained as if under duress until she returns to her door exhausted by postponement and incapable even of saying good night and, 'The limit of resistance was reached'. This brief sentence acts in the text almost like a trigger to release the cry of self-centred demand that Dorothea has been suppressing since the first chapter and that here she finally allows herself to feel. The power of thought leaves her ('Then came the hour in which the waves of suffering shook her too thoroughly to leave any power of thought') and the narrator takes over so completely that Dorothea is momentarily a speck on the horizon of human history and its generic sorrow ('In that hour she repeated what the merciful eyes of solitude have looked on for ages in the spiritual struggles of man'). Conflicting energies of longing and loss are described 'that tore her heart in two, as if it had been the heart of a mother who seems to see her child divided by the sword, and presses one bleeding half to her breast while she gazes forth in agony towards the half which is carried away by the lying woman that has never known the mother's pang'. The terms here are both very distanced in biblical rhythm and very immediate in evocative detail.

But at this moment of individual crisis the passage sustains composed distance from Dorothea's grief and from her eventual awakening and restoration of social and active intent toward the rival Rosamond, whom she quixotically but commendably sets out to 'save'.

The narrative voice shifts from a vantage point nearest Dorothea's self-absorption ('Why had he come obtruding his life into hers. . . . Why had he brought his cheap regard. . . . He knew that he was deluding her') to the vantage point farthest from her ('But she lost energy at last . . . [and] sobbed herself to sleep'), all the while maintaining a much higher profile than in the immediately preceding scenes of dialogue. For Dorothea and for the reader there is almost literally a struggle for consciousness. Dorothea disappears momentarily, but she soon re-emerges with 'the clearest consciousness that she was looking into the eyes of sorrow' but without that 'besotted misery of a consciousness that only sees another's lot as an accident of its own'. She resumes the power of consciousness that the narrator has sustained conspicuously through the passage, and to the extent she does the narrator's distinct presence disappears. The compelling metaphor of the passage as she looks out her window in the dawn comes from very near her individual mind:

> On the road there was a man with a bundle on his back and a woman carrying her baby; in the field she could see figures moving – perhaps the shepherd with his dog. Far off in the bending sky was the pearly light; and she felt the largeness of the world and the manifold wakings of men to labour and endurance. She was a part of that involuntary, palpitating life and could neither look out on it from her luxurious shelter as a mere spectator, nor hide her eyes in selfish complaining. (ch. 80)

The judgement is self-judgement, directed from within as well as from without; the uncertainty about the shepherd suggests no omniscient presence beyond Dorothea yet the past-tense locution ('She was a part of that involuntary, palpitating life') maintains a close doubling between figural and narrative voice so that the passage can *only* be read in more than one way: that she recognizes her partnership with this involuntary life; and that she again recognizes what she used to know but temporarily forgot. The complexity of this negotiation between I and Thou, in solitude but not alone, is then relieved somewhat by an action and a dialogue. 'Presently she rang for Tantripp, who came in her dressing-gown. "Why, madam, you've never been in bed this blessed night," burst out Tantripp'. The difficult matters of consciousness and connection rest for a moment as affairs take a new direction, but the narrator never disappears altogether because the medium of consciousness that was especially evident during the solitary crisis remains even in the daily dialogue, telling neutrally what happened next.

Lydgate is a fascinating counterpart to Dorothea because his chief failing is precisely his refusal to make that reach beyond the moment which enables her to stabilize her mind and steady her action. She takes

advantage of her divided mind while Lydgate's merely paralyses him and
he watches his own decline from one state of being to another as if powerless to avert the disaster he is bringing on himself. The following passage
demonstrates the shifts in consciousness from focused to expansive, from
particular to generic, that distinguish the narrative voice from Lydgate's
and measure his practice relative to it. The passage is from Book Seven,
'Two Temptations', just after the New Year's Day party given by Mr
Vincy. Farebrother, making his own series of interpretations concerning
Lydgate, has offered Lydgate financial help and has been rejected.

> Naturally, the merry Christmas bringing the happy New Year, when
> fellow-citizens expect to be paid for the trouble and goods they have
> smilingly bestowed on their neighbours, had so tightened the pressure
> of sordid cares on Lydgate's mind that it was hardly possible for him to
> think unbrokenly of any other subject, even the most habitual and soli-
> citing. He was not an ill-tempered man; his intellectual activity, the
> ardent kindness of his heart, as well as his strong frame, would always,
> under tolerably easy conditions, have kept him above the petty uncon-
> trolled susceptibilities which make bad temper. But he was now a prey
> to that worst irritation which arises not simply from annoyances, but
> from the second consciousness underlying those annoyances, of wasted
> energy and a degrading preoccupation, which was the reverse of all his
> former purposes. "*This* is what I am thinking of; and *that* is what I
> might have been thinking of," was the bitter incessant murmur within
> him, making every difficulty a double goad to impatience.
>
> Some gentlemen have made an amazing figure in literature by
> general discontent with the universe as a trap of dullness into which
> their great souls have fallen by mistake; but the sense of a stupendous
> self and insignificant world may have its consolations. Lydgate's
> discontent was much harder to bear; it was the sense that there was a
> grand existence in thought and effective action lying around him, while
> his self was being narrowed into the miserable isolation of egoistic fears,
> and vulgar anxieties for events that might allay such fears. His troubles
> will perhaps appear miserably sordid, and beneath the attention of lofty
> persons who can know nothing of debt except on a magnificent scale.
> Doubtless they were sordid; and for the majority, who are not lofty,
> there is no escape from sordidness but by being free from money-
> craving, with all its base hopes and temptations, its watching for death,
> its hinted requests, its horse-dealer's desire to make bad work pass for
> good, its seeking for function which ought to be another's, its compul-
> sion often to long for Luck in the shape of a wide calamity. (ch. 64)

Here the narrator provides, as in Dorothea's critical moment, a wider
horizon of implied consciousness, but here Lydgate does not negotiate the
gap between self and other, between consciousness and 'second consciousness', that would give him access to that available wider life. This passage
mentions Lydgate's conditions very specifically, itemizing the mercenary
rituals whereby he has tied himself, thread by thread, in Lilliput. The

'second consciousness' held out for readers by the narrator, is also a reflex of Lydgate's own mind, one that is capable of recognizing what is happening to him, but apart from the stress it produces it spurs no liberating action. For Lydgate this second consciousness, with its creative awareness of the boundary between self and other, has been all but submerged by Rosamond's torpedo contact and has been reduced at this point to a small reflex in quotation (' "*This* is what I am thinking of; and *that* is what I might have been thinking of" '). Largely overbalanced by the forces of materialistic world and wife, this small voice has no play; its hopeless wail contrasts with the narrative voice that comments on his character ('he was not ill-tempered') and on the course of integrity in his case and in general ('his self was being narrowed into the miserable isolation of egoistic fears'). These comments are, to Lydgate's credit, not far from his own bitter ruminations, but the narrator goes on where Lydgate does not, and does so by turning to the reader whose actual existence is brought suddenly close to this fictional world so that the distinction between actual and fictional becomes lost temporarily in the flow of consciousness from one individual case to a whole series of implied cases ('His troubles will perhaps appear miserably sordid').

In both these passages the extension of consciousness that restores, by extension or by irony, the play between individual and other, does not exhaust the whole effect of the narrative voice. The most powerful impression is that the continuing consciousness present here does not merely preside over Dorothea's self-abandonment or over Lydgate's temporizing: it actually sustains temporality; in the process it becomes the *site* of temporality. Moving from Dorothea's suppression, to her feeling, to the grief of ages; or moving through Lydgate to money-craving in general; and moving in both cases to the reader, lofty or ordinary, the narrative voice never stops until the end of the text. The process which links events and which is expressed both in spatial and temporal metaphors is indistinguishable from this omnipresent narrative consciousness, and that consciousness in turn, a representation of the self-awareness of the human species, is indistinguishable from the process of historical time. The narrator may be nobody but, like Odysseus in the cave of Polyphemus, it has the power of the generically human. The main 'plot' in *Middlemarch*, as of other nineteenth-century novels with versions of this narrator, is the extended plot of consciousness maintained by the narrative voice in and between particular narrated events.

The power represented by the narrator has a fascinating and still unwritten history. Comparison between the passages just discussed and the soliloquies of *Hamlet* helps to bring into relief the discourse within which such a conception of consciousness has had play. Steven Mullaney has summarized admirably one essential feature in his discussion of *The Merchant of Venice*, where he finds evidence of forces in European Renaissance culture that operated to produce 'new forms of internal constraint and self-apprehension – that is to say to produce something like the modern subject'. The radical originality of these new forms and of the theatrical productions that began in the 1570s with the construction of James Burbage's theatre, have been blurred by four centuries of assimilation. By comparing Shakespearian character with the personified abstractions of medieval drama, we can see how 'a new mode of dramatic representation' had evolved that blurred the boundary between observation and enactment, with the result that the audience, accustomed perhaps to reassuring repetitions, was now made apprehensive of seeing themselves, of being called into the action if only vicariously. Imaginary and real became covalent; the actual and artificial person indissolubly linked. As Professor Mullaney summarizes it, 'The destabilizing dialectic between self and other, audience and play, social and psychological constitutions of the subject which defined the complex theatrical transaction we know as Elizabethan and Jacobean drama was in itself an influential forum and laboratory for the production of what would become the modern subject.'[4] That subject, conceived not in individual but in generic terms, inhabits the foreground of *Middlemarch*.

With such new drama unfolding on stage, the audience finds itself in a new relation to what passes before it, becoming more immediately implicated as potential performers, as observers who can be observed. This is not only because of the deep theatricality inherent in the Elizabethan exercise of power but more directly because the play puts the audience in sight of itself. The fictional construction of character underway on stage had its consonance in what Professor Mullaney calls the 'social construction of the self' and, I would argue, the plays themselves, especially in the system of soliloquies and asides, force upon an audience a very particular sense of its own powers of interpretation and of its powerful aegis as the body for which the play is played out. The soliloquies in particular are little plots of 'conscience' very similar to the extended plot of consciousness evident in the narrator of *Middlemarch*; by implicitly acknowledging the presence of the audience soliloquies implicate viewers in the very problems of interpretation that the players confront more thematically. The character in soliloquy shares a power of mutual consciousness not only with himself or herself (the other half of a divided mind, or of one's private audience), but also obliquely with the theatre audience for whom thought is made audible.

In *Hamlet*, the soliloquies are formally distinct from the action in progress, formally delivered at marked stages of plot development, and distinctly the privilege of the hero, who delivers most of them. They punctuate the play with speeches that have become as familiar as religious texts, for example, 'O that this too, too solid flesh would melt' (I, ii, 129–59); 'O what a rogue and peasant slave am I!' (II, ii, 534–91); 'To be or not to be – that is the question' (III, i, 56–90). All these speeches are addressed to nobody, as if the audience were absent, yet its presence is most clearly invoked at such moments. The power to soliloquize belongs to a

[4]Steven Mullaney, 'Brothers and Others, or the Art of Alienation,' in *English Institute Essays for 1985*, Marjorie Garber, ed., (Baltimore, Johns Hopkins University Press, 1986).

character with special powers and in special relation to the audience. Claudius lapses into soliloquy only twice (III, iii, 36–72; IV, ii, 57–67), once when he is failing to pray. Besides Hamlet, no one else even tries. Ophelia's speech, 'O, what a noble mind is here o'er-thrown!' (III, i, 150–61) does not qualify because she knows that the king and Polonius are eavesdropping, although the two men do make up a kind of audience-within-the-audience. The soliloquy involves an exchange between the speaker and an invisible other, between an I addressing a Thou beyond the individual characters of the play. No one but Hamlet has the power of conscience to debate with themselves the very dilemmas of conscience that the soliloquy characteristically presents.

The term 'conscience' in this play has an informative geneology. From the Latin *conscientia*, the word at root means a knowing with, or consciousness, or knowledge within oneself. Only latterly did it mean conscience in the more restrictive sense of moral judgement – and that meaning grew only gradually to its present primacy as the idea of consciousness itself exchanged its properties from general and external to individual and internal. In the sixteenth century 'conscience' is not the property of individuals but a common, even an external common, fund of reasonableness that individuals inhabit and live by. Conscience is consciousness and not some mere policing faculty. In *Hamlet* the term 'conscience' implies that wider fund, or consciousness *with*. Knowing *with*, in turn, implies that self-division later defined by Feuerbach as the key to distinctively human consciousness, that is, consciousness defined in generically human terms. In this conception of consciousness, one knows 'I' by knowing 'Thou', even the Thou within. By the nineteenth century this self-division (and this other) was conceived mainly in social terms; Shakespeare obviously conceived it in another sense; but despite their differences both he and George Eliot locate the crux of individual conscious life in this all-important nexus between self and other. Even in her post-Romantic modernity, George Eliot keeps the root usage that makes consciousness and conscience nearly synonymous.

In *Hamlet* the emergent idea of consciousness belongs to a broad cultural problematic having to do with action and temporality. 'Conscience doth make cowards of us all' (III, i, 83) because before we act, we think, and the moment for action passes. Yet to act without thinking means the moment of action can become grotesque in its logic. The king in the play-within-the-play is quite astute about this:

> What to ourselves in passion we propose,
> The passion ending, doth the purpose lose. (III, ii, 186–7)

How to maintain a constant will between moments of passion is the problem – a problem Hamlet and Claudius both know well. It is a problem Hamlet frequently discusses in soliloquy, a moment of knowing-with himself and with the audience. By contrast, the guilty Claudius knows that when his murderous act continues its life in his enjoyment of its fruits (his crown, his ambition, his wife) then repentence means little; there is no talking with himself, or with God or with anyone else. His wretched mind yanks him back and forth between guilt and confidence, quite literally deranging his syntax to fit his consciousness:

> What then? What rests?
> Try what repentance can. What can it not?
> Yet what can it when one cannot repent?
> O wretched state! O bosom black as death!
> O limèd soul, that struggling to be free
> Art more engaged! (III, iii, 64–9)

A moment later this theme is redoubled when Hamlet enters behind the kneeling king and reflects on this chance to act out his revenge. No sooner does he think this than he recoils upon himself with the thought that to kill a man in prayer will only send him to heaven. One feels for Hamlet at this moment, wrought up for action and confronted by the bent unsuspecting back and bowed head of a solitary man. What Hamlet faces is not merely a problem of action in the bald sense. He can act, as he proves when the pirates board his ship or when he disposes of Rosencrantz and Guildenstern with ingenious efficiency. It is acting deliberately that is the problem, acting with consciousness or 'Conscience'. It is the problem of a subject asserting its power over temporality. To act when the moment unexpectedly brings a need is one thing; to act with forethought quite another, even when the plan is so little open to question as the plan of Hamlet's revenge is in this play with its eloquent ghost. Readiness takes care of Rosencrantz and Guildenstern and the pirates; but plotting for control of history is not something that ever works out very well in *Hamlet*.

The best laid plans, such as those laid in the first four acts, backfire in Act V when outcomes are repeatedly unexpected, surprising, and impossible to plan for. Readiness for the moment is all, yet readiness is not a product of calculation. To force the event by forethought is foolishness or worse. Whatever it is that shapes our ends, its mystery makes most human plots small by comparison. Temporality is in the hands of a shaping divinity – something perhaps part of 'conscience' but also beyond it. Hamlet's final achievement can be read in his recognition that events, like temporality itself, are not motivated primarily by human powers and that even the best interpretation needs to wait upon that mystery.

Of all the dramatis personae, only Hamlet in soliloquy demonstrates a matured power to act on this recognition and to become his own audience. At these privileged moments he can present by himself a full, unfolded and reflexive consciousness. The other characters are lost in their more modern dramas of plot and influence; thus engaged they simply do not exercise the power of consciousness, the doubleness of knowing-with oneself that enables Hamlet to die instructively. For these characters the power of reflexiveness is held for them in trust by the audience. Ophelia, Polonius, Gertrude engage in no soliloquies. The extension of their consciousness towards that doubled power Hamlet exhibits is made by the audience which sees them as they do not see themselves. To the extent that there is a completing, co-ordinating consciousness in each case, and for that matter in the play as a whole, that power of completion belongs to the audience; it outstrips even Hamlet in omnipresence. The audience knows collectively about Gertrude's complicity, Ophelia's innocence, Polonius's ephemeral wisdom. The audience interprets (so does a narrator) and temporalizes an action that otherwise would be incompletely readable, incompletely rationalized (so does a narrator temporalize action). The audience does not 'get into' the minds of Gertrude and Polonius so much as it *is* their minds, in the sense of 'conscience' or extended power of human consciousness, doubled and taken in knowledge-with. After Hamlet declares himself 'mad' (although the audience knows he is only 'mad in craft') Ophelia laments his overthrow in terms that suggest both the resemblances between the situation of consciousness in the play and in later traditions, and also the different emphasis given to the power of consciousness in each:

> O, what a noble mind is here o'erthrown!
> The courtier's, soldier's, scholar's eye, tongue, sword,
> Th'expectancy and rose of the fair state,
> The glass of fashion and the mould of form,
> Th'observed of all observers, quite, quite down! (III, i, 150–4)

Hamlet alone in the play's economy represents the power of mind or consciousness that belongs to all as a common quality. The fact that 'conscience' is not common is a measure of the state of things in Denmark. With that power extinguished, as Ophelia supposes it has been extinguished in Hamlet, all hope of political sanity is lost. With the loss of the central observed observer goes the power to mirror and mould, the power to sustain 'conscience' beyond the moment of enactment, the power to create free from determination by events. In his rightful role Hamlet should focus the social order. When all observers observe him he collects their gaze as, in his princely role, he collects their active allegiance.

In its role as *un*observed observer the audience extends through the play the reflexive power of the private mind in soliloquy, and this function resembles that of the nineteenth-century narrator, another *un*observed observer whose palpable presence is all-important and all-empowering and whose effect is to temporalize the action, that is, give it an interpretable unity. The complicity between real and imaginary is thus made explicit in this complicity between audience or reader and artifical voice. The audience complements individual awareness of characters in *Hamlet* in much the same way the narrator does in *Middlemarch*. The transcendent nature of this invisible power is its greatest asset. The intangible, dematerialized consciousness strengthens in proportion to its freedom from simple location. It defies material limitation, even the limitation of death.

The power of this agency, human yet effaced from physical existence, is a subject thematized in the plays and in interpretations of them. In her discussion of the authorship controversy in Shakespeare studies, Marjorie Garber shows how the absence of historical information has made room for open-ended controversy about the true author of the plays, controversy so persistent that it can be read as an emblem of power. 'It is as though Shakespeare *is* beyond authorship, beyond even the "plurality of egos" that Foucault locates in all discourse that supports the "author-function".' Professor Garber finds this function thematized in the plays themselves in such 'ghost writers' as (to name only two) the ghost of Hamlet's father, and the ghost of Julius Caesar. The more effaced the ghostly conscience, the more powerful it can be; in Caesar's case, 'It is clear from the moment of the assassination that the conspirators have killed the wrong Caesar, the man of flesh and blood and not the feared and admired monarch. They have, so to speak, killed the wrong author-function.' Caesar's works are his signature, physical testimony to the power of the absent signer; and in *Hamlet* as in many of Shakespeare's plays strategy often 'locates power in absence – absence of personality, absence of fact, absence of peculiarity'. The power of absence – absent ruler, absent father, absent historical Shakespeare – is a power that stimulates substitution and hence continues the discourse of interpretation. The unobserved observers, whether audiences or narrators, participate in this power of absence. At the centre of the discourse, shared in such different ways by George Eliot and Shakespeare, is the importance, even the being, conferred on the interpreter by the need (generated by lack, by absence) for interpretation.[5]

The need for interpretation that appears with different emphases and different definitions both in *Hamlet* and in *Middlemarch* initiates and sustains a distinctively modern process of consciousness. The birth of the modern subject and its process of substitution is demonstrably at work in *Hamlet* both thematically and, where the audience carries responsibility for the doubling 'conscience', also structurally. Thus distributed, that power of consciousness can be disabled if only temporarily, but when it becomes institutionalized in the narrator of *Middlemarch* it loses any tenuousness it might have had. The all-powerful Nobody, human but not individual, that broods between 'events' of the novel and extends the mental reflexes of characters, is inescapable as the flow of time, and is inseparable from that temporality. The audience reflex, its collective gaze, becomes incorporated in a narrator that does what the Shakespearian audience does, only more consistently: it focuses the action as one and, in so doing, interprets and temporalizes it. In *Middlemarch*, human consciousness remains a power of 'conscience' in the expanded sense that involves more than narrow judgement, but that power is entirely social, involving the continuous exchange between self and other, I and Thou,

[5]Marjorie Garber, 'Shakespeare's Ghost Writers', in *English Institute Essays for 1985*. I am grateful to Thomas Vargish for suggestions, and to Marjorie Garber and Steven Mullaney for permission to quote from the manuscripts of their lectures for the 1985 English Institute session on Shakespeare.

that takes place in dialogue or private thought. Consciousness remains a knowing-with, but the Thou or other has social definition and lacks the providential valences that 'conscience' has in *Hamlet*.

As the definition of consciousness becomes more resolutely human and social and less susceptible to cosmic interference, the representation of temporality becomes more emphatically historical. A symbiosis appears between the birth of the modern subject and the birth of historical time: neither the time of cycle, nor monumental time, but instead the atmosphere of 'human' history with its continuous process of exchange and negotiation between self and other. In *Hamlet*, where temporal discontinuity has a place and where human powers of interpretation and consciousness can be radically questioned, this historical time can be avoided; it is inescapable in *Middlemarch*. The time it takes to discover facts or decide how to act, the 'slack' time between the bald events of plot – the time that has attentuated importance in *Hamlet* especially in the last act – in *Middlemarch* largely *is* the object of representation. The narrator sustains that temporality so that to read the novel at all means to accept the historical medium with all its entailed powers of consciousness and interpretation. The little plots of conscience that in *Hamlet* are occasional and problematic in *Middlemarch* become the commanding motive of the fictional order.

Note

The most easily available editions are those in the OUP World's Classics series and the Penguin English Library. Only a minority of the 47 novels have been adequately edited, though some modern editions reprint fairly reliable or identified earlier editions. Of the works referred to in this article, *Framley Parsonage*, *Can You Forgive Her?* and *Phineas Finn* in Penguin, and *Orley Farm* in *World's Classics* have reliable texts. The Dover edition of *The Claverings* reprints the original serial text without corrections.

Anthony Trollope (1815–82) made a successful career as a Civil Servant in the Post Office, after a youth of deprivation and neglect. The first of his many novels was not published until 1847, and he became well-known only after the publication of his fourth and fifth novels, *The Warden* and *Barchester Towers* in 1855 and 1857. He became a fashionable best-seller in 1860, with *Framley Parsonage*, and throughout the 1860s rode high in public esteem. His later novels frequently enter into more problematic social and moral areas. His *Autobiography*, which was published posthumously, gives a fascinating account of his working life, including details of his earnings and his relations with his publishers. As well as the 47 novels, his output included half a dozen collections of shorter tales and eight or nine books of non-fiction. The major works of the years principally under discussion in this article are: *Castle Richmond*, 1860; *Framley Parsonage*, 1860–61; *Tales of All Countries*, 1860–1; *Tales of All Countries* (second series), 1861–3; *Orley Farm*, 1861–2; *The Struggles of Brown, Jones, and Robinson*, 1861–2; *North America*, 1862; *Rachel Ray*, 1863; *The Small House at Allington*, 1862–4; *Can You Forgive Her?*, 1864–5; *Miss Mackenzie*, 1865; *Hunting Sketches*, 1865; *Travelling Sketches*, 1865, *The Belton Estate*, 1865–6; *Clergymen of the Church of England*, 1865–6; *The Last Chronicle of Barset*, 1866–7; *The Claverings*, 1866–7; *Nina Balatka*, 1867; *Lotta Schmidt and Other Stories*, 1867.

The following critical works bear particularly on the subject of this article: John W. Clark, *The Language and Style of Anthony Trollope* (London, Andre Deutsch, 1975); A.O.J. Cockshut, *Anthony Trollope* (Glasgow, William Collins, 1955); P.D. Edwards, *Anthony Trollope: His Art and Scope* (St Lucia, University of Queensland Press, 1977); James R. Kincaid, *The Novels of Anthony Trollope* (Oxford, OUP, 1977); Michael Sadleir, *Trollope: a Bibliography* (London, 1928, reprinted Dawsons, 1964); *Trollope: a Commentary* (London, Constable, 1927); David Skilton, *Anthony Trollope and His Contemporaries: a Study in the Theory and Conventions of Mid-Victorian Fiction* (London, Longman, 1972).

9

The Trollope Reader

David Skilton

The art of reading is, we may assert, a performance art, and involves the reader in accepting certain rules or guidelines for the nonce for the production of a performance. In return the reader enjoys certain privileges of entry into the world of the literary work. 'There is implied', wrote Charles Lamb on the process of understanding a novel, 'an unwritten compact between Author and reader'.[1] The reader's pleasure will sometimes derive in part from a close identity with the assumptions built into the work about who should be reading it, and from this may follow a ready acceptance of the nonce rules; or, in the contrary case, a stimulating or amusing distance between these assumptions and the actual reading self, and an associated strangeness of the rules, may be a major source of gratification. We might speak of the *distance* between the actual reader and the work's assumptions about its readers – what, loosely following Wolfgang Iser, is often called 'the implied reader', though the bundle of qualities implied more reasonably requires a plurality of addressees.

The object of this article is both historically to establish something about the actual readers of Trollope, and to examine their representatives in his novels; and in the process to investigate the modern reader's relationship with these readers and their fictional counterparts. I shall deliberately concentrate on the 1860s, the period of Trollope's greatest popularity, when his style of fiction became established as one of *the* types of the age – a period too when, it seems, there was in respect to many of the greatest novelists an unusually well-sustained identity of standards between writer and public – a coincidence well worth investigating for its own sake.

A novel-reader of the early 1860s, when Trollope was reaching the height of his market success, was blessed with a rich list of works to chose from. Prose fiction was, as the mid-Victorians never tired of telling themselves, *the* literary form of the period: this was indeed 'the age of the novel', just as Shakespeare's had been the age of the drama. At no time in

[1] Letter to Wordsworth, 30 January 1801, in Roy Park, ed., *Lamb as Critic* (London, Routledge and Kegan Paul, 1980), p. 201.

143

our literary history were more good novels being published and read, and to some commentators it seemed that the public could not have enough of it: 'a novel-reader will go on reading novels to all eternity, and sometimes even will have several in hand at once – a serial of Mr. Trollope's here, a serial of Mr. Dickens's there, and the last three-volume tale into the bargain'.[2]

At no time, moreover, was the middle-class public better served by the institutions designed to bring fiction into its drawing-rooms. Recent advances in the techniques of printing, stereotyping and illustration had made the production of attractive books on a large scale easier. Various fiscal changes had helped a new wave of periodicals of all kinds, and an increasing number of novels now ran as magazine serials, alongside the still vigorous part-issue system by which most of Dickens's and Thackeray's great novels to date had reached the public. And the great circulating libraries, even if they had a damaging effect on book-prices and the trade discount system, certainly ensured a flood of fiction into middle-class homes.

The circulating-library giants, Mudie and W.H. Smith, and the lesser entrepreneurs who aspired to compete with them, such as the Library Co. Ltd of Pall Mall, were not yet bitterly at odds with authors and publishers over the question of the moral tone of the works they would stock. The time would come in the 1880s and 1890s when George Moore's claim that the 'narrow-minded tradesman', Mudie, was responsible for 'an appallingly low ebb' in English fiction, would represent the mood of a large proportion of important novelists.[3] But many of the notable disputes in which the circulating libraries were involved in the early 1860s, such as Mudie's with John Blackwood and G.H. Lewes over the price of George Eliot's *Mill on the Floss*, concerned the level of discount allowed by the publisher, and not the morality of the work of literature. M.E. Braddon's sensational *Lady Audley's Secret*, for example, a novel about bigamy, blackmail and murder, was so written that it could be stocked in large numbers in 1862 by Mudie and the Library Co. Ltd, who, according to Braddon's publisher, William Tinsley, competed to buy the greater quantity of the book.[4] About Trollope's subjects and attitudes there was rarely much serious doubt: he was 'the mighty monarch of books that are good enough to be read . . . the Apollo of the circulating library' to one critic, and to another, 'a writer who is born to make the fortune of circulating libraries'.[5]

Of course occasional works fell foul of the exacting standards of the

[2] E.S. Dallas [anon.], 'Lady Audley's Secret', *The Times* (18 November 1862),p. 8.

[3] See George Moore, *Circulating Morals or Literature at Nurse* (London, 1885), and his 'A New Censorship of Literature', *Pall Mall Gazette* XL (10 December 1884), p. 1.

[4] See Guinevere L. Griest, *Mudie's Circulating Library and the Victorian Novel* (Newton Abbot, David & Charles, 1970), p. 23.

[5] E.S. Dallas [anon.], 'Anthony Trollope', *The Times*, (23 May 1859),p. 12, and review of *Framley Parsonage, Saturday Review*, XI, (4 May 1861), 451–2. See Skilton, *Trollope and His Contemporaries* pp. 17–18.

guardians of public morality. In 1857 Trollope had been forced by Longman's reader to make a number of changes in the manuscript of *Barchester Towers* for the sake of delicacy, and consented to substitute 'deep chest' for 'fat stomach', and delete the phrase 'foul breathing'.[6] In 1861 he received what he described as 'A wonderful letter' from Laurence Oliphant, one of the proprietors of the *London Review*, complaining of the public's 'disapprobation' of two of his short tales, which were considered rather too 'strong',[7] but which seemed inoffensive enough to some of the author's other contemporaries. There was always someone to object to any fiction on some ground or other. In 1863 *Rachel Ray* ran into difficulties with the editor of *Good Words*, for whom it had been written, and who refused to print it. Trollope disingenuously reports that the trouble lay in 'some dancing in one of the early chapters, described, no doubt, with that approval of the amusement which I have always entertained'. The problem in fact came from the unsympathetic portrayal of an evangelical clergyman, his faults stemming, Trollope makes clear, from his evangelicalism. This was not well calculated to suit a periodical 'in the field of cheap Christian literature', whose editor, Norman Macleod, was a Scottish presbyterian divine, and one of the founders of the Evangelical Alliance.[8] In fact, the rejection of *Rachel Ray* would actually reinforce the claim that Trollope spoke for many middle-class members of the Church of England. In any case, the sorts of objections to fiction we most frequently meet with in the period give no impression of middle-class morality under real threat. Most authors, editors and publishers were operating a voluntary moral censorship or self-restraint which accorded happily with much middle-class public opinion, and there seems to have been a temporary, though surprisingly broad consensus – morally suffocating though it would later seem – about what should and should not go into a novel.

As so often, it is Dickens who first and most memorably expresses the absurdities of a particular phase of middle-class ideology. Mr Podsnap, the embodiment of bourgeois philistinism in *Our Mutual Friend* (1864–5), requires his literature to be 'large print, respectfully descriptive of getting up at eight, shaving close at quarter past, breakfasting at nine, going to the City at ten, coming home at half-past five, and dining at seven'. He places, moreover, severe moral restrictions on what may be expressed in art or conversation:

> A certain institution in Mr Podsnap's mind which he called 'the young person' may be considered to have been embodied in Miss Podsnap, his daughter. It was an inconvenient and exacting institution, as requiring everything in the universe to be filed down and fitted to it. The

[6]For a full account of this incident see Sadleir, *Trollope*, pp. 160–6.

[7]N. John Hall, ed., *The Letters of Anthony Trollope* (Stanford, Stanford University Press, 1983), pp. 140–1.

[8]See A. Trollope, *An Autobiography* (Oxford, Oxford University Press, 1950), p. 188, and Donald Macleod, *Memoir of Norman Macleod, D.D.* (London, William Isbister, 1882), p. 330.

question about everything was, would it bring a blush into the cheek of the young person? And the inconvenience of the young person was, that, according to Mr Podsnap, she seemed always liable to burst into blushes when there was no need at all.[9]

What is striking is the variety and quality achieved in the early and mid 1860s without undue offence to the cheek of the 'young person'. *The Woman in White* from Wilkie Collins, *Great Expectations* and *Our Mutual Friend* from Dickens, *Mill on the Floss*, *Silas Marner* and *Romola* from George Eliot, *Sylvia's Lovers* and *Wives and Daughters* from Gaskell, and *Philip* from Thackeray – these indicate an indisputable standard. And Trollope's novels of the period can stand beside them, including *Framley Parsonage*, *The Small House at Allington*, *Orley Farm*, *The Claverings* and *Can You Forgive Her?* Whatever effort of voluntary restraint was required to make fictional subjects and styles acceptable to the public and its moral guardians, seems for the time being to have been an aesthetically profitable one.

This list is not, of course, intended to be exhaustive, but even allowing for the bias introduced by the particular interests of the present writer, it is striking that of the fourteen novels mentioned, no fewer than seven first appeared as serials in the *Cornhill Magazine*, a journal which has a special place in Trollope's career. It was through its pages that he first rose from the status of a well-read and successful novelist to the great fame and prosperity he enjoyed throughout the 1860s.

The story of how *Framley Parsonage* was commissioned in the eleventh hour as the first novel for the new *Cornhill Magazine* has often been told, and the records of its reception leave no question as to its popularity. Sales reached 100,000, and the novel 'ranked almost as one of the delicacies of the season' with the magazine's extensive readership.[10] The *Cornhill* was aimed at an educated middle-class readership, with eclectic interests, but no particular pretensions to learning. Thackeray, as editor, expressed the matter clearly in 'A Letter from the Editor to a Friend and Contributor', which appeared in the first number of the *Cornhill Magazine*:

> It may be a Foxhunter who has the turn to speak; or a Geologist, Engineer, Manufacturer, Member of the House of Commons, Lawyer, Chemist, – what you please. . . . If our friends have good manners, a good education, and write good English, the company, I am sure, will be glad to be addressed by well-educated gentlemen and women. A professor ever so learned, a curate in his country retirement, an artisan after work-hours, a schoolmaster or mistress when the children are gone home, or the young ones themselves when their lessons are over, may

[9] *Our Mutual Friend* (Harmondsworth, Penguin, 1971), pp. 174 and 175.
[10] For the commissioning and publication of *Framley Parsonage* see *Autobiography*, pp. 136–44, and P. Miles and D. Skilton, 'Introduction' and 'The Writing and Printing of *Framley Parsonage*', in A. Trollope, *Framley Parsonage* (Harmondsworth, Penguin, 1984), pp. 7–28. For the reception, see Skilton, *Trollope and His Contemporaries*, pp. 19–20.

like to hear what the world is talking about, or be brought into friendly communication with persons whom the world knows.

This passage not only defines the public aimed at, but promotes the important notion that the magazine made possible a personal association between its readers and celebrities in many walks of life.

When Trollope was asked to write 'an English tale, on English life, with a clerical flavour',[11] it was to gratify this public's taste and to give it a fictional world with which it could comfortably identify. The novel he was already engaged on at the time was judged unsuitable, since, having an Irish subject and being set during the famine, it could not be the vehicle for the easy social intercourse which Thackeray was looking for. Thackeray's 'Letter' explains that political and religious controversy was not to appear in his pages, and the broad tolerance of existing social, political and religious institutions this implies enables us further to recognize his readers as in many senses predominantly conformist; subscribers too to Mr Podsnap's standards of decency, who can be assured that 'At our social table, we shall suppose the ladies and children always present.' It is no surprise to us to find marketing managers promising to flatter their customers' prejudices, but the generally unstrained acquiescence of so many literary producers – Gaskell, George Eliot, Thackeray and Trollope among them – marks the period from 1860 to about 1867 as a striking interval of harmony between all branches of the novel industry.

Most Victorian novelists directly address one or more fictional persons in their novels, who are outside the story, and who for rhetorical purposes stand in from time to time as the readers' representatives. The habit was old then – older than Fielding's conversational narrator, who had much of the discursive essayist about him, and at least as old as the 'Curious Reader' addressed in 1623 at the opening of James Mabbe's *The Rogue*. The differentiation between categories of readers, which Sterne carries to great creative lengths in *Tristram Shandy*, is a device in even the least self-conscious story-tellers, and Scott for one is often to be found explaining a point to a particular section of his audience. Here is a characteristic example from Chapter Nine of *The Heart of Midlothian*: 'The more youthful part of my readers may naturally ask, whether Jeanie Deans was deserving of this mute attention of the Laird of Dumbiedikes; and the historian, with due regard to veracity, is compelled to answer, that her personal attractions were of no uncommon description.'[12] Scott's 'more youthful' readers are typical of the rhetorical lay-figures we are speaking about, and which are arranged in attitudes of novelists' choosing, and dressed in any prejudice or ignorance they may wish to have displayed. Actual readers will be able to take on the roles prescribed, or alternatively may assume an effortless superiority to the limited understanding thus

---

[11]*Autobiography*, p. 142.
[12]W. Scott, *Waverley Novels* (48 vols., *Magnum opus edition*, Edinburgh, Cadell, 1830–3) XI, p. 308.

implied. In either case they will then have been manoeuvred by the narrator into consciously considering a matter which might otherwise have been passed 'on the nod'.

In this unchallenging example from Scott no great effort is needed for any likely reader to adjust to the views required to understand the subsequent narrative, but two examples from Trollope's *The Claverings* (written 1864 and serialized in the *Cornhill* in 1866–7) will show how the same phenomenon can take us into an area of potentially problematic morality, where this rhetorical nudging of the reader may be a stage in his or her Trollopian education. Julia Brabazon has jilted Harry Clavering in order to marry the wealthy, dissipated and aging Lord Ongar, and, returning to London a rich and beautiful widow, she once more captivates Harry, who is now engaged to the quiet, modest daughter of a civil engineer:

> The reader, perhaps, will hardly have believed in Lady Ongar's friendship [for Harry]; – will, perhaps, have believed neither the friendship nor the story which she herself had told. If so, the reader will have done her wrong, and will not have read her character aright. The woman was not heartless because she had once, in one great epoch of her life, betrayed her own heart; nor was she altogether false because she had once lied; nor altogether vile, because she had once taught herself that, for such a one as her, riches were a necessity.[13]

Implicitly what is challenged here is a set of assumptions about how human nature should be displayed in a novel, and hence a larger question about realism is raised. When Harry's emotions are examined, the aesthetic point is put more firmly:

> I fear that he will be held as being too weak for the role of hero even in such pages as these. Perhaps no terms have been so injurious to the profession of the novelist as those two words, hero and heroine. In spite of the·latitude which is allowed to the writer in putting his own interpretation upon these words, something heroic is still expected; whereas, if he attempt to paint from Nature, how little that is heroic should he describe! How many young men, subjected to the temptations which had befallen Harry Clavering, – how many young men whom you, delicate reader, number among your friends, – would have come out from them unscathed? A man, you say, delicate reader, a true man can love but one woman, – but one at a time. So you say, and are so convinced, but no conviction was ever more false.[14]

The education of the reader does not involve any great change in mental attitudes as regards life, but a modification of the rules for incorporating the experience of life into art. The narrator of *The Last Chronicle of Barset* (1866–7) makes the point clearly, in an example which is insistent in

---

[13]*The Claverings* (Oxford, OUP, The World's Classics, 1986), p. 129.
[14]*op. cit.*, pp. 295–6.

locating the reader in the same social circumstances in his or her world as
the characters are in theirs:

> People are so much more worldly in practice than they are in theory, so
> much keener after their own gratification in detail than they are in the
> abstract, that the narrative of many an adventure would shock us,
> though the same adventure would not shock us in the action. One girl
> tells another how she has changed her mind in love; and the friend
> sympathizes with the friend, and perhaps applauds. Had the story been
> told in print, the friend who had listened with equanimity would have
> read of such vacillation with indignation. She who vacillated herself
> would have hated her own performance when brought before her
> judgment as a matter in which she had no personal interest. Very fine
> things are written every day about honesty and truth, and men read
> them with a sort of external conviction that a man, if he be anything of a
> man at all, is of course honest and true. But when the internal convic-
> tions are brought out between two or three who are personally
> interested together . . . those internal convictions differ very much
> from the external convictions. This man, in his confidences, asserts
> broadly that he does not mean to be thrown over, and that man has a
> project for throwing over somebody else; and the intention of each is
> that scruples are not to stand in the way of his success. The '*Ruat
> coelum, fiat justitia*,' was said, no doubt, from an outside balcony to a
> crowd, and the speaker knew that he was talking buncombe. The '*Rem,
> si possis recte, si non, quocunque modo*,' was whispered into the ear in a
> club smoking-room, and the whisperer intended that his words should
> prevail.[15]

The narrator's mild dissent from his readers' stock reactions is a world away
from the accusing tone of 'hypocrite lecteur!'; he is not shocking them but
benignly explaining that they are more closely linked to his realistic fiction
than they are to novels which purport to reach towards human perfection.
With motives quite different from Baudelaire's or T.S. Eliot's, Trollope
would have been perfectly comfortable to recognize his reader as '*mon
semblable, mon frère*'.

In *Framley Parsonage*, the novel whose first instalment opens the first
number of the *Cornhill Magazine*, the narrator's relationship with his
readers is at its closest. He treats them as acquaintances and social equals,
and presents the image of a middle-class readership of modest means,
earning (we may note) the sort of income Trollope himself had recently
been earning, and defining a group he was fast leaving with the aid of
promotion and a burgeoning income from his fiction. The narrator appeals
to the class sense of his fellows not to imitate the titled and wealthy in
adopting the new, aristocratic style of serving dinners:

---

[15]*The Last Chronicle of Barset* (2 vols bd. as one, Oxford, OUP, The World's Classics, 1946)
II, pp. 156–7.

And indeed this handing round has become a vulgar and an intolerable nuisance among us second-class gentry with our eight hundred a year – there or thereabouts; – doubly intolerable as being destructive of our natural comforts, and a wretchedly vulgar aping of men with large incomes. The Duke of Omnium and Lady Hartletop are undoubtedly wise to have everything handed round. . . . But we of the eight hundred can no more come up to them in this than we can in their opera-boxes and equipages.[16]

The style of service known as *service à la russe* had become fashionable in Paris during the 1850s, and spread across the Channel into those households able to field the army of servants required to dispense with all passing and serving of dishes by the diners themselves. The very wealthy, like the Russian aristocracy from whom the procedure was derived, might be able to afford one servant per diner, but it was not adaptable to more modest middle-class circumstances, as Trollope makes clear in a hilarious chapter of *Miss Mackenzie* of 1865, where a dinner is ruined by the attempt. If hostesses of modest means feel that they must give such dinners, the narrator says, 'ordinary Englishmen must cease to go and eat dinners at each other's houses'. He then goes on, half-humorously, to clarify that this 'ordinary Englishman . . . has eight hundred a year; he lives in London; and he has a wife and three or four children'.[17] This is the ideal reader humorously imaged in most of Trollope's novels of these years.

Mary Elizabeth Braddon wrote to her upper-class mentor, Sir Edward Bulwer Lytton, that she liked *Miss Mackenzie* 'very tolerably, especially that description of the dinner *à la Russe*, which may be Greek to an inhabitant of Park Lane – but which is very true to the life of Bloomsbury'.[18] Trollope's ideal reader for most of his novels of these years is 'Bloomsbury' and not 'Park Lane'. In contrast, his *Autobiography* reports that he consciously chose to aim more selectively at Mayfair and Parliament when he wrote his political novel, *Phineas Finn* (1867–9). This book sold less well than the *Chronicles of Barsetshire*: 'But the men who would have lived with Phineas Finn read the book, and the women who would have lived with Lady Laura Standish read it also. As this was what I had intended, I was contented'.[19]

Few periods of fiction can demonstrate such a clear assumption that there exists a close social identity between narrators and readers as that which was commonplace in the 1860s. Trollope's narrators go further and insist on involving the principal characters too in the relationship, which is indicative of the identity of interest between writer and public which we have already noted. Whether writing *Framley Parsonage* in the character of

[16]*Framley Parsonage*, p. 217.
[17]*Miss Mackenzie* (Oxford, OUP, The World's Classics, 1924), p. 106.
[18]Letter of March 1866; see Robert L. Wolff, 'Devoted Disciple: The Letters of Mary Elizabeth Braddon to Sir Edward Bulwer-Lytton, 1862–1873', *Harvard Library Bulletin* XII (1974), pp. 133–4.
[19]*Autobiography*, p. 318.

a typical *Cornhill* reader, or writing *Phineas Finn* and its successors as a 'method of declaring myself' politically, after failing to get elected at the Beverley election of 1868,[20] Trollope was a middle-class gentleman addressing his equals. A later generation would be unable to understand the unproblematic relationship which was possible at this time between the writer and his society, and it is worth contrasting the attitude of Robert Louis Stevenson, in an essay composed in 1887–8 and published posthumously under the title 'On the Choice of a Profession'. Stevenson is clear not only that a parent would resist a son's desire to become a creative artist (this would have been true in the 1860s), but that to become an artist provided an attractive answer to the terrible alternative of being asked to become successfully middle-class. 'You are now come to that time of life,' writes Stevenson's typical father to his son, 'and have reason within yourself to consider the absolute necessity of making provision for the time when it will be asked, Who is this man? Is he doing any good in the world? Has he the means of being "One of us?" '.[21]

For Stevenson and many of his contemporaries, nothing worse could be contemplated than this 'being "One of us" '. In contrast, Trollope's dearest wish, and one of his obvious motives in writing fiction, was exactly to be considered respectably bourgeois. He puts the matter poignantly in his *Autobiography*:

> I have long been aware of a certain weakness in my own character, which I may call a craving for love. I have ever wished to be liked by those around me, – a wish that during the first half of my life was never gratified . . . It was not till we had settled ourselves at Waltham that I really began to live much with others. The Garrick Club was the first assemblage of men at which I felt myself to be popular.[22]

He was 46 at this time. The social and economic estrangement – that feeling of being 'something of a Pariah' – which would be the very stuff of the artistic life of many a later author, was precisely what Trollope spent half a lifetime fleeing from. His aim of 'belonging' was triumphantly achieved during the 1860s, a period when he was an acknowledged leader among 'realistic' novelists, and sought after by the editors and publishers of London. But he was typical of these years in a profounder way, in that his close identification with his public produced a first-class body of fiction.

Taken in a perfectly straightforward way, Trollope's plots during these years often propose the steady advance of the middle-class in their power struggle with the aristocracy. *Doctor Thorne* (1858) elevates the doctor's adopted daughter as far financially as she already is morally above the aristocratic De Courcys. In *Framley Parsonage* the unglamorous, 'brown' Lucy Robarts, a physician's daughter, wins the heart of Lord Lufton, and,

---

[20]*Autobiography*, p. 317.
[21]R.L. Stevenson, 'On the Choice of a Profession', *Essays Literary and Critical* (*Tusitala Edition*, London, Heinemann, 1923), p. 17.
[22]*Autobiography*, p. 159.

more importantly, that of his mother too, as a needful preliminary in obtaining his hand; while the conventionally beautiful Griselda Grantly sells herself into a cold, worldly and 'successful' marriage in the higher reaches of the aristocracy. In *Orley Farm* Felix Graham deservedly wins his way to the judge's daughter by his brains and not his birth. In *The Claverings* Florence Burton is yet another example of the superiority of middle-class females as mates. The 'second-class gentry' do well, indeed. Luke Rowan in *Rachel Ray* (1863) even succeeds in making a living from brewing beer in Devon. Such examples on their own might prove nothing; but added to the accumulation of other evidence, we can see a middle-class public sufficiently confident in its moral, financial and electoral power to enjoy tales which immortalize its successes. If Virgil celebrated the establishment of Roman civilization by the force of arms, these new epics record Victorianism as the product of the middle-class virtues of work, moderation and sense, at a time when neither these qualities nor their success were in doubt. It is appropriate that Mowbray Morris, the manager of *The Times*, should praise Trollope after his death for accurately registering this world:

> By the clear light of sense
> He drew men as they are, without pretence
> To re-gild virtue, or to lash offence.[23]

If we go further and look at the cultural heritage and experience Trollope assumes his readership to share, we find once more the image of the primary public[24] as educated and middle-class. An acquaintance with Shakespeare, stopping well short of scholarship, is taken for granted, and Shakespearean tags, like miscellaneous quotations from Milton, Pope, Gray, Burns and elsewhere, are rendered with no greater degree of accuracy than cultured conversational use would require. Many of the shared, acceptable references will have been familiar to the primary readership, even when it is unlikely that more than a handful of them would have known the source. Examples such as Trollope's habitual quotation from Tusser's *Five Hundred Points of Good Husbandry*

> 'Tis merry in hall
> When beards wag all

would be known to those who had not heard of the work, while a misquotation he often uses from Nicholas Rowe's *The Rival Queens*, 'When Greek meets Greek, then comes the tug of war', was almost proverbial. Such tags are habitual in Trollope. Meanwhile lower-status characters place

[23]Mowbray Morris, 'Anthony Trollope', *Graphic* (30 December 1882) p. 719.
[24]The term 'primary public', or 'det primære publikum', derives from Sven Møller Kristensen, *Digteren og samfundet* (2 vols, Copenhagen, Munksgaard, 2nd edn, 1965) vol. 1, p. 13.

themselves outside the privileged circle of the narrator and his chosen readers by uneducated mistakes and faulty references, such as Mrs Greenow's 'furious Orlando' in *Can You Forgive Her?*[25]

Biblical references are mainly fairly obvious, and such as an educated person or church-goer would know, who had no particular pretensions to devotion. The frequent allusions to the Book of Common Prayer, of course, limit our ideal readers to adherents of the Established Church. There are numerous quotations from the liturgy, while the psalms are usually quoted accurately from the Prayer Book and not from the Authorised Version. (Hardy, who also learnt his psalms in Church, habitually quotes them from the same source, and, like Trollope, has been wrongly accused of misquotation in consequence.) Far from limiting the range of meanings of a Trollope novel by narrowing the permissible subjects to be treated, the common culture of the Church of England can enlarge it. Elsewhere I point out an example from the first paragraph of Chapter Four of *Framley Parsonage* where the narrator is found at once 'making light of Mark's temptations and failings, and giving them a deeper resonance', by using the word 'naughty' so that it simultaneously has its modern, rather trivial and childish sense, and hints at Original Sin through an evocation of the word as it occurs in, for example, the homily 'Of the Misery of Man': 'We have sinned, we have been naughty'.[26] It is not necessary to subscribe to Church of England doctrine or indeed any Christian beliefs at all, or even to posit in Trollope any consistent theological opinions, in order to identify a layer of meaning which depends upon these ecclesiastical resonances.

The case of Latin reference and quotation is fairly straightforward in the novels we are dealing with. Little active or scholarly knowledge of Latin language and literature is required in the primary public, but a residue of school learning is implied – at least in male readers – and in the female, we may suppose, a willingness to accept quotations because they are part of the mental furniture of the men in the family. The males of the primary public have been through the ritual amount of classical education which has long been held in Britain to guarantee respectability. The point comes into prominence if we consider the title of the first chapter of *Framley Parsonage*, '*Omnes omnia bona dicere*', and remember that these are the first words to greet the reader in the first number of the new *Cornhill Magazine*, which aims to be so welcoming to its consumers. Though perfectly simple to understand, the four words themselves – 'All men all things good to say' – do not form a complete message, and might provoke disproportionate thought or speculation, were it not that they are familiar not only to those who have studied and conned passages of Terence's *Andria*, from which they come, but to any schoolboy who has had to learn them off-by-heart (with a few words' extra context), as a grammatical

---

[25]*Can You Forgive Her?* (Harmondsworth, Penguin, 1972), p. 663.
[26]Introduction to *Framley Parsonage*, p. 17.

example in such a text-book as the so-called *Eton Latin Grammar*.[27] The chapter heading does not stand in the way of the novel, as a pedantic obstacle would, but is a gesture of class recognition – a sign that the narrator is, like the novelist, 'one of us'. Having thus greeted his fellows, the narrator goes on at once to give us a near translation of the whole passage as listed in the grammar: 'all men began to say all good things to him, and to extol his fortune in that he had a son blessed with so excellent a disposition'. Having established their social credentials, the reader and narrator can now proceed on a friendly basis. No inconvenient amount of learning has been called for, though it is useful to be able to remember that the father in the *Andria* is about to see his son go to the bad. Characteristically *Framley Parsonage* contains a joke at the expense of those who believe that this amount of Latin is a significant accomplishment, when Mr Green Walker gives a public lecture on 'the grammarians of the Latin language as exemplified at Eton school'.[28] Most of Trollope's Latin is as familiar as this example and, though we know that he was well-read himself, and read Latin authors for pleasure, he uses them in the novels we are discussing largely to form the desired link between his narrator and his readers. The example from the *Andria*, mentioned here in fact, is unusually rich in intertextual significance for this period of Trollope's work.

It remains for the modern reader to make contact with Trollope's fiction by negotiating with the implied readers in it. The chief resistance to the fiction of Trollope comes, one suspects, from a problem in the relationship of the present-day reader not so much directly with Trollope the author or his oeuvre as with his original public as represented so faithfully in his books. The works on which his reputation was to a large extent based seem so unchallenging or unproblematic, and the original public so undemanding, that a claim for greatness has usually been supported by those books in which he was least successful in captivating his contemporaries. Yet to value chiefly those of his works – such as *He Knew He Was Right, The Way We Live Now* or *The Prime Minister* – which were least well received in his own day, may be to surrender (negatively) to the judgements of others – and, in such a case, to the judgements of a consuming public held rather in intellectual despite.

Some of Trollope's later novels continue in his sunniest vein, but many have challenging subject-matter and attitudes. The extreme example is *The Way We Live Now* of 1874–5, which shows a breakdown in the shared confidence in the adequacy of the middle-class virtues, and an awareness of the powerful forces of international finance in moulding the world into inimical forms. The easy collusion of narrator, characters and readers has given way to a problematic recognition – expressed in the 'we' of the title – that all are in the same predicament, and that run-of-the-mill

[27] *The Eton Latin Grammar, or an Introduction to the Latin Tongue* (11th edition, London, 1822), p. 88.
[28] *Framley Parsonage*, p. 95.

commonsense is inadequate to cope with the situation.[29] The very rejection of standard Victorian optimism, and the fact that it was ill-received by its original reviewers, make the novel attractive to today's commentator. I am far from suggesting that this great novel should be ignored. Rather it should be seen in conjunction with other important fiction which, while less startling, is still insistently unconventional – such as *Is he Popenjoy?* (1878) or *Lady Anna* (1874)[30] – and against other novels no less great in their way, written during the high season of middle-class confidence.

'We should go so far as to say that it is a natural law that literature which has not offended at least one generation stands no chance of being valued by the next'. While the modern reader is unlikely to grant unqualified support to this heroic post-Romantic sentiment from the great Danish critic, Georg Brandes, we must admit that we have habitual strategies for dealing with works which offended a good proportion of their original middle-class Victorian readers. We are suspicious of the Victorian bourgeoisie and its attitudes to its own cultural consumption, remembering J.S. Mill's strictures about the middle-classes paying others to do their thinking for them, and finding in our backward look at such matters, the grotesque figure of Mr Podsnap uncomfortably prominent in the scene. We are so used to approving of literature which was at odds with a dominant ideology of the day, that there is still, through habit, a certain strangeness in looking at fiction which was received with enthusiasm and understanding by the consuming public. This very unease is surely needless now. We can look at Victorian attitudes today without fear of being thought to subscribe to them. It is the task of the editor to bring sufficient information before the modern reader to enable him or her to become partly identified for the nonce with the bundle of attributes called the 'implied reader'. The adaption this calls for will be soothing for some – the escapists, perhaps – and intellectually stimulating for others. It will in any case send us to read the Trollopian output from *Framley Parsonage* to *The Last Chronicle of Barset* with new pleasure, admiration and understanding.

[29]See D. Skilton, ' ''Des êtres blets'': quelques techniques de récit dans la présentation de la grande bourgeoisie chez Dickens, Trollope et Meredith', trans. P. Citron, *Romantisme* XVII–XVIII (1977), pp. 174–94.
[30]See Skilton, *Trollope and His Contemporaries*, pp. 97–8.

Note

Text. The New Wessex Edition (paperback) of *Tess of the D'Urbervilles: a Pure Woman* (London, Macmillan, 1984).

Criticism. Four of the best book-length studies of Hardy are, in chronological order, J. Hillis Miller, *Thomas Hardy: Distance and Desire* (Cambridge, Mass., Harvard University Press, 1970); Michael Millgate, *Thomas Hardy: His Career as a Novelist* (London, The Bodley Head, 1971); Ian Gregor, *The Great Web: the Form of Hardy's Major Fiction* (London, Faber & Faber, 1974) and John Bayley, *An Essay on Hardy* (Cambridge, CUP, 1978). Hillis Miller's more recent *Fiction and Repetition: Seven English Novels* (Oxford, Basil Blackwell, 1982) has two excellent chapters on *Tess* and *The Well-Beloved*.

Two useful collections of essays are R.P. Draper, ed., *Thomas Hardy: the Tragic Novels* (London, Macmillan, 1975) and Dale Kramer, ed., *Critical Approaches to the Fiction of Thomas Hardy* (London, Macmillan, 1979). The standard biography of Hardy is Michael Millgate, *Thomas Hardy: a Biography* (Oxford, OUP, 1982). A recent theoretical study which incorporates an interesting section on Hardy is Mary Ann Caws, *Reading Frames in Modern Fiction* (Princeton, Princeton University Press, 1985).

Draper's edition includes Tony Tanner's justly famous essay 'Colour and Movement in *Tess of the D'Urbervilles*' (pp. 182–208), which first appeared in *Critical Quarterly* in 1968. Arnold Kettle discusses *Tess* in chapter 4 of his *An Introduction to the English Novel: Volume II Henry James to 1950* (London, Hutchinson, 1953, 1967). In his edition of *The Nineteenth-Century Novel: Critical Essays and Documents* (London, Heinemann, 1972) Kettle offers a reconsideration of Hardy. One of the most influential essays on *Tess* is David Lodge, 'Tess, Nature, and the Voices of Hardy', in his *Language of Fiction: Essays in Criticism and Verbal Analysis of the English Novel* (London, Routledge & Kegan Paul, 1966, 2nd edn 1984), pp. 164–88. Lodge's *Working with Structuralism: Essays and Reviews on Nineteenth- and Twentieth-Century Literature* (London, Routledge & Kegan Paul, 1981) includes three fine essays on Hardy. A helpful study of the shaping, composition and publication of *Tess* is J.T. Laird, *The Shaping of Tess of the D'Urbervilles* (Oxford, Clarendon Press, 1975).

10

Hardy's Authorial Narrative Method in *Tess of the D'Urbervilles*

Jakob Lothe

As Daniel R. Schwarz has shown,[1] several of the most valuable critical insights in Dorothy Van Ghent's *The English Novel* are closely related to the author's consistent focus on the narrative and thematic functions of 'method' in narrative fiction. In Van Ghent's suggestive discussion of Thomas Hardy's *Tess of the D'Urbervilles* (1891), one implication of this kind of critical focus is to emphasize the necessity of freeing 'ourselves from the temptation to appraise Hardy by his "philosophy" – that is, the temptation to mistake bits of philosophic adhesive tape, rather dampened and rumpled by time, for the deeply animated vision of experience which our novel, *Tess*, holds'.[2]

As the 'bits of philosophic adhesive tape' would seem synonymous with the authorial comments and reflections scattered throughout *Tess*, there is an obvious sense in which Van Ghent's point is connected with the critical concern indicated by the title of this essay. Now an investigation of Hardy's narrative method in *Tess* is already a substantial critical venture: it is a working hypothesis of this consideration that although qualitatively uneven, the authorial narrative method of *Tess* is more sophisticated, nuanced and productive than most commentators on the novel have noted. An exhaustive analysis of this complex method cannot be attempted here. My more modest aim is to draw attention to, and critically to discuss, some selected constitutive aspects of the novel's all-embracing, authorial narrative. As I regard the authorial reflections as an integral, if sometimes awkwardly explicit, part of this narrative, it follows that my approach dissents from one of Van Ghent's main points: I do not consider the authorial commentary as belonging to 'another order of discourse' in the novel.[3] The narrative aspects to be considered can be summarized thus:

[1]Daniel R. Schwarz, ' "The Idea Embodied in the Cosmology": The Significance of Dorothy Van Ghent', *Diacritics* VIII (1978), pp. 72–83.
[2]Dorothy Van Ghent, *The English Novel: Form and Function* (1953; rpt. New York, Harper & Row, 1961), p. 196.
[3]Van Ghent, *The English Novel*, p. 197.

variations of the authorial narrator's knowledge and perspective, and authorial distance and reflection.

In order to establish a starting-point and textual basis for our discussion, it might be helpful to outline the main action of *Tess*. The following summary condenses that given in the latest edition of the *Oxford Companion to English Literature*:

> Tess Durbeyfield is the daughter of a poor villager, whose head is turned by learning that he is descended from the ancient family of D'Urberville. Tess is seduced by Alec, a young man of means, whose parents, with doubtful right, bear the name of D'Urberville. Tess gives birth to a child, which dies after an improvised midnight baptism by its mother. Later, when working as a dairymaid on a farm, in a beautiful summer, she becomes engaged to Angel Clare, a clergyman's son. On their wedding night she at last confesses to him the seduction by Alec, and Angel consequently abandons her. Misfortunes and bitter hardships come upon Tess and her family, and accident/coincidence throws her once more in the path of Alec D'Urberville. He has become an itinerant preacher, but his temporary religious conversion does not prevent him from persistently pursuing Tess. As her appeals to her husband remain unanswered, she is driven for the sake of her family to become the mistress of Alec. Angel, returning from Brazil and repenting of his harshness, finds Tess living with Alec in Sandbourne. Maddened by this second wrong that has been done her by Alec, Tess stabs and kills him. After a brief halcyon period of concealment with Angel, Tess is arrested at Stonehenge, tried, and hanged.

Although such a crude summary of action is bound to be simplifying, there is an interesting sense in which this outline of the action in *Tess* is less distorting than that of, say, Conrad's *Nostromo*. One obvious reason for the relative accuracy of this summary is suggested by the form of chronological progression *Tess* evinces: as the seasons change and as Tess grows older, the 'phases' of the book succeed one another with a strange but effective inevitability. This is another way of saying that the distinction which the Russian formalists urge between story and plot (or *fabula* and *sjužet*) in narrative fiction is less apparent in *Tess* than in *Nostromo*, but it does not follow that the distinction is unproductive if applied to the former novel. The essential point to make here is to stress to what extent the difference between the story and plot of *Tess* is dependent upon the diverse functions of the novel's authorial narrator, who not only repeatedly emphasizes the various aspects of causality commonly associated with plot, but also extends and enriches the thematic scope of the novel in a number of ways.

Interestingly, the apparent (though in one sense devious) proximity of story and plot in *Tess* confirms the critical suggestiveness of Peter Brooks' understanding of plot in his recent *Reading for the Plot*. For Brooks, plot can be best understood as 'the dynamic shaping force of the narrative discourse'.[4] This description is influenced by Paul Ricoeur's emphasis on 'the plot's connecting function between an event or events and the story. A story is *made out of* events to the extent that plot *makes* events into a story. The plot, therefore, places us at the crossing point of temporality and narrativity'.[5] If this general description is applied to Hardy, Brooks would seem justified in stressing the critical usefulness of Ricoeur's notion of the shaping function of plot. We might think of Hardy's plots as instances of dynamic structuring: it is the manner in which the numerous fictional elements of *Tess* are accumulated, combined and commented upon by the authorial narrator which serves to constitute a plot (and by implication a thematics) that is infinitely richer and more complex than the rather simplistic and melodramatic plot we are in a position to postulate on the basis of the story of *Tess* presented above.

To say that the narrative method of *Tess* is 'authorial' is to imply that the narrator does not participate in the action of the novel and does not refer to himself by the use of 'I': his ontological status is different from that of a personal narrator. 'Everything that is told in the I-form', says Franz Stanzel in *Theorie des Erzählens*, 'is somehow of existential relevance to the personal narrator'.[6] Yet the position and function of Hardy's authorial narrator provide a good illustration of the theoretical complications associated with the basic distinction between authorial and personal narrative. For although the typical Hardy narrative can be described, to adopt Gérard Genette's concept, as 'nonfocalized',[7] with an omniscient narrator outside the story, still this authorial narrator is paradoxically and problematically involved in the lives of the characters he presents. One suggestion to be made in this essay is that this kind of narrative involvement has an interesting existential dimension which goes some way to explain the various inconsistencies and contradictions pertaining to the authorial narrator's position and function in *Tess*.

Although it is now a commonplace of narrative theory that it is essential not to confuse author and narrator, some critics of Hardy continue to do so. One reason for the confusion might be sought in the overtly explicit character of some of the authorial commentary in Hardy's fiction – the 'bits of philosophic adhesive tape' Van Ghent warns us not to isolate from their narrative and thematic context. What needs to be recognized, however, is that in Hardy the distinction between author and authorial narrator is not just a question of sophistication of narrative terminology: although separated from the characters he describes, the narrator performs

[4]Peter Brooks, *Reading for the Plot: Design and Intention in Narrative* (Oxford, Clarendon Press, 1984), p. 13.
[5]Paul Ricoeur, 'Narrative Time', in W.J.T. Mitchell, ed., *On Narrative* (Chicago, University of Chicago Press, 1981), p. 167.
[6]Franz K. Stanzel, *Theorie des Erzählens* (Göttingen, Vandenhoeck & Ruprecht, 1979), p. 132, my translation. See also Tzvetan Todorov, *Introduction to Poetics*, trans. Richard Howard (Brighton, Harvester, 1981), pp. 39–40.
[7]Gérard Genette, *Narrative Discourse*, trans. Jane E. Lewin (Oxford, Basil Blackwell, 1980), p. 189.

a crucial function as integral part of the fictional universe Hardy creates in his novels. As Hillis Miller puts it in his excellent study of Victorian fiction:

> [The narrator] is a voice Hardy invented to tell the story for him; or, to put this another way, the narrator is a personality created by the tempo, diction, and tone of the words Hardy chose to put down on paper. Hardy's narrator . . . stands outside the events of the novel in the sense of existing at a time when they have all passed. He looks back on the action after it is over or down on it from a height which is outside of time altogether. He has ubiquity in time and space and knows everything there is to know within that all-embracing span. Moreover, from his point of view the events of the story are real events which he describes not as they were for Hardy (imaginary, fictive), but as if they had a substantial existence independent of the narrator's knowledge of them.[8]

This is perhaps the most accurate description of the typical Hardy narrator that we have. However, it is also a very condensed characterization; and as Hillis Miller himself notes in the chapters on *Tess* and *The Well-Beloved* in his more recent *Fiction and Repetition*,[9] both authorial knowledge and perspective vary more in Hardy than the quoted passage might make us expect. Although Hardy's detached, authorial narrator typically 'looks back on the action after it is over or down on it from a height which is outside of time altogether', still there are noticeable, and thematically significant, variations of Hardy's method which can all be subsumed under his nonfocalized authorial narrative. One reason why critics of *Tess* have not paid sufficient attention to the variations I am thinking of is suggested by their inelegant or unpolished form: paradoxically, the explicit character of the modulations often seems to have distracted critical attention from them by inviting rather adverse commentary on Hardy's 'bad' writing. However, as David Lodge demonstrates in his chapter on *Tess* in *Language of Fiction*,[10] the narrative variations in Hardy, though variously successful, still serve, *qua* variations, as essential constitutive elements of the complex authorial narrative method through which his novels are shaped.

In order to give a preliminary specification of the authorial narrative variation in *Tess* we might refer to Genette's distinction between narrative 'voice' and 'mood'. As he points out, voice is related to the question of *who speaks* in the narrative text, mood to the question of *who sees*.[11] In a strictly technical sense, then, there seems at first to be little narrative variation in *Tess*: as the predominant narrative voice of the novel is that of

[8]J. Hillis Miller, *The Form of Victorian Fiction* (1968; Cleveland, Arete Press, 1979), pp. 10–11.
[9]Hillis Miller, *Fiction and Repetition*, chs. 5–6.
[10]Lodge, *Language of Fiction*, ch. 4.
[11]Genette, *Narrative Discourse*, p. 186. For Genette, the concepts of 'distance' and 'focalization' can both be subsumed under mood, which is one of his five main narrative categories. In this essay I substitute the term 'perspective' for focalization. For a clarifying discussion and specification of literary perspective, see Todorov, *Introduction to Poetics*, pp. 32–7.

the authorial narrator, so his perspective also seems to be the controlling and authoritative one. In spite of the apparent stability of voice and mood, however, the characteristic flexibility and range of the authorial narrative in *Tess* enable Hardy to diversify both the voice and the perspective of the authorial narrator. Several accents mingle in his voice; and, along with the predominant focus on Tess, he may adopt the perspective of other characters too in addition to his own.

The accents of the authorial voice – it would seem more accurate to speak of accents of one voice than of 'voices' – have been ably discussed by Lodge. As he observes, the narrator of *Tess* may often appear to be 'a combination of sceptical philosopher, and local historian, topographer, antiquarian, mediating between his "folk" – the agricultural community of Wessex – and his readers – the metropolitan "quality" '.[12] Lodge's reference to chapter 47 here is illustrative enough. The chapter opens with a descriptive, strikingly visual, first paragraph: 'It is the threshing of the last wheat-rick at Flintcomb-Ash Farm. The dawn of the March morning is singularly inexpressive, and there is nothing to show where the eastern horizon lies' (p. 372). However, as Tess and Izz Huett arrive in this beautiful setting, the kind of work awaiting them is not of the habitual, manual sort described earlier in the novel, but instead work conditioned by the newly introduced 'red tyrant that the women had come to serve . . . the threshing-machine which, whilst it was going, kept up a despotic demand upon the endurance of their muscles and nerves' (p. 372). The metaphor of 'red tyrant' and the adjective 'despotic' leave the reader in little doubt as to where the sympathy of the narrator lies here. Both metaphor and adjective adumbrate the characterization of the engineer which the narrator goes on to give in the fourth paragraph:

> What he looked he felt. He was in the agricultural world, but not of it. He served fire and smoke; these denizens of the fields served vegetable, weather, frost, and sun. He travelled with his engine from farm to farm, from county to county, for as yet the steam threshing-machine was itinerant in this part of Wessex. (p. 373)

On one level, this passage offers a good illustration of what Lodge calls the voice of the 'second Hardy' – characterized by 'a quality of distance, both of time and space, through which the characters can be seen in their cosmic, historical, and social settings'.[13] For Lodge, this 'second voice' – or, as I would prefer to put it, this second accent of the authorial narrator's all-embracing voice – is distinguished from that of Hardy as 'local historian'. However, while this broad distinction is suggestive and valid enough in itself, and while it is also true that the transitions from the discourse of the 'local historian' to that of the 'sceptical philosopher' can be too abrupt, the quotations we have given from chapter 47 also reveal the extent to which both accents (and that of the 'sceptical philosopher' in

[12]Lodge, *Language of Fiction*, p. 169.
[13]Lodge, *Language of Fiction*, p. 168.

particular) can be modified and attuned to each other, so that the persua-siveness of the combined effect of the two is considerably enhanced. Let me try to illustrate this point in a tripartite comment.

First, although the voice of the narrator as 'local historian' is more immediately noticeable in other sections of *Tess*, and especially in those which modulate towards narrated monologue and quoted monologue (both these narrative variations will be discussed below), there are elements of this voice or accent detectable in the narrative of the opening of chapter 47 as well. What is interesting about the accent as it functions here is that it is not so much indicated through vocabulary and idiom as through what might be described as the narrator's understanding or sympathy. This is another way of saying that the accent of the narrator as local historian is here suggested through a *perspectival* modulation: although the opening description of scenery is rendered by the narrator, and effectively intensi-fied by the use of the present tense, the second paragraph invites us to relate the perspective of the narrator to those of Tess and Izz Huett. The suggestion is strengthened if we think of the numerous descriptions of Tess's attitude to nature and manual work earlier in the narrative. And it is confirmed in the comment on the engineer who operates the threshing-machine; in contrast to Tess, 'He was in the agricultural world, but not of it.'

Second, there would seem, in these paragraphs, to be a linkage or logical connection between the authorial narrator's strong sympathy for Tess – and, as a corollary, the kind of attitude, work and lifestyle she represents – and the description of the threshing-machine and the engineer. It is certainly true, as Lodge observes, that there are aspects of the narrator's reflections as sceptical philosopher noticeable in the description. At the same time, however, there can be no doubt that the kind of scepticism voiced here is of a rather simplifying kind compared to other passages of authorial reflection in *Tess*. The main reason why we do not, as readers, react more strongly to the simplifications connected with the sarcastic and scornful elements in the characterization of the engineer is suggested by Hardy's success in manipulating us into sharing the authorial narrator's sympathy for Tess: by virtue of logical entailment we thus also come to share his contempt for the machine Tess has to serve. We could rephrase this observation by saying that the potentially damaging effects of the sarcasm and simplifications associated with the description of the threshing-machine are reduced, if not wholly eliminated, by a productive perspectival modulation.

This comment is closely related to the final one to be made on this passage. Critics of *Tess* have frequently emphasized the omniscience of the authorial narrator. As we shall see shortly, this omniscience can be striking indeed. However, the excerpt from the novel that we have been consi-dering here would seem to lend some support to the proposition that the understanding or insight of the authorial narrator in *Tess* might more accurately be described as a combination of omniscience and variations of knowledge. In one sense the omniscience of the description of the engineer is surely obvious enough – 'What he looked he felt'. At the same time, though, the affinity between the authorial perspective and that of Tess would appear to delimit authorial knowledge here, and especially if this attitudinal affinity is related to the categorical simplifications we have noted. More interestingly, perhaps, the perspectival and attitudinal affinity of the narrator and Tess might be extended to include a frustrating uncertainty as to the long-term effects of the mechanizing process of agricultural life in Wessex. This kind of uncertainty, which in itself offers a partial explanation of a somewhat hostile attitude to what is new and threatening, might suggest one limitation of authorial knowledge in *Tess*.

An illustrative example of authorial knowledge of a more precise and unmodified kind is provided by the comment in chapter 36 which offers a partial explanation of Angel's abandonment of Tess after she has confessed her seduction by Alec:

> She broke into sobs, and turned her back to him. It would almost have won round any man but Angel Clare. Within the remote depths of his constitution, so gentle and affectionate as he was in general, there lay hidden a hard logical deposit, like a vein of metal in a soft loam, which turned the edge of everything that attempted to traverse it. It had blocked his acceptance of the Church; it blocked his acceptance of Tess. Moreover, his affection itself was less fire than radiance, and, with regard to the other sex, when he ceased to believe he ceased to follow: contrasting in this with many impressionable natures, who remain sensuously infatuated with what they intellectually despise. (p. 284)

The predominant narrative and thematic thrust of *Tess* provides substantial internal motivation for the kind of authorial omniscience presented in this passage. Although less shocked than Tess, the reader, too, is surprised by Angel's reaction (part of our surprise originates in the attitudinal affinity between the narrator and Tess that we have already noted); and our surprise makes the need for a convincing authorial explanation of Angel's reaction more acute. On this level of narrative motivation and explanation, the passage achieves much. However, it also illustrates some of the problems actualized by this kind of authoritative authorial evaluation. For instance, though the fourth sentence follows logically from the third, the latter is clearly the more successful. While 'like a vein of metal in a soft loam' is a rich and suggestive image, the equation of Tess and the Church seems forced and unconvincing, even though it is related to the great weight Angel attaches to 'principle'.

Although there is a sense in which the authorial omniscience of a passage such as this one makes it relatively independent or self-contained, still its thematic impact and persuasiveness rely heavily on the manner in which it is integrated into the immediate narrative context. On this level too, the passage we are considering is variously successful. At the end of the chapter, significant thematic elements of the passage are effectively related to an omniscient authorial description of Tess's understanding of Angel's reaction: 'He was pale, even tremulous; but, as before, she was appalled by the determination revealed in the depths of this gentle being she had married – the will to subdue the grosser to the subtler emotion, the substance to the conception, the flesh to the spirit' (p. 288). This is a productive and convincing modulation of the earlier authorial evaluation of Angel: focusing on Tess's intelligence and disillusionment, it also serves to shape the reader's final evaluation of Angel. As Michael Millgate puts it, 'If Alec sacrifices Tess to his lust, Angel sacrifices her to his theory of womanly purity. The one obeys a natural law, the other a social law, and Hardy has no hesitation is assigning to the latter the greater blame'.[14]

More problematic, however, is the relation of the passage to the authorial comments on Angel later in the narrative. I am thinking of the last paragraph of chapter 39, which stresses the gap between the narrator's omniscience and Angel's severely limited self-understanding:

> But over them both there hung a deeper shade than the shade which Angel Clare perceived, namely, the shade of his own limitations. With all his attempted independence of judgement this advanced and well-meaning young man, a sample product of the last five-and-twenty years, was yet the slave to custom and conventionality when surprised back into his early teachings. (p. 309)

There is both irony and authorial pity in this characterization of Angel. What is problematic in relation to the former passage we have discussed, however, is that while Angel was there portrayed as exceptional, he is here described as 'a sample product of the last five-and-twenty years'. In one sense this contradiction is a rather obvious example of narrative inconsistency or imprecision. An alternative (or additional) explanation might be to regard it as an instance of paradoxical limitation of authorial knowledge: if the content of the two authorial statements, both of which seem omniscient when considered in isolation, appears inconsistent or contradictory, then surely the omniscience of both becomes more questionable.

The passages discussed so far can all be seen as variations of the authorial narrator's referential discourse. But *Tess* also contains further narrative modulations which supplement those of accent and perpective associated with referential narrative statements. I am thinking of the numerous instances of narrated monologue and quoted monologue in the novel.[15] As both these variations serve to enrich and diversify the authorial narrative in *Tess*, we shall briefly consider some illustrative, selected examples. Broadly, the vocabulary and syntax of the narrated and quoted monologues strikingly resemble the referential and reflective discourse of the authorial narrator. This observation confirms a point already made: in spite of the inclusion of various aspects of language – ranging from dialect to rather elaborate literary quotations and allusions – the language of all of

14Millgate, *Thomas Hardy*, p. 276.
15For an extended discussion of these terms, see Dorrit Cohn, *Transparent Minds: Narrative Modes for Presenting Consciousness in Fiction* (1978; Princeton, Princeton University Press, 1983), chs. 2–3, esp. pp. 99–107.

Tess is influenced by the idiom of the authorial narrator. This predominance of authorial accent is not always unproblematic. Lodge draws our attention to a sentence in chapter 13 where the authorial narrator seems to be aware of the artificiality of his own language if it is applied to Tess's thought: 'She thought, without exactly wording the thought, how strange and godlike was a composer's power, who from the grave could lead through sequences of emotion . . . a girl like her who had never heard of his name' (pp. 119–20). It is as though the narrator is offering his excuse for polishing and rephrasing Tess's thought here, but in actual fact this is precisely what he does over and over again throughout the novel.

Although retaining the syntax of referential narrative statement, the sentence just considered modulates towards narrated monologue. In order to illustrate how this narrative variation can function as constitutive part of the authorial narrative method of *Tess*, we might refer to the penultimate paragraph in chapter 38 which describes Tess's reaction after she has arrived home and told her parents that Angel has left her:

> Poor Tess, who had heard as far as this, could not bear to hear more. The perception that her word could be doubted even here, in her own parental house, set her mind against the spot as nothing else could have done. How unexpected were the attacks of destiny! And if her father doubted her a little, would not neighbours and acquaintance doubt her much? O, she could not live long at home! (p. 303)

The three last sentences of this passage all qualify as narrated monologue: the mental verb is deleted, but the third-person reference and the past tense are retained. There is certainly a sense in which the phrasing of these outbursts and questions seems artificial, and neither should we overlook the danger of sentimentalism in such an exclamation as the last one of the passage. Still it would seem that the narrated monologue as presented by the authorial narrator provides an effective rendering of Tess's despair at this stage of her painful life. Moreover, there is an interesting sense in which this narrative device here serves both to suggest what Tess *might have said* (the omission of quotation marks implies that she did not actually employ the words the narrator has chosen to describe her feelings) and to reaffirm the narrator's sympathy and pity – an attitude to Tess that we as readers are being asked to share.

If the narrated monologue of this passage both expresses and offers a partial, authorial justification of Tess's despair, it can also be used to indicate, and confirm the importance of, other characteristic thoughts and feelings of hers. Early in chapter 44, for instance, as Tess embarks on her futile trip to Angel's parents, her hope and uncertainty are suggested in questions presented as narrated monologue: 'Why had her husband not written to her? . . . Was he really indifferent? But was he ill? Was it for her to make some advance?' (p. 341). In my reading, however, the most successful instance of narrated monologue in the novel occurs towards the end of chapter 51. At this stage of the narrative the 'convert' Alec is again eagerly pursuing Tess who, sensing her vulnerability and recognizing that she is not immune to his arguments, explodes in an angry outburst directed at her absent husband:

> Tess remained where she was a long while, till a sudden rebellious sense of injustice caused the region of her eyes to swell with the rush of hot tears thither. Her husband, Angel Clare himself, had, like others, dealt out hard measure to her, surely he had! She had never before admitted such a thought; but he had surely! Never in her life – she could swear it from the bottom of her soul – had she ever intended to do wrong; yet these hard judgements had come. Whatever her sins, they were not sins of intention, but of inadvertence, and why should she have been punished so persistently? (pp. 404–5)

Considering the inherent quality of modification in narrated monologue, the intensity of this narrative variation is remarkable in this passage. The attitudinal distance between the authorial narrator and Tess seems momentarily suspended; not only sharing her anger, he also appears to understand the frustrations arising from her inability to answer her last question. This is hardly surprising – Tess's question is also the central one put by *Tess* as a novel – and yet the blending of authorial and personal voice and perspective is exceptionally suggestive here. It seems right that the outburst should come just at this point, as a reaction to Alec's tormenting questions. Moreover, it economically and logically provides a basis for her second letter to Angel (p. 405, cf. p. 417).

If narrated monologue characteristically blends the voice and perspective of narrator and character, quoted monologue generally attempts to render the thought or reflection of a character more directly and unambiguously than the former narrative modulation. As Dorrit Cohn puts it, the 'dubious attribution [in narrated monologue] of language to the figural mind, and its fusion of narratorial and figural language charge it with ambiguity'.[16] In contrast, quoted monologue presents the thought of a character in quotation marks, in the present tense and with first-person reference. But while the accent of the authorial narrator is thus less noticeable here, the fact that it may be detectable even in the quoted monologues of *Tess* reveals much about the all-inclusive character of the voice of the authorial narrator in the novel. Chapter 44, which I have referred to already as illustration of narrated monologue, also elucidates how the authorial narrator's account of a character's successive encounters and experiences can be accompanied by direct citations of his or her own thoughts. I have argued above that an essential function of the narrated monologue at the beginning of this chapter is to draw the reader's attention to Tess's stubborn hope. This hope is related to her stamina and refusal to give in; coexisting with her despair, it has almost become a precondition for her progress through this life of mishap and hardships. Further on in the chapter the omniscient narrator confirms the existential importance that Tess semi-consciously attaches to hope: 'and there is no doubt that her dream at starting was to win the heart of her mother-in-law, tell her whole history to that lady, enlist her on her side, and so gain back the truant' (pp. 342–3). The narrator's use of the noun 'dream' here not only characterizes his typically mixed attitude of scepticism, pity and disillusionment, but also implies a warning to the reader about the outcome of Tess's most recent undertaking. 'Dream' thus prefigures the disappointment of hers which is intensified through the use of quoted monologue towards the end of the chapter:

> 'Ah!' she said, still sighing in pity of herself, '*they* didn't know that I wore those [Tess's walking boots] over the roughest part of the road to save these pretty ones *he* bought for me – no – they did not know it! And they didn't think that *he* chose the colour o' my pretty frock – no – how could they? If they had known perhaps they would not have cared, for they don't care much for him, poor thing!' (p. 347)

It is of course most unlikely that Tess, in such a despairing and hopeless situation, should be formulating complete sentences to herself. But while her fragmented thoughts are organized into grammatically correct speech by the authorial narrator, he takes care to retain a rather simple idiom. Dramatizing Tess's reaction to the problems she is repeatedly confronted with, this quoted monologue functions as a productive variant on the narrated monologue on page 303 (see above, p. 163). Furthermore, the danger of sentimentalism is better controlled here than in the last exclamation of the narrated monologue on page 303. In this quoted monologue, the narrator explicitly informs us that Tess 'knew it was all sentiment . . . which had caused her to read the scene as her own condemnation' (p. 347). Broadly, it is the combination of authorial distance and omniscience which serves to counteract the elements of sentimental melodrama which underlie the story of Tess. Not surprisingly, then, these elements may become disturbing if no authorial comment is attached to the dialogue (or to narrated or quoted monologue), witness the quoted monologue which concludes chapter 28: 'I can't bear to let anybody have him but me! Yet it is wrong to him, and may kill him when he knows! O my heart – O – O – O!' (p. 219).

A more complex variant of quoted monologue in *Tess* is that related to the narrator's resigned irony. The most illustrative example of this variation occurs at the very end of chapter 46, a key chapter in which Tess, in order to protect herself from Alec, angrily turns the arguments of the sceptic Angel against the convert Alec. The irony here is closely connected with Tess's unintentional success; and it is made quite explicit in the quoted monologue which brings the chapter to conclusion:

> The drops of logic Tess had let fall into the sea of his enthusiasm served to chill its effervescence to stagnation. He said to himself, as he pondered again and again over the crystallized phrases that she had handed on to him, 'That clever fellow little thought that, by telling her those things, he might be paving my way back to her!' (p. 371)

The crudity of this thought seems wholly consonant with Alec's scheme and character. Again, we note to what great extent the effect of the quoted monologue depends on the authorial comment which precedes it. I have quoted just the concluding paragraph, but actually the referential statements of all three last paragraphs of the chapter point towards the quoted monologue which effectively concludes it. The last sentence of the penultimate paragraph is particularly suggestive. Its use of 'perhaps' modifies authorial knowledge, but the sentence as a whole illustrates the narrator's attempt to understand all his major characters, including Alec: 'Reason had had nothing to do with his whimsical conversion, which was perhaps the mere freak of a careless man in search of a new sensation, and temporarily impressed by his mother's death' (p. 371). The concluding quoted monologue goes some way to confirm the validity of this reflection, but still the qualification of authorial knowledge suggested by 'perhaps' enhances, though modestly, the complexity of Alec as character.

Broadly, narrated monologue and quoted monologue serve as important additions to the referential statements and dialogue of *Tess*. There are variations of authorial knowledge and perspective attached to both these kinds of monologue. Although the omniscience of the authorial narrator often is striking, he does not pretend to know the reasons for everything that happens; indeed the keenness of his interest and the stability of his narrative focus seem in part to result from the sense of inexplicability and inevitability which characterizes the pattern of action in which the major characters of the novel are engaged. Although I have noted some of the ways in which Hardy modulates the voice of his authorial narrator, there can be no doubt that, on balance, the perspectival variations are more important than those of voice. Combined with the narrator's great distance from his characters, his narrative flexibility and immense superiority of knowledge enable him to adopt a number of perspectives by virtue of which the action is illuminated, though not necessarily explained, from a variety of angles. In addition to the narrator's own perspective, the most important one is that of Tess. But this recurrent authorial slanting into Tess's perspective should not make us overlook the narrative and thematic significance of the observations minor characters can make – even from vantage points only peripherally connected with the main action of the novel. In *Tess* such perspectival modulations are generally more successful than those of narrative accent, at least in the sense of being less obtrusive in the narrative structure.

One of the best examples of this kind of perspectival variation occurs in chapter 35, and reads like a silent, outside comment on the estrangement of Tess and Angel after Tess's confession:

They wandered on again in silence. It was said afterwards that a cottager of Wellbridge, who went out late that night for a doctor, met two lovers in the pastures, walking very slowly, without converse, one behind the other, as in a funeral procession, and the glimpse that he obtained of their faces seemed to denote that they were anxious and sad. (p. 275)

Simply by reporting what 'was said afterwards' this authorial description, while retaining the narrative focus on Tess and Angel, temporarily adopts the perspective of an outside observer. Lodge has interpreted 'Hardy's reliance on specified and unspecified observers as evidence of the importance he attached to visual perspective – it is as though he is trying to naturalize devices of presentation that would require no such explanation or justification in film.'[17] In the passage just quoted, the sudden slanting into the perspective of an anonymous observer not only helps the reader to visualize the relevant scene, but also incorporates elements of interpretation and prefiguration that influence and shape our understanding of the novel as a whole. We may note how, on the stylistic level, the observation that the 'lovers' are 'walking very slowly' is correlated with a sudden influx of commas, which slows down our reading of the sentence. Second, the image of the two walking behind one another 'as in a funeral procession' is strikingly suggestive, and more on a second reading of *Tess* than on a first. The image becomes one of the numerous 'omens' (to adopt Tony Tanner's well-chosen term[18]) in the novel; and it also draws attention to the potentially very serious consequences of Angel's abandonment of Tess. Finally, I also find the use of 'seem' suggestive here: it suggests a paradoxical affinity between this unidentified observer and the authorial narrator. Both rely heavily on visual observation, and they both attempt to interpret what they see. In one obvious sense, the superior knowledge of the authorial narrator would of course seem vastly removed from the ignorance of this unidentified observer. At the same time authorial knowledge, however superior, does vary; and one implication of this variation is, in my reading, an accentuation of the novel's strong and distressing sense of the unavoidability and inexplicability of human action. The narrator can observe his characters with amazing precision, but he is in no position to influence the courses of their problematic lives. The narrator's detachment is one of the basic sources of his knowledge, but it also prevents him from making this knowledge effective.

Broadly, the narrator's distance from the characters and from the action could be specified as an uneasy combination of necessary detachment and painful involvement. This problematic combination is related to, if it does not exactly create, several of the narrative and thematic inconsistencies in *Tess*; and it serves to make the narrative discourse of the novel less unified and more fragmented. What needs to be stressed, however, is that though problematic, the kind of combination of narrative detachment and involvement dramatized in *Tess* is not necessarily, and definitely not only, a narrative 'weakness' of Hardy's authorial narrative method. The main thematic elements presented and dramatized by the authorial narrator are intrinsically difficult and multi-faceted; and there is an intriguing sense in which the narrative inconsistencies of the novel confirm, rather than

---

[17]David Lodge, 'Thomas Hardy as a Cinematic Novelist,' in *Working with Structuralism*, ch. 7.
[18]Tanner, 'Colour and Movement in *Tess of the D'Urbervilles*'.

suppress, the contradictions and unresolved problems associated with the aspects of human life *Tess* portrays.

The detachment of the narrator could be seen as an implication of the omniscience and flexibility which characterize the authorial narrative of the novel. But while variations of the narrator's knowledge may reduce his distance from the characters, the remarkable flexibility of his narrative paradoxically confirms this distance. Although the narrator may, as we have seen, temporarily adopt the perspective of Tess, he is in no position to influence or change the direction of her action. In Tess's life each event or stage, however unexpected in itself, seems to conform to an 'immanent design'[19] which has no source, but in which she and the other characters are inextricably involved.

The narrator is both outside and inside the design which shapes and determines the lives of his characters. Although removed from the characters by virtue of his knowledge, flexibility and different ontological status, he is as unable as Tess is to answer the crucial question: 'why should she have been punished so persistently?' (p. 405). The narrator's reflections provide an attempt at an answer, but the failure of the attempt interestingly confirms the attitudinal affinity between the narrator and the characters of *Tess*. It is certainly true, as several critics have noted, that many of the authorial reflections (along with the numerous quotations and literary allusions) are not only awkwardly explicit, but also, in a number of cases, problematically removed from the basic thematics of the novel. Still, if we ask why these reflections – such as that embedded in the reference to Aeschylus in the very last paragraph – do not seriously impair the thematic impact of *Tess*, a possible riposte might be to emphasize the existential dimension of the narrator's need for explanation of the fates of his characters. This is another way of suggesting that there is a linkage between the narrator's numerous references to the thoughts and theories of others (theories which in part contradict one another) and his own inability to comprehend the lives of the characters he describes. In my reading, this kind of limitation of authorial knowledge enriches the thematics of *Tess* by giving the narrator's detached irony an exceptionally humble quality.

---

[19]Cf. Hillis Miller, '*Tess of the D'Urbervilles:* Repetition as Immanent Design,' ch. 5 of *Fiction and Repetition*, pp. 116–46.

Notes on Contributors

Marjorie Burns is an associate professor at Portland State University in Portland, Oregon, specializing in nineteenth-century British literature. Her recent publications include an article on Goethe's *Faust*, and *Cataclysms on the Columbia* (Portland, Oregon, Timber Press, 1986).

Angus Easson, who is Professor of English at the University of Salford, has previously taught at the University of Newcastle and the Royal Holloway College (University of London). His publications include *Elizabeth Gaskell* (London, Routledge, 1979), and editions of works by Dickens and Gaskell, as well as articles on Romantic and Victorian literature.

Elizabeth Deeds Ermarth is Professor of English at the University of Maryland, Baltimore County. She is the author of *Realism and Consensus in the English Novel* (Princeton, Princeton University Press, 1983), and of *George Eliot* (Boston, G.K. Hall, 1985). She is currently writing a book on contemporary fiction.

Kate Flint is Fellow and Tutor in English at Mansfield College, Oxford. A graduate of Oxford and the Courtauld Institute, London, she previously taught at Bristol University. *Dickens* was published by the Harvester Press in 1986, and she has edited *Impressionism in England: the Critical Response* (London, Routledge, 1984). A study of the language and function of late-nineteenth-century art criticism is forthcoming, and she is writing *The Woman Reader, 1830–1920*. She is the author of numerous reviews and articles on nineteenth- and early-twentieth-century fiction and painting.

Jakob Lothe was born in 1950 and has studied at the universities of Bergen, California (Santa Barbara), Sussex and Oxford. He is presently teaching at the University of Oslo. He has recently completed a study of Conrad's narrative method, and has published several reviews and articles in Norwegian and English journals.

D.A. Miller is an associate professor (English and Comparative Literature) at the University of California, Berkeley. His first book, *Narrative and its Discontents* (Princeton, Princeton University Press, 1981) was widely reviewed and well received.

Stein Haugom Olsen is Professor in the Department of English, University of Oslo. His first book *The Structure of Literary Understanding* was published by Cambridge University Press in 1978 and reissued in paperback in 1985. A second book is due out in 1986. He has published very widely in journals and collections, mainly on the topic of literary aesthetics.

J.M. Rignall is a lecturer in the Department of English and Comparative Literary Studies at the University of Warwick. His main interest is the novel in the nineteenth and twentieth centuries in English and European Literature, and he has published essays and articles on both English and German fiction.

Roger D. Sell is Professor of English at the University of Gothenburg, Sweden. He has edited the shorter poems of Sir John Beaumont, and has written book-length studies of Andrew Young, Henry Fielding, and Robert Frost. His most recent publications include editions of unpublished work by Frost – prose, plays and children's stories. At present he is writing a series of articles on literary pragmatics.

David Skilton is Professor of English at the University of Wales Institute of Science and Technology, Cardiff, and has edited or introduced a number of Trollope's novels, including *The Warden, Doctor Thorne, Orley Farm* and *The Claverings* for the Oxford University Press World's Classics series, and (with Peter Miles) *Framley Parsonage* for the Penguin English Library. He is the author of *Anthony Trollope and his Contemporaries* (London, Longman, 1972) and *Defoe to the Victorians: Two Centuries of the English Novel* (Harmondsworth, Penguin, 1985).

Name Index